Presented Saonak
Kanjilal & Asis Kanjilal
with good wishes
& Prayer.

Swami Lokeswaranda

9. 10. 97

The
Vedanta Society
of
NEW YORK

A Brief Survey

The
Vedanta Society
of
NEW YORK

A Brief Survey

SWAMI TATHAGATANANDA

THE VEDANTA SOCIETY OF NEW YORK
34 WEST 71ST STREET
NEW YORK, NEW YORK 10023

Copyright © 2000 The Vedanta Society of New York

Library of Congress Cataloging-in-Publication Data

Tathagatananda, Swami

The Vedanta Society of New York : A Brief Survey
by
Swami Tathagatananda — 1st ed.

p. cm.

Includes bibliographic references and index.

ISBN 0-9603104-1-X

1. Ramakrishna Mission—History
2. Vedanta Societies in America—History
Library of Congress Control Number 00-133008
I. Title.

Copies can be had of
Advaita Ashrama
5 Dehi Entally Road, Calcutta 700 014

Printed and bound in India at
Trio Process, Calcutta
First Edition, October 2000

Those who wish to learn in greater detail about the teachings contained in this book may write to:
Spiritual Leader, Vedanta Society of New York,
34 West 71st Street, New York, New York 10023, U.S.A.

☎ 654-9581/9681
654-1144/1180
FAX : 654-4346

RAMAKRISHNA MATH
P.O. Belur math 711 202
Dist. Howrah, West Bengal

3rd June, 1999

My dear Tathagatananda,

I am very glad to know that you are going to bring out a book by name *The History of the Vedanta Society of New York* for which you want my benedictions.

I am sure the book will contain many interesting and valuable details about the start and the early years of the Vedanta Society of New York. I also hope this book will be a great help to the young generation of America as well as other countries to know the nature and growth of the Vedanta Movement in the West initiated by Swami Vivekananda.

I convey my love and blessings to you for all success in your efforts and for the wide circulation of the book which will be a valuable addition to the story of Vedanta in America.

Ranganathananda

(Swami Ranganathananda)
President
Ramakrishna Math and
Ramakrishna Mission

Swami Tathagatananda
Vedanta Society
34 West 71st Street
New York, NY 10023
U.S.A.

DEDICATION

In loving memory of all friends, admirers,
and followers past and present, of Vedanta.

---

*Swami Vivekananda had learned the need of the
West for the philosophy of Vedanta and he had seen
how that philosophy could be applied to every problem
of modern man. He was now ready to nurture the seed
he had planted into a sturdy tree whose roots would
strike deep and whose branches would give shelter to
the world.*

— Marie Louise Burke

Sri Ramakrishna

Sri Sarada Devi

Swami Vivekananda

Swami Saradananda, 1896

CONTENTS

ILLUSTRATIONS

INTRODUCTION

In the last years of the nineteenth century Swami Vivekananda came from India to America and shed an abundance of powerful spiritual light over the land. Many people, thousands of people, who came in contact with him, received that light unto themselves. Some few became illumined; many others gained hope and direction; still others set out on a course that would lead them straight and sure to the eventual goal of all life. But unless light is somehow captured and held, it will in time become dispersed and fade. Swami Vivekananda knew that he was sowing the seeds of spirituality over this land of America, but he also knew that for those seeds to sprout and grow into sturdy trees, they would need protection and nourishment—in short, they would need guardians and a home—an organization.

But the Swami was leery of organization. He knew its potential to strangle the very ideals for which it exists. Still, he also knew that in the world—*particularly* in the Western world—nothing can thrive without being organized. Therefore, in November of 1894, he founded a Vedanta society in New York, the first Vedanta society in the West in which his ideas, his spirit, and his power would be preserved without being watered down or so misconstrued as to be entirely lost. He founded this organization as gingerly as possible. To be sure, the society had officers—a president, a vice president, a secretary and a treasurer—but it had no membership roll, and mast certainly it had no bylaws or articles of association—nothing like that. Nevertheless, the Vedantic ideals that the Swami had been teaching now had a place from which the light that he had brought to the West would shine undiluted and strong.

In a few years after that small, almost amorphous, beginning, the Vedanta Society of New York became legally, officially, incorporated and has had an unbroken growth up to the present time. Guarded and nourished by swamis of the Ramakrishna Order, it has been faithful to its ideals and to its great founder. No watering down, no adulteration, no misinterpretation.

How precious today would be an authoritative history of the first Christian community established two thousand years ago! How precious in years to come will be an authoritative and well-researched history of the first Vedanta society in the West!

Swami Tathagatananda has written such an account. Nor do we have to wait two thousand years to enjoy it and benefit from it. Here in the pages of this book is a treasure of religious history which can inform and inspire everyone who cares about preserving the spiritual light that is given periodically to the world—most recently, and perhaps most powerfully and universally by Sri Ramakrishna and his great apostle Swami Vivekananda.

May 31, 2000   Marie Louise Burke

PREFACE

The phenomenal progress of science and technology in modern times is not matched by a similar development of our wisdom, sense of purpose or vision of a meaningful life. The speed, complexity of life and the incredible variety of available options in our time are without any precedent. We have more courage than integrity of character, more knowledge that agitates our mind without illuminating it, more comfort than contentment, and more excitement than peace and harmony. A materialistic philosopher looks upon the world as a huge, casually governed, automatic, lifeless machine. Materialism has degraded our mind and made us cynical, aimless. Excessive material power has made us disinterested, restless, domineering and violent. Spiritual blindness has brought forth chaos, wars and disharmony. Our experience of the materialistic outlook of life expresses the tragedy of Macbeth—"a tale told by an idiot full of sound and fury signifying nothing." Life is a driblet of woe and weal and plagued by confusion, fear and anxiety. We are tired of being the plaything of the forces of life, of being pushed by pleasure here and pulled around by pain there. Our age lacks a single overarching purpose and consistent direction. Vedantic spiritual orientation alone can restore the balance and give us peace and harmony. Mystics proclaim that we live not—as secularism suggests—in a clockwork mindless universe, but in a universe which is alive and in which thought and Consciousness are paramount forces. Infinite Consciousness exists behind finite objects. This is a philosophy which is spiritually inspiring and intellectually satisfying, bringing us optimism, faith and enthusiasm to lead a life in quest of Truth.

Scientific materialism and religious provincialism—these two ideas of modern life combine to make us like a one-eyed giant with its characteristic split and blindness. We are confused by the radical dualism between man and nature, God and the world or even matter and energy. We are tired of analysis; we are hungry for synthesis. Material prosperity and spiritual poverty coexist in the same person. This dichotomy between the two worlds—spirit and matter—demands a synoptic comprehension of Truth embracing both the worlds. To overstep the limited area of human knowledge and embrace Truth in its totality and entirety has been the supreme longing of philosophers in all ages and climes. To this supreme task, Vedanta, as interpreted by Swamiji, provides the best solution by bringing harmony, freeing the mind of nagging confusion and giving modern people a philosophy of life that can satisfy them intellectually, emotionally and spiritually. It was a good synthesis, from the Absolute to the relative and from the relative to the Absolute. Shri Ramakrishna is the incarnation of this synthetic genius of philosophy and religion in modern times.

History is the eternal story of humanity's seeking freedom from bondage. History is the drama of "Universal Intelligence" enacted against the backdrop of Eternity. The high watermark of human excellence in history is preeminently a revelation of "Creative Intelligence" or the Divine. Great ideas appear in life silently. H.G. Wells says that "the beginnings of such things are never conspicuous. Great movements of the racial soul come at first like a thief in the night, and then suddenly are discovered to be powerful and worldwide. Religious emotion—stripped of corruptions and

freed from its priestly entanglements—may presently blow
through life again like a great wind, bursting the doors and
flinging open the shutters of individual life and making many
things possible and easy that in these days of exhaustion seem
almost difficult to desire."

The most remarkable epoch-making incident in our age
is the appearance of Swami Vivekananda at the Parliament of
Religions. Swami Vivekananda was an "unconscious tool of
History."

Life is a great gift of "Nature," and true living is the
outcome of wisdom born of spiritual insight. Any really cultured
person of awakened consciousness seeks the goal of life in
freedom, enlightenment and perfection. The destiny of any
society depends upon the living principles of the cultural ethos
of that society. Noble, healthy and living ideas play a great
role in human progress in the development of the inner life.
These ideas, given to us by the great spiritual giants, move
history. Spiritual giants are the epoch makers. As matter in
motion is energy, similarly, the great ideas exemplified by the
lives of saintly persons are ideas in action.

Vedanta—the spiritual wisdom, the whole museum of
Truth—is a timeless philosophy. Vedanta is mainly a
philosophy of inquiry into the mysteries of life. It is absolutely
non-dogmatic. It abhors the non-critical attitude. Vedanta is
a philosophy *par excellence*. It harmonizes all faiths by
discovering the unity behind the diversity of faiths. It definitely
provides the basic attitude for inner-religious fellowship. The
true religion is based on this integral view of life and the world.
Therefore, the Vedantic idea gives a soul to the growing world
consciousness. The Vedantic spirit should be emulated for
mutual benefit of mankind. It provides us an enduring wisdom,
a widsom resistant to the fluctuation of time. It is comprehensive, incredibly flexible and essentially responds to the vital
needs of the people. Vedanta is broad and all encompassing
in its attitude as Mother Earth. It does not neglect any belief
or dogma and gives support to everyone's faith in his or her

onward journey. Vedanta provides an impersonal background
to different theistic conceptions of existing religions. Vedantic
ideas find a welcome in every broad philosophic mind. One
can find in Vedanta the spiritual ideals of different religions.
Vedanta is so broad-based and universal in its outlook and so
resourceful in its philosophy that it can supply the spiritual
needs of everyone under the sun. The message of Swami
Vivekananda at the historic Parliament is the essence of Indian
wisdom. Wisdom is intuitive experience and, therefore,
irreducible conviction. His message is indeed an epoch-making
incident in view of its saving power. Reality is one in essence
and plurality in appearance.

Swami Vivekananda asks us to see the Divine in this
universe. The universe is "deified." All indeed is Divine. This
attitude of a unitary vision of life is an eternal source of
inspiration to actively participate in life. The wide gap between
the secular and the spiritual is bridged here. Swamiji's synthetic
vision of Vedanta was lucidly expressed in his famous
statement:

> Each soul is potentially divine.
> The goal is to manifest this Divinity within by
> controlling nature, external and internal.
> Do this either by work, or worship, or psychic control,
> or philosophy—by one, or more, or all of these—and be
> free.
> This is the whole of religion. Doctrines, or dogmas, or
> rituals, or books, or temples, or forms, are but secondary
> details. (*Complete Works*, I: 124)

We will see the full sweep of this magnificent insight in
the future.

These ideas—divinity of the soul, universality of Truth,
unity of existence and harmony of religions—certainly can
provide confused civilization a viable philosophy of life, and
humanity a soul and principle to live by.

Vedanta demands a radical change of perspective. In this age, educated people with a scientific cast of mind and believers in reason as the arbiter in all controversies must see the relevance of changing our old, outmoded perspective. The temper of the age desperately demands it.

The greatest gains are not those of material success and scientific discovery but that of insight about humanity and the world. The greatest gains are in the sphere of an understanding and enlightened view. The expanding knowledge of the physical world and the superficial study of the human being do not take note of the presence of cosmic intelligence behind man and nature. When that is understood, the human mind will blossom, attaining something far beyond the realm of matter.

We stated earlier that life is a gift of "Nature." Vedanta gives us a comprehensive view of nature. It is inclusive of the physical, biological, neurological and spiritual. God in Vedanta is both personal and impersonal. Everything originates from God, is sustained by Him and ultimately is absorbed by Him. Secular scholarship only knows the superficial aspect of man and nature. It lamentably lacks insight about the spiritual dimension of man—the man in depth.

Unlike Vedanta, popular religions are "culture-centered rather than humanity-centered." Vedanta preaches unity of mankind. The idea of world civilization is now taking roots in the minds of thoughtful people both in the East and in the West. The days of "East is East and West is West and never the twain shall meet" are now happily passing away. Various conferences and programs for inter-religious and intercultural understanding are the order of the day. Lewis Mumford writes: "He who is one hundred percent an American or a Russian ... or an Asiatic, is only half a man; the universal part of his personality, equally essential to his becoming human, is still unborn. Every act that softens the egoistic claims of nations and accentuates the unity of mankind adds another foundation stone to the new world that we must now build" (*This is My*

Philosophy, ed. by Whit Burnett, 33). This broadening of our outlook is a great gain. Toynbee is of the opinion that "on the spiritual plane ... one inch gained is of greater consequence for mankind than a mile gained in supererogatory additions to man's command over non-human nature...." (Arnold J. Toynbee, *A Study of History*, VII: 488).

Through this enlightened living model, humanity can establish harmony between spirituality and science, reason and faith, mysticism and logic, East and West, for the mutual benefit of a reciprocal relationship.

Since its inception, the Vedanta Society has been unceasingly preaching the sublime universal and dynamic philosophy of Vedanta for the enlightenment of humanity. Vedantic concepts are revolutionary; they are bound to make an impact in the course of time on rational-minded people having scientific temperament. We do firmly believe that the impact of the preaching does not necessarily help only the congregation, it also does produce a tremendous impact on the entire humanity through its pure thoughts, holy living, and books and other literature pertaining to Vedanta. Great ideas take time to germinate in the collective mind; they inspire people gradually. But the universal ideas of the Vedanta, consciously or unconsciously, already have moulded the human mind. These ideas are no longer new—they have become an established conviction of the general humanity. We do hope, in due course, the essential ideas of Vedanta will continue to color the human mind and gradually change man's outlook to bring about religious harmony and peaceful living. This humble work may be appraised as a compilation of the source materials of a very important chapter of the Vedanta Movement in this country.

I have included two essays, respectively—"Practical Vedanta" (Appendix A) and "The Concept of Soul or Self in Vedanta" (Appendix B)—with the intention of helping readers to understand the viewpoint of Vedanta, which is extremely difficult for every one of us. "The Concept of Soul or Self in Vedanta," if read patiently and sincerely, may help the reader to comprehend the central principle of Vedanta vis-à-vis other philosophies.

I also intended to include two additional essays, "The Fundamental Teachings of Vedanta" and "Vedanta and Its Special Features," but these were excluded—I did not want to increase the bulk of the book. These two essays are to be separately published immediately after the publication of this book.

I am grateful to Revered Swami Ranganathanandaji, President of Ramakrishna Math and Mission, for his kind blessing which appears in the book.

I am indebted to Marie Louise Burke for her monumental works on Swamiji in the West. These books were, to say the least, the main source of information. Her painstaking, long-sustained effort stretching almost for a decade or more, her Herculean labor in unearthing the unknown stories lying buried in the newspapers of that period, her scholarship in marshalling those facts, are all unique. Her enduring sincere love and genuine loving dedication to Swamiji and Vedanta are also unique. I am grateful to her for writing the introduction in spite of her failing health and pressing work.

When I came to the Society in 1977, I thought about writing the history of the Vedanta Society of New York and requested Miss Jean McPhail, a Vedanta student and a voracious reader, to collect materials from available sources. She collected many materials from different sources about our Society. She has become a nun, known by the name Pravrajika Gayatriprana, and her present home is the convent in Northern California. I express my gratitude for her labor of love in her effort to collect materials.

During the Centenary period, as I was busy writing another book for publication, I could not afford to give any time to writing this history. So I requested many friends, insiders as well as outsiders. Our dear friend Mr. Noriman Dhalla earnestly began to form a sketch in his own style, which did not satisfy me, so it was abandoned. Professor Jayanta

Sirkar of Maryland University, College Park, a great friend and supporter of the Center, was requested, and he did finally publish two short articles in the Bulletin of the Ramakrishna Mission Institute of Culture, one of which appeared in its May 1997 commemorative issue of the Centenary of the Ramakrishna Mission and the other in the following month's issue.

Now, I myself tried to write the history. In this work, I received very substantial help from Helen; her sincerity and wholehearted painstaking labor of love helped me in many ways, apart from typing in the computer and preparing the Index. Mahesh Tirunkudulu, a Ph.D. candidate at New York University, helped particularly in setting the computer aright, off and on again as needed. Dora Barbera gave me many books from the University Library of Columbia University. Barbara Horton read some portions of the manuscript. Professor Jayanta Sircar gave me constant inspiration to finish the book and Professor Tapan Sarkar of Syracuse University, a great friend of the Society, also gave moral support for the publication. I am grateful also to Swami Bodhasarananda of Advaita Ashrama in Calcutta for helping to get the book printed. I express my hearty thanks to all of them.

One thing still bothers me—I have used the personal pronoun in this book. I consulted some of our friends, in my effort to avoid it, but there was a consensus in favor of the personal pronoun in spite of my dissatisfaction.

May this book be a source material about the nascent Vedanta Movement for future historians.

Phalaharini Kali Puja   Swami Tathagatananda
June 1, 2000
The Vedanta Society of New York

PROLOGUE

Shri Ramakrishna was a God-intoxicated man with manifold spiritual experiences of the rarest quality. His intimate experiences of many facets of Truth, his all-encompassing wideness, his extraordinary range and depth of mind, his wholehearted acceptance of the Truth in all religions—a broad outlook that was unknown in any revelation in religious history—is a historical fulfillment of the ideal of religious harmony. His was an enigmatic personality, deep as the ocean, wide as the blue sky, forbearing as Mother Nature, lofty as the mountains and soothing as the rays of the morning sun. The impressive spectrum of admirers ranging from different disciplines—Max Müller, Romain Rolland, Arnold Toynbee, Pitirim A. Sorokin, Harlow Shapley, J. R. Oppenheimer and Aldous Huxley—is indicative of Shri Ramakrishna's uniqueness in the history of world religions.

We quote the opinions of only two such admirers. In his article, "A Real Mahatman," Professor Max Müller wrote that "Sri Ramakrishna seems to have been not only a high souled man, a real Mahatman, but a man of original thought." In the introduction to his book *The Life of Ramakrishna*, Roman Rolland wrote "I am bringing to Europe, as yet unaware of it, the fruit of a new autumn, a new message of the Soul, the symphony of India, bearing the name of Ramakrishna … The man whose image I here evoke was the consummation of two thousand years of the spiritual life of three hundred million people … It is my desire to bring the sound of the beating of that artery to the ears of fever-stricken Europe, which has murdered sleep. I wish to wet its lips with the blood of Immortality."

He sailed in the wide ocean of Truth like an adept sailor; he dived deep and collected many rare gems of Truth. He said to his disciples: "I have practiced all religions in Hinduism, Islam, and Christianity and I have also followed the paths of the different Hindu sects ... I have found that it is the same God towards Whom all are directing their steps, though along different paths." The uniqueness of Shri Ramakrishna lies in his possession of such a wide spectrum of Self-knowledge. He has become a model of religious harmony for men of diverse creeds and beliefs. He was a synthetic genius.

His birth was a historical necessity. There was great need for a prophet of religious harmony. Shri Ramakrishna laid the foundation for a new concept of universal religion based on mutual understanding, acceptance, and friendship among the followers of different religions. A great flowering of religious harmony has taken place since 1893, and that year has become a symbol for the harmony of faiths. Swami Vivekananda implemented that grand insight of his master throughout his spiritual ministry.

No religious tradition can enjoy long endurance without a powerful Noumenal support. By placing before humanity the incontrovertible evidence of Divinity that has manifested the world, he rendered a signal service to assure the people that the world is rooted in Divinity Who is Existence, Knowledge, and Bliss Absolute.

Through his direct spiritual experience in different faiths, Shri Ramakrishna has taught humanity the following principles of religious harmony:

(1)   *His famous dictum "As many faiths, so many paths to God."*
      Therefore, one single faith, however lofty, can never
      become a universal religion, or, there can never be a
      single religion for all humanity. On this coordinating
      thread he sought to string together the gems of

different religions. He may be regarded as the real founder of harmony of religions for cooperation and mutual understanding among warring faiths.

(2) *Each faith has one unique mode of living, leading to God.* This shows that each faith is distinct in its character and differences among religions are therefore real and have a definite significance in the economy of enriching divine life.

(3) *Religion is Realization—not talk.* The true basis of religious harmony stems from spiritual experience. "Phenomenological" views, tolerance, or social exigency cannot be the real and enduring way of understanding different religions.

(4) *None is capable of knowing God in all His dimensions unless one experiences the Truth by practicing other faiths.* This is illustrated by Shri Ramakrishna's famous parables of the chameleon and the blind men's report about the elephant. Collective life has been enriched through his unique contribution. The spiritual seeker is highly benefited by such a variety of experiences, without forsaking his own.

Shri Ramakrishna's special contribution to the harmony of religions has been highlighted by Arnold Toynbee, a great historian-philosopher of the modern age: "Sri Ramakrishna's message was unique in being expressed in action. The message itself was the perennial message of Hinduism ... In the Hindu view, each of the higher religions is a true vision and a right way, and all of them alike are indispensable to mankind, because each gives a different glimpse of the same truth, and each leads by a different route to the same goal of human endeavors. Each, therefore, has a special value of its own which is not to be found in any of the others. To know this is good, but it is not enough.

"Religion is not just a matter for study; it is something that has to be experienced and to be lived, and this is the field in which Sri Ramakrishna manifested his uniqueness. He practiced successively almost every form of Indian religion and philosophy, and he went on to practice Islam and Christianity as well. His religious activity and experience were, in fact, comprehensive to a degree that had, perhaps, never before been attained by any other religious genius, in India or elsewhere. His devotion to God in the personal form of the Great Mother did not prevent him from attaining the state of 'contentless consciousness'—an absolute union with absolute spiritual Reality" (Arnold J. Toynbee, in foreword to Swami Ghanananda, *Sri Ramakrishna and His Unique Message* [London: Ramakrishna Vedanta Centre, 3rd ed., 1970], vii-ix).

The life of Ramakrishna is itself a blessing to humanity. He looked upon human beings as the children of God. To Ramakrishna, man is divine. This image of man is very helpful. Man's idea of man is very vital for the growth of civilization and its continuity—"The same Greek idea of man, which accounts for the Greek civilization's rise and culmination, is also the explanation of its strange and tragic fate. Hellenism was betrayed by what was false within it" (Arnold J. Toynbee, *The Ancient Mediterranean View of Man*, 3-4).

All his life, Ramakrishna lived an exemplary pure life. Purity itself is extremely beneficial for the spiritual motivation of humanity, as it is a great source of inspiration for living a higher spiritual life. Children of light in all ages never come with the bag of dollars to give to the poor people and make them happy. They have invariably given to humanity precious bread for living by their simple, exalted, illumined lives.

Bertrand Russell in his *Principles of Social Reconstruction* says, "The power of thought in the long run is greater than any other human power." In all great epochs of history, such greatly illumined souls who move men, move the world, for absolute peace and security. "The only real revolution is in the enlightenment of the mind and the improvement of character; the only real emancipation is individual and the only real revolutionists are philosophers and saints" (Will and

Ariel Durant, *The Lessons of History*, [New York: Simon and Schuster, 1968], 72).

Hegel says, "The great man of the age is one who can put into words the will of his age, tell his age what its will is, and accomplish it. What he does is the heart and essence of his age; he actualizes his age" (E. H. Carr, *What is History?* 48).

Albert Einstein says, "I am absolutely convinced that no wealth in the world can help humanity forward, even in the hands of the most devoted worker in this cause. The example of great and pure characters is the only thing that can produce fine ideas and noble deeds. Money only appeals to selfishness and always tempts its owner irresistibly to abuse it" (*The Great Scientist*).

Pitirim A. Sorokin says, "If we ask ourselves what kind of individuals have been most influential in human history, the answer is the person like Lao-tse, Confucius, Buddha, Zoroaster, Mahavira, Moses, Jesus, St. Paul, St. Francis of Assisi, Mahatma Gandhi, and other creators and leaders of altruistic religions and morality ... In contrast to the short-lived, and often destructive influences of the autocratic monarchs, military conquerors, revolutionary dictators, and potentates of wealth, the great apostles of love have most tangibly affected the lives, minds, and bodies of untold billions during the millennia of history, and still affect us." The spirit of this excerpt can be found out in Toynbee's writings in *Civilization on Trial and the World and the West* (New York: Meridian Books, Inc., 1958), 141.

Toynbee further says, "Sri Ramakrishna made his appearance and delivered his message at the time and the place at which he and his message were needed. This message could hardly have been delivered by anyone who had not been brought up in the Hindu religious tradition. Sri Ramakrishna was born in Bengal in 1836. He was born into a world that, in his lifetime, was, for the first time, being united on a literally worldwide scale. Today we are still living in this transitional chapter of the world's history, but it is already becoming clear that a chapter which had a Western beginning will have to have an Indian ending if it is not to end in the self-destruction of the human race. In the present age, the world has been united on the material plane by Western technology. But this Western skill has not only 'annihilated distance'; it has armed the peoples of the world with weapons of devastating power at a time when they have been brought to point-blank range of each other without yet having learnt how to know and love each other. At this supremely dangerous moment in human history, the only way of salvation for mankind is an Indian way. The Emperor Ashoka's and the Mahatma Gandhi's principle of nonviolence and Sri Ramakrishna's testimony to the harmony of religions: here we have the attitude and the spirit that can make it possible for the human race to grow together into a single family—and, in the Atomic Age, this is the only alternative to destroying ourselves ... The survival of the human race is at stake. Yet even the strongest and the most respectable utilitarian motive is only a secondary reason for taking Ramakrishna's and Gandhi's and Ashoka's teaching to heart and acting on it. The primary reason is that this teaching is right—and is right because it flows from a true vision of spiritual reality" (A. J. Toynbee, in foreword to Swami Ghanananda, *Sri Ramakrishna and His Unique Message*, vii-ix).

ELEVATION OF THE STATUS OF WOMEN:
A TRUE PICTURE OF WOMAN
MOTHERHOOD OF GOD

Shri Ramakrishna regarded and addressed the personal God (God with name, form and attributes) as Divine Mother whose power has manifested the universe. She, the Power (Sakti) of the Absolute, is identified with the personal God of Vedanta, and is not a mere female counterpart of a male deity. Shri Ramakrishna's Mother Kali was his beloved loving and gentle Mother. She is the blissful Mother of the universe, the principle of Sakti, the very genesis and power behind existence.

She is the dynamic aspect of the Godhead. She is not an inert deity but is in the form of a luminous sea of Consciousness, which with its surging waves, invades and saturates everything. She is not merely a living presence, but the living, loving, blissful Mother Herself, All-Consciousness, with hands that offer boons and freedom from fear. Shri Ramakrishna spelt out the "Great Revelation" of the new religion of Vedanta: "Mother has become everything."

This is the new gospel that evokes our longing for spiritual life. God is neither in heaven, nor is the world illusory—commonly understood as maya. "God is everything." Swami Vivekananda says: "This is the central message of the Master's Mother-worship"—a message which was destined to rejuvenate the sensate culture of the day and bring a resurrection of spirit everywhere. "Light comes to individuals through the conscious efforts of their intellect; it comes slowly though, to the whole race through unconscious percolations. The philosophers show the volitional struggles of great minds; history reveals the silent process of permeation through which truth is absorbed by the masses" (*The Complete Works of Swami Vivekananda* [Calcutta: Advaita Ashrama, 1972], IV, 258).

Swami Vivekananda also says, "At the present time God should be worshipped as 'Mother,' the Infinite Energy. This will lead to purity, and tremendous energy will come here in America. Here no temples weigh us down, no one suffers as they do in poorer countries. Woman has suffered for aeons, and that has given her infinite patience and infinite perseverance. She holds on to an idea. It is this which makes her the support of even superstitious religions and of the priests in every land, and it is this that will free her. We have to become Vedantists and live this grand thought; the masses must get it, and only in free America can this be done. In India these ideas were brought out by individuals like Buddha, Sankara, and others, but the masses did not retain them. The new cycle must see the masses living Vedanta, and this will have to come through women" (*C. W.*, VII, 95).

RESURRECTION OF MOTHER POWER

Shri Ramakrishna, by worshipping God as feminine, experienced the Truth that She is a living presence in all women regardless of their status in society, and equated womanhood with motherhood. His attitude and behavior toward women has infinite significance in modern life nurtured in a sensate culture. This exalted place of womanhood as a symbol of Divine Motherhood can be very useful in finding a workable solution to the problems in our individual and social life. Women's place will be immensely elevated in the estimation of man and a new dignity will be given to woman herself. Social life will be ennobled, giving us a new, healthy perspective to deal with crucial problems of our world. The emancipation and rise of women, awakened by the new idea of their being imbued by the spiritual vision of life, will bring forth a new element of cohesive force in the emerging social structure, balancing the inadequacies of the existing patriarchal system.

In Shri Ramakrishna's life of spiritual practices we find a unique combination and unification of innumerable spiritual experiences and realizations. He was the living embodiment of almost all types of spiritual realizations—a fact that established him as a universal man. He himself was a "Parliament of Religions." His unique life was the real ground of the reconciliation of all the different creeds and spiritual paths. Sri Aurobindo has said, "Sri Ramakrishna represents a synthesis, in one person, of all the leaders. It follows that the movements of his age will unify and organize the more provincial and fragmentary movements of the past. Ramakrishna Paramahamsa is the epitome of the whole. His was the great superconscious life, which alone can witness to the infinitude of the current that bears us all oceanwards. He is the proof of the power behind us and of the future before us. So great a birth initiates great happenings." He was really an "Epoch-Maker."

SWAMI VIVEKANANDA: WORLD TEACHER

Swami Vivekananda, the prophet of the age, or "the pilot and guide to the needs of the age," as Romain Rolland says, was the chief disciple of Shri Ramakrishna. Under his direction he struggled hard and experienced the highest Truth of Advaita Vedanta—Unity of Existence, or, oneness of matter and energy—the ultimate oneness of God, man, and nature. He assimilated it in his great character at a very young age. Shri Ramakrishna also transmitted his power to Swami Vivekananda and commanded him to teach the world and serve people as God. Swami Vivekananda's deep and vast secular knowledge of East and West, his extensive travel in India as an itinerant monk, his massive intellect, his pure character, his great heart and, above all, his unitary vision based on his spiritual experience, made him a rare class of world teacher.

Shri Ramakrishna's mandate was urging Swami Vivekananda to fulfill his mission. He was sent abroad by the expanding spiritual consciousness of India in its wholeness through his disciples in Madras: "To their unbounded faith, it never occurred that they (the disciples) were demanding what was, humanly speaking, impossible. They thought that Vivekananda had only to appear and he would be given his chance. The Swami himself was as simple in the ways of the world as these his disciples; and when he was once sure that he was divinely called to make the attempt, he could see no difficulties in the way. Nothing could have been more typical of the unorganisedness of Hinduism itself than this going forth of its representative unannounced, and without formal credentials, to enter the strongly-guarded doors of the world's wealth and power" (Sister Nivedita, in *The Life of Swami Vivekananda* by His Eastern and Western Disciples [Calcutta: Advaita Ashrama, 1974], 294).

Swami Vivekananda actually came to teach the West how to spiritualize its material culture and enjoy peace and enlightenment. Four years later, on July 9, 1897—close to the anniversary of his arrival in America—Swamiji was to write from Almora to Miss Mary Hale: "I had to work till I am at death's door and had to spend nearly the whole of that energy in America, so that the Americans may learn to be broader and more spiritual" (*C. W.*, V, 135). That is why he decided to attend the Parliament of Religions. Before embarking for the United States of America, Swami Vivekananda said to Swami Turiyananda: "The Parliament of Religions is being organized for this [striking his own chest] alone. My mind tells me you will see it verified in the not-so-distant future."

On May 31, 1893 Swami Vivekananda took the ship *Peninsular* at Bombay and visited Sri Lanka, Penang, Singapore, Hong Kong, Nagasaki, Kobe, Yokohama, Osaka, Kyoto and Tokyo. On July 14, 1893, he embarked from Yokohama for Vancouver, Canada on the 6,000-ton Canadian Pacific Line steamship, *Empress of India. The Empress* docked at Vancouver on Tuesday, July 25 at 7:00 P.M. Swamiji's friends gave him only light summer clothing and he suffered terribly from the cold of the Pacific. The next morning, Swamiji took the train and traveled through the scenic Canadian southwest, reaching Winnipeg on Friday night, July 28. There, he transferred to another train that carried him into the United States, to the city of St. Paul, Minnesota. A third train took him the last four hundred miles to Chicago, which he reached, most probably, on July 30.

On that part of his journey, Swamiji met "this Providential woman," Miss Kate Sanborn, a leading American poet, humorist, author, and lecturer. Her father, a learned professor, entertained many guests and she had met many talented and great thinkers of her day. She described the encounter with Swami Vivekananda: "I had met him in the observation car of the Canadian Pacific where even the gigantically grand scenery of mountains, canyons, glaciers, and the Great Divide could not take my eyes entirely from the cosmopolitan travellers, all en route for Chicago ... I talked with all ... I alluded to the

distinguished men and women in Boston and the vicinity who
were frequently my guests ... But most of all was I impressed
by the monk ... He spoke better English than I did, was
conversant with ancient and modern literature, would quote
easily and naturally from Shakespeare or Longfellow or
Tennyson, Darwin, Müller, Tyndall; could repeat pages of our
Bible, was familiar with and tolerant of all creeds. He was an
education, an illumination, a revelation! I told him, as we
separated, I should be most pleased to present him to some
men and women of learning and general culture, if by chance
he should come to Boston" (*Western Women in the Footsteps of
Swami Vivekananda*, Pravrajika Atmaprana, ed. [New Delhi:
Ramakrishna Sarada Mission, 1995], 8-9).

Swami arrived in Chicago and received several shocks
all at once. From the vast serenity of India he was now plunged
into the excited mood of the Fair and the exuberance of the
American way of life. "Burdened with unaccustomed
possessions, not knowing where to go, conspicuous because
of his strange attire, annoyed by the lads who ran after him in
amusement, weary and confused by the exorbitant charges of
the porters, bewildered by the crowds, chiefly visitors to and
from the World's Fair, he sought a hotel. When the porters
had brought his luggage and he was at last alone and free
from interruptions, he sat down amidst his trunks and satchels
and tried to calm his mind" (*The Life of Swami Vivekananda*, by
His Eastern and Western Disciples [Calcutta: Advaita Ashrama,
1974], 292). Another shock was his discovery that the
authorities of the Parliament of Religions required all its
delegates to produce credentials—of which he had none.
Wisdom had bade him stay at a first-class hotel to begin with,
at three dollars or more a night, and he realized his small
finances could never carry him through the cold American
winter at the rate of about five dollars a day, on which he was
surviving.

The depressed national economy and widespread
unemployment of that spring had caused a general panic, and

therefore, generosity was scarce in the people—a stark contrast to the broadcasting of glad industrial news at the Exposition. Though he was never altogether without the acquaintance of "people belonging to the highest Chicago society," he realized that he would have to remain alone and without financial support for the five weeks before the opening of the Parliament. As Swami Vivekananda wrote in a letter to India, "They were so very kind to me, but here they want to make much of foreigners, [just] for a fun and no farther. When it comes to their pocket, they all almost step back, and this is such a bad year here, commercial failures everywhere." So, he "took [his] departure forthwith and came to Boston" from Chicago after having spent twelve days or so at the World's Fair. The Wonder of India, poked and stared at with impertinent curiosity, having seen the "wonders" of the Exposition, left disheartened, for Boston and a lower cost of living.

His visit to Boston was providential. He sent a telegram to inform Miss Kate Sanborn that he had arrived and was at Quincy House awaiting her orders. She asked him to come that very same day to "Breezy Meadows," her home near Boston. He was invited to address a local, women's club. Soon after, Miss Sanborn introduced him to Professor John Henry Wright, a distinguished professor of Greek at Harvard University. After a four-hour conversation with Swami Vivekananda, Professor Wright recognized his extraordinary talent and genius; he gave him the much-needed credentials to become an official delegate to the Parliament of Religions. Earlier, the Professor's response to Swamiji's remark about his lack of such credentials was: "To ask you, Swami, for your credentials is like asking the sun to state its right to shine!" In his letter of introduction the Professor wrote, "Here is a man who is more learned than all our learned professors put together." Professor Wright then kindly presented Swamiji with the railway ticket to Chicago and additional letters of introduction to the committees responsible for housing and provisions for the Oriental delegates.

Swamiji came to Chicago, but his trials were not over. He had misplaced the address of the Chairman of the Parliament Committee. Language difficulty stood in his way and he again failed to get any clues from the people in that predominantly German quarter of the city, for they could not understand his accent. Tired and exhausted, he spent the night in the railroad freight yard, sleeping in an empty boxcar. In the morning, he ventured forth onto Lake Shore Drive, the winding length of which was populated by millionaires and powerful business-men. Relying with faith on his sannyasin tradition, he went door-to-door for food, asking for directions to the Parliament Committee. He received only rude talk and insults from servants who opened the doors at the homes of the wealthy. Exhausted by hunger and anxiety, he sat down at the steps of a church and resigned himself to God. A refined soul was watching him through a window across the street. She came to him with regal bearing—and providential relief: "Sir, you seem to be in some trouble; are you a delegate to the Parliament of Religions? Can I be of any help to you?" She was the noble lady, Mrs. Mary W. Hale. She took him to her house and refreshed his spirit by offering him a bath and breakfast. She then conducted him to the Parliament and secured his admission as a delegate.

The year 1893 found the United States of America undergoing much economic suffering. The financial crisis had led to industrial chaos, culminating in many bank failures, in 23,000 miles of railway being passed under receivership, and many other hardships. Chicago, the greatest railway center in the United States and rated second in U.S. population, manufacturing and commerce, was in the grip of a severe financial crisis, due to various economic and political reasons. Swami Vivekananda's letter to Alasinga, dated the 20th of August 1893, may be read to get a hint. The Parliament of Religions was held in the midst of agitation, confusion, and disturbance.

The Parliament of Religions was really a part of the World's Columbian Exposition held at Chicago to celebrate

the fourth centenary (1493-1893) of the discovery of America
by Christopher Columbus. As a part of the Exposition, twenty
different congresses met between May 15 and October 28,
1893. The favored topics of the day were represented at these
congresses. Among them were law reform, commerce and
finance, economic science, women's progress, the public press,
medicine and surgery, temperance, music, and "Sunday rest."
Thus, the entire range of human achievements was covered.

     Surprisingly, the religious congress—the Parliament of
Religions—stole a march over the others and aroused universal
interest from the very beginning. In the words of Reverend
John Henry Barrows, "No one gathering ever assembled was
awaited with such universal interest." For the most part,
Protestant Christians dominated the Parliament delegation,
but all Christian sects were represented, and among them,
some were broad-minded and welcomed Swamiji's message.
The most expansive Christian view came from Reverend E. L.
Rexford of Boston, who stated in the course of his paper: "And
the great religious teachers and founders of the world ... have
lived and taught and suffered and died and risen again, that
they might bring us ... to God. 'God-Consciousness,' to borrow
a noble word from Calcutta, has been the goal of them all"
(Marie Louise Burke, *Swami Vivekananda in the West: New
Discoveries, His Prophetic Mission* [Calcutta: Advaita Ashrama,
1983], vol. 1, 120).

     Burke perceptively observes that despite "whatever the
divine motives may have been, the human motives lying behind
the organization were mixed... . never before had the
representatives of the world's great religions been brought
together in one place ... It was an unparalleled meeting, and
when first proposed in that day of intolerance and materialism
it seemed to many impossible of human achievement... .
Swamiji later wrote in a letter: "The Parliament of Religions
was organized with the intention of proving the superiority of
the Christian religion'." Burke makes the same observation,
pointing out that "a reading of the accounts of both the

preparations and the proceedings leaves one without a doubt that the Parliament was permeated with Christian prejudice. That Christianity would gloriously and unequivocally prove its superiority was a foregone conclusion in the minds of many of its promoters" (Burke, *Swami Vivekananda in the West*, vol. 1, 67-68).

Moreover, Burke informs us that "up until the very last day of the Parliament, the Hall of Columbus rang with such pronouncements as: 'Christianity is absolutely superior in its motive power, its purifying influence and its uplifting inspiration from any and all other religions with which it comes in competition. The greasy bull of Madura and Tanjore has little in common with the Lamb of God who taketh away the sins of the world,' or, 'The attitude ... of Christianity towards religions other than itself is an attitude of universal, absolute, eternal, unappeasable hostility; while toward all men everywhere, the adherents of false religions by no means excepted, its attitude is an attitude of grace, mercy, peace, for whosoever will.' That is, for whosoever will become a Christian... . papers [at the Parliament], indicative of a broad and liberal outlook, were rare" (Burke, *Swami Vivekananda in the West*, vol. 1, 119-120).

Thus—although the main objective of the Exposition had been to exhibit material prosperity and the progress of science and technology, and obviously, to highlight the material prosperity of the West—to their surprise, through Swamiji's presence at the Parliament, the doors to interfaith dialogue and sharing the views of others were opened, and the Parliament actually became the prominent event of the World's Columbian Exposition.

The Chicago Parliament was also the occasion when America came to know about India: "The United States recognized in some official way the existence of India, for the first time, at the Columbian Exposition opened in Chicago in 1893" (Dale Reipe, *The Philosophy of India and Its Impact on American Thought* [Illinois: Charles C. Thomas, 1970], 73).

WESTERN MOOD

Despite the façade of agnosticism and indifference towards religion, it was generally believed that "faith in a Divine Power ... has been like the sun, a light-giving and fructifying potency in man's intellectual and moral development." Therefore, the religious congress gained much attention. Time was quite appropriate for having an open-minded dialogue between the East and the West and, also, between science and religion. Really speaking, the United States of America and the entire western world were at the crossroads. As Burke writes, "There was without question a sincere and open-minded search in America for spiritual truth and an eagerness to welcome it wherever it might be found. But while this need existed, a truly liberal attitude could not, in those days, obtain acceptance among the clergy or the public as a whole. Ironically, however, the Parliament, which could be convened only through a spirit of Christian evangelism, became in spite of itself an instrument for the destruction of bigotry" (Burke, *Swami Vivekananda in the West*, vol. 1, 74).

America was the youngest nation, free from Colonial rule and endowed with a secular Constitution. America was prosperous, liberal-minded, inquisitive, free from the stronghold of traditional Christian culture, and bubbling with youthful zest. A section of the people was desperately searching for the bread of life that could satisfy their intellect, inspire their heart and fulfill their spiritual hunger. Swamiji was the right person at the right time to offer them the right philosophy of life. Swamiji, the true ambassador of the ancient spiritual culture of India, met the fresh, youthful mind of America: "Such was the psychological area, such the sea of mind, young, tumultuous, overflowing with its own energy and self-assurance, yet inquisitive and alert withal, which confronted Vivekananda when he rose to speak. Behind him, on the contrary, lay an ocean, calm with long ages of spiritual development.... These, then, were the two mind-floods, two immense rivers of thought, as it were, Eastern and modern, of which the yellow-clad wanderer on the platform of the Parliament of Religions formed for a moment the point of confluence" (*C. W.*, I, Introduction, xi). He made an astounding impact, as no one of his spiritual eminence had ever before appeared in America. As Burke points out, "Never before had the people of America seen one in whom spiritual truths had been fully realized" (Burke, *Swami Vivekananda in the West*, vol. 1, 101).

Here may be told what Swamiji afterwards thought about the rich potentiality of the American culture. People were ready for his teaching about a new image of man as potentially Divine, a new conception of *experiencing* the truth of religion, a new moral philosophy based upon the concept of Brahman, which manifests, permeates, interpenetrates, and controls the entire Creation—visible and invisible—and again transcends everything! They were ready for Swami Vivekananda's teachings that the One Supreme Being (Brahman or Impersonal God) is the Soul of all souls; that the human being is a combination of matter, mind, life, reason, ego, and Atman; that man is a unity or synthesis of all these; that the individual soul is only an "abridged edition," as it were, of Brahman. True religion, Swamiji said, proclaims the identity of the individual soul and the Supreme Soul in their pure, essential nature as Pure Consciousness. The unity and divinity of all souls forms the raison d'être of all ethics and morality. Spiritual unity is all-embracing. When we recognize Truth, we establish a spiritual relationship with all. This is the real foundation of moral laws and is not based on fear, or, mere belief. The eternally pure, ever free, and Immortal Atman is an inseparable part of Brahman. The impulse of ethics and morality comes from within when we are spiritually awakened to realize the world of multiplicity as the manifestation of One Supreme Divine addressed in many names.

Swamiji's ideal was to preach unto mankind their inherent and inalienable divinity and Swamiji exhorted us to make that a supreme fact manifesting in every breath of our life. Moral life is closest to spiritual life. Swamiji made the doctrine of the "Divinity of Man" the main pivot from which all excellencies of life will emerge. Hence, Swamiji in modern times created a new concept of ethics having universal relevance. This is a universal moral philosophy giving a unitary vision of life and a new concept of religious harmony as spelled out by Shri Ramakrishna, the Great Prophet of religious harmony. The main emphasis of Swamiji's message was to provide a viable philosophy of life that, at once, is intellectually satisfying, emotionally inspiring, and spiritually fulfilling. To Swamiji, the American climate is the real climate, where freedom of thought and prosperity of life will give infinite scope to actualize human potentialities. Swamiji spoke eloquently about this in his inspired talks at Thousand Island Park (C. W., VII, 95).

Swami Vivekananda's opening speech at the historic Parliament of Religions on the eleventh of September 1893 was his truly first public lecture to a large assembly—the Hall of Columbus had a seating capacity of 4,000 and it was filled with 7,000 persons. Swamiji spoke only five words—"*Sisters and Brothers of America!*" and history was created. At that supreme moment of spontaneous fraternity he took the Parliament by storm. Behind these electrifying words was the power of his illumined self that quickened and transformed others. Shri Ramakrishna's prophecy, "Naren [Swamiji] shall shake the world to its foundations," was fulfilled. Burke elaborates on this: "His entrance onto the scene of the West was dramatic and impressive. Through hindsight it almost seems to have been planned by a master planner in response to the profound need of the age" (*Prabuddha Bharata* [Calcutta: Advaita Ashrama, March 1979], Burke, "Science, Religion, and Swami Vivekananda—I," 95).

His speech, to quote Romain Rolland, "was like a tongue of flame. Hardly had he pronounced the very simple opening words: 'Sisters and Brothers of America!...' than hundreds arose in their seats and applauded." The subsequent words that followed were like a cool, soothing breeze in the dry summer or like rainwater upon a parched earth. It was a brief speech but it touched the hearts of an audience haunted by fear, prejudice and sin. He literally gave a spiritual jolt to the people. "Among the grey wastes of cold dissertations it fired the souls of the listening throng," Romain Rolland says.

India, entire and ancient, teems with gods, yet these but form the unbroken chain of the varied expressions of one God. Swami Vivekananda realized that one spiritual unity pervades and unites in itself all races, all religions, the east and the west, the north and the south, all life and all actions, and that this spiritual unity is eternally creative in all periods of time. When, prior to 1894, his extraordinary pilgrimage over the whole of the continent of India came to a pause in Kanyakumari, Swami Vivekananda had not only become the "conscience of India," he had become the embodiment of the unity of the entire humanity. Romain Rolland describes Swamiji's unity with all as "world unity as well; and unity of action and reason, love and work, unity of a hundred races of India with their hundred different tongues and hundred thousand Gods, springing from the same religious centre, the core of the present and future reconstruction. Unity of a thousand sects of Hinduism. Unity within the vast ocean of all religious thought and all rivers past and present, western and eastern" (Romain Rolland, *The Life and Gospel of Vivekananda* [Calcutta: Advaita Ashrama, 1979], 287).

Swamiji's three-minute extempore speech in response to his welcome mesmerized the audience because as Nivedita says, "it was the religious consciousness of India that spoke through Swamiji, the message of his whole people as determined by their whole past." Or, it was Shri Ramakrishna, who spoke through him.

In that very opening speech, he gave the main theme of his message, which was the unity of religions: "We believe not only in universal toleration, but we accept all religions as true

... Sectarianism, bigotry, and its horrible descendant, fanaticism have ... destroyed civilization and sent whole nations to despair ... But their time is come; and I fervently hope that the bell that tolled ... in honour of this convention may be the death-knell of all fanaticism, of all persecutions with the sword or with the pen, and of all uncharitable feelings between persons wending their way to the same goal" (*C. W.*, I, 3-4).

This idea was hammered with a parable in his second talk, highlighting the religious and ethnic bigotry that is responsible for a narrow outlook. In this address he called the Parliament a "great attempt ... to break down the barriers of this little world of ours." Speaking first against bigotry and exclusiveness he boldly opened the door to interreligious dialogue and sharing. All his addresses had one recurrent theme, "the universality of religious truth, a dangerous topic in communities which still clung to a rigid Christian fundamentalism," according to Christopher Isherwood.

But it was his third talk on September 19 that is regarded as his main address on Vedanta. He had been entered in the official records at the Parliament as a representative of Hinduism and he belonged to the Hindu community. The assembly expected him to talk on Hinduism as it had always been talked about, but his unforeseen message brilliantly transcended all the categories of the richly diverse religion of which he was now the modern representative. Sister Nivedita says that "when he began to speak, it was of 'the religious ideas of the Hindus,' but when he ended, Hinduism had been created" (*C. W.*, I, x). Burke observes, "perhaps in that moment not only was Hinduism created but a new religion for the world was given its first enunciation." She gives it the name of Universal Religion, "a living religion springing from the very soul of humanity itself."

The voices of all religions spoke in his one voice in a new revelation: "From the high spiritual flights of the Vedanta philosophy of which the latest discoveries of science seem like echoes, to the low ideas of idolatry with its multifarious mythology, the agnosticism of the Buddhists and the atheism of the Jains, each and all has a place in the Hindu's religion" (*C. W.*, I, 6). Swami Vivekananda never mentioned the different rituals and beliefs of any of its many sects, but went straight to his point and said that experience was superior to learning, which he properly understood to be an aid to realization: "the whole religion of the Hindu is centred in realization." Towards the end of his address he said, "If there is ever to be a universal religion, it must be one which will have no location in place or time, which will be infinite like the God it will preach, and whose sun will shine upon the followers of Krishna and of Christ, on saints and sinners alike."

This brilliant talk was a written paper on Hinduism, with a well-planned foundation for his entire message in the West, and he delivered it in a succinct manner. It highlighted the infinite capacity of the vigorous, all-inclusive religion of Hinduism, with its tremendous capacity to absorb and assimilate the various sects that arose from ancient days. He erased the common misconceptions about Hinduism's vast inclusive pantheon by explaining the role of imagery in the spiritual approach to the Divine. He spoke of the happy relationship between Hinduism and science, which is again due to Hinduism's inherent capacity of inclusiveness. His every fiery word was a demonstration of the parallel between religion and science. An epoch maker he became, recognizing the importance of both to the future foundation of the entire human society. Both science and religion seek rigorously through a spirit of enquiry the same goal of unity or Truth.

In this memorable paper, Swamiji introduced the essence of Advaita Vedanta: the immortality, infinity, immutability of the Soul which is Divine; the perfection of the apparent Self which is "non-created"; the law of Karma and its corollary, reincarnation, that pertains to the individual soul; the truth of harmony between religion and science; and the fact that "art, science, and religion are but three different ways of expressing a single Truth." He emphasized the need for spiritual strength to attain the inherent purity of mind that brings the grace of God for final emancipation from bondage and the attainment of eternal peace. He also discussed the obsession of the western mind with sin and punishment, and attributed it to the non-scientific acceptance of theories of religion without a serious search for Truth in inner life through intense spiritual struggle. With powerful grace, he set forth the main thrust of his message: humanity has limitless opportunities for self-realization; immense possibilities are inherent in the human soul. In so many ways, he presented his message of religious harmony.

In his incisive fourth address, his lone voice nobly and bravely tolled against the insufficiency of the Christian missionary work in the East, its neglect and exploitation of the poorer nations: "You Christians, who are so fond of sending out missionaries to save the soul of the heathen—why do you not try to save their bodies from starvation?" In the fifth address he spoke of the relationship of Buddhism and Hinduism, for "Hinduism cannot live without Buddhism, nor Buddhism without Hinduism." They are mutually fulfilling: "Let us then join the wonderful intellect of the Brahmin with the heart, the noble soul, the wonderful humanizing power of the Great Master."

He spoke very specifically about the need for integrating into one's own religion the best elements of other religions. He did this at the final session of the Parliament: "The Christian is not to become a Hindu or a Buddhist, nor a Hindu or a Buddhist to become a Christian. But each must assimilate the spirit of the others and yet preserve his individuality and grow according to his own law of growth." Proclaiming religious harmony in many ways, he showed again and again that the various religions were but different expressions of one eternal universal religion. He felt it was the duty of the Parliament of Religions to "proclaim to all quarters of the globe that the Lord is in every religion." Incisive and unforgettable are his

words: "Upon the banner of every religion will soon be written
... Help and not Fight, Assimilation and not Destruction,
Harmony and Peace and not Dissension." This was his great
plea to humanity.

He spoke ten times in all at the Parliament and each
time he gave emphasis to the universal aspect of religion.
These are the main points of his talks at the Parliament: (1)
the Spiritual Unity of Existence, i.e., one Divine Principle
dwells in all hearts and that Principle has manifested as the
whole universe; (2) the Universality of Truth; (3) the Divinity
of the human spirit as the main radiating source of all spiritual
values, ethics and morality; (4) the Harmony of Religions, i.e.,
the purpose of religion is to find and realize the infinite divinity
underlying all apparent religious differences—religion is
realization, not talk; (5) the Truth that spiritual realization
can be attained in our life; (6) the law of Karma and its
corollary, the doctrine of reincarnation, i.e., inequality in life
is due to our past Karma.

HOW SWAMIJI WAS RECEIVED

About the impact of his personality, Burke points out that
"the spiritual status of Vivekananda was such that he could
not live among men without altering, enriching and
illuminating the very texture of world thought." Her six
volumes on his life in the West are replete with excerpts from
U.S. newspapers describing his "most fascinating personality,"
his "penetrating eye," and his capacity to be "master of his
situation" (*Chicago Advocate*, September 28, 1893). Further she
says, "it is undeniable that the American people had not been
merely intellectually impressed by the nobility and the wisdom
of the eastern doctrines ... but had been touched by and had
responded to the tremendous power of living spirituality that
Swamiji embodied." In another context Burke writes, "when
a Prophet of the stature of Vivekananda inaugurates a work
on the visible level, a tremendous creative current is set in

motion at deeper and more subtle levels, which nothing can stop from becoming a historic force."

When an illumined soul of Swami Vivekananda's stature speaks from his heart the audience is totally captivated, uplifted, and gets a foretaste of blissful life. The reception Swamiji received began with several minutes of hearty spontaneous applause and when his first address was over, Mrs. S. K. Blodgett "saw scores of women walking over the benches to get near him," and said to herself, "Well, my lad, if you can resist that onslaught you are indeed a God." But though, in the words of Burke, he was adored for his "towering spiritual eminence," he ever yearned for his solitary wandering mendicant's life.

Harriet Monroe, who first published Tagore's poems in the United States some twenty years after the Parliament, wrote of that first address in her autobiography: "The handsome monk in the orange robe gave us in perfect English a masterpiece. His personality, dominant, magnetic, his voice rich as a bronze bell, the controlled fervor of his feeling, the beauty of his message, to the Western world he was facing for the first time—these combined to give us a rare and perfect moment of supreme emotion. It was human eloquence at its highest pitch." And, presiding over the Scientific Section of the Parliament, Merwin-Marie Snell gave testimony that Swamiji was "by far the most important and typical representative of Hinduism ... in fact was beyond question the most popular and influential man in the Parliament ... [who] on all occasions ... was received with greater enthusiasm than any other speaker, Christian or 'Pagan'."

The *New York Herald* proclaimed, "He is undoubtedly the greatest figure in the Parliament of Religions. After hearing him we feel how foolish it is to send missionaries to this learned nation." The *Boston Evening Transcript* heralded that "Vivekananda's address before the Parliament was broad as the heaven above us, embracing the best in all religions, as the ultimate universal religion—charity to all mankind and good works for the love of God, not for fear of punishment or hope of reward. He is a great favourite of the Parliament.... If he merely crosses the platform he is applauded.... At the Parliament of Religions they used to keep Vivekananda until the end of the programme to make people stay till the end of the session.... The four thousand fanning people in the Hall of Columbus would sit smiling and expectant waiting for an hour or two to listen to Vivekananda for fifteen minutes. The Chairman knew the old rule of keeping the best until the last" ("What They Said of Swamiji and His Speeches at the Parliament of Religions, Chicago," *Prabuddha Bharata*, September 1993, 430).

Christopher Isherwood has said that, for the West, Swami Vivekananda's presence was inspiring and convincing beyond the power of any book because he was the example of a life solely dedicated to the practice of Vedanta and enlivened by the very breath of Shri Ramakrishna. Never did he mention his Master in any of his talks at the Parliament, but Shri Ramakrishna, together with the deep and haunting sorrow of his own suffering and humiliated people, graced Swamiji with an eloquence to speak on Vedanta and the glory of its eternal message from India. Swamiji was convinced of the power of Vedanta practiced in daily living to redeem people from their misfortune and misery. His eloquence, born of conviction and deep feeling, was his power in the Parliament. Even though Reverend Barrows and the orthodox Christians felt that Swamiji was an infidel in the Christian-dominated Parliament, it is undeniable and true that in Swamiji's comprehensive message the old conflicts between science and religion, reason and faith, the secular and the sacred, the modern and the ancient, the East and the West, were satisfactorily resolved.

Basically, Swamiji presented Vedanta philosophy, which can be understood by rational-minded people having a scientific temperament. His presentation was completely free from the academic accent of a teacher of philosophy. Eschewing the orthodox vocabularies of the so-called scholars—his message was not just an echo of the great Sankara's philosophical analysis that gives tremendous emphasis to Nirguna Brahman. He was lucid, understandable to the common man, very practical in his approach to our daily life, and touched the hearts of the listeners. He was a man of great spiritual experience. His own conviction of Truth, not his scholarship, was articulated through his simple language, touching the essence of Vedanta, free from scholastic jargon. It can be called humanistic Vedanta, geared to uplift human life to the highest truth through gradual transformation of life.

Swami Vivekananda actually gave a completely new interpretation of Vedanta than was known, up to that time, to the Indian people. His passion for universalism and his great love for the people helped him to formulate the essence of Vedanta, thus avoiding a cold, life-negating, world-negating Monism. Universal religion for a new humanity found a new dimension, a new meaning of Advaita Vedanta in all his talks. Burke attests to this: "Never before Swamiji's time had the term [Vedanta] been given such universal significance as he gave it. Never before had it been broadened into a philosophy and religion which included every faith of the world and every noble effort of man—reconciling spirituality and material advancement, faith and reason, science and mysticism, work and contemplation, service to man and absorption in God. Never before had it been conceived as the one universal religion, by accepting the principles of which the follower of any or no creed could continue along his own path and at the same time be able to identify himself with every other creed and aspect of religion" (Burke, *Swami Vivekananda in America: New Discoveries*, 608). Merwyn-Marie Snell, President of the Scientific Section at the Parliament, wrote a letter to the editor of *Hope* that included his impression that "Never before has so authoritative a representative of genuine Hinduism as opposed to the emasculated and Anglicized versions of it so common in these days—been accessible to American inquirers... . America thanks India for sending him, and begs her to send more like him..." (cited in *The Indian Mirror*, March 9, 1894).

The impact of Swamiji's presence in the Parliament has been assessed by Burke: "The descriptions we have of Swamiji at the Parliament of Religions show him as colorful and dynamic, dominating the scene with the force of his personality and the utter purity of his message. He was in the full vigor of his youth, ready to face the entire world and to sacrifice his life for 'the poor, the ignorant, the oppressed' of his motherland. And there was yet another reason for his phenomenal popularity. Never before had the people of America seen one in whom spiritual truths had been fully realized. Though the fact that Swamiji was such a one was not consciously known by the thousands who flocked to hear him speak, who waited interminable hours for even a few words and who applauded when he simply crossed the platform, the people through some inner knowledge unerringly recognized him for what he was, and, from start to finish, instinctively sensed that his very presence conferred a blessing. *Darshan* was unheard of in America, but here at the Parliament was a spontaneous and unconscious manifestation of the attraction of the human soul to the spiritually great" (Burke, *Swami Vivekananda in America: New Discoveries*, 67). She further adds, "It is undeniable, moreover, that the American people had not been merely intellectually impressed by the nobility and supreme wisdom of Eastern doctrines, which hitherto, in the words of Dr. Alfred Momarie, 'they had been taught to regard with contempt,' but that they had been touched by and had responded to the tremendous power of living spirituality that Swamiji embodied. Something far more important and more far-reaching had taken place than an intellectual appreciation of Eastern religions. It was as though the soul of America had long asked for spiritual sustenance and had now been answered" (Ibid., 83).

PART ONE

SWAMI VIVEKANANDA'S WORK IN AMERICA
AND THE FOUNDATION OF
THE VEDANTA SOCIETY OF NEW YORK

1

AFTER THE PARLIAMENT:
SWAMI VIVEKANANDA'S WORK IN AMERICA
BEGINS, ATTRACTING FRIENDSHIP AND
SUPPORT FOR THE MISSION OF VEDANTA

"AN ARDUOUS LECTURE TOUR"

After the Parliament of World Religions, in October 1893, Swami Vivekananda started giving lectures in and around Chicago. At this time he signed a three-year contract with the Slayton Lyceum Lecture Bureau, and leaving Chicago on November 12, 1893, he began his "arduous lecture tour" of the mid-western, southern, and eastern states. He lectured in Illinois, Indiana, Michigan, Wisconsin, Minnesota, Iowa, Tennessee, Massachusetts, New York, Maine, Maryland, and Pennsylvania. The Lecture Bureau embarrassed and cheated him shamelessly. On February 20, 1894, Swamiji wrote a letter to Mrs. Hale: "I am thoroughly disgusted with this Slayton business and am trying hard to break loose. I have lost at least $5,000 by joining this man... Through the help of Mr. Palmer ... [I] got the fraudulent contract annulled." The Lecture Bureau compelled Swamiji to pay a heavy price for the cancellation. It is most probable that he was free by the 20th of March when he was in Detroit.[1] This freedom is an important event in his post-Parliament life in America.

SWAMIJI'S EARLY INFORMAL "PARLOUR LECTURES"

From Detroit Swamiji came to New York around the first of April at the invitation of Mrs. Arthur Smith, Dr. and Mrs. Egbert Guernsey and Miss Helen Miller Gould, who were interested in Vedanta philosophy. Swamiji wrote a letter to Mrs. Hale on April 2, 1894 from the Guernsey residence at 528 Fifth Avenue, between Forty-third and Forty-fourth Streets. While staying there, he gave a few "parlour lectures."

FIRST PUBLIC LECTURES ATTRACT
SWAMIJI'S FIRST FRIENDS AND SUPPORTERS

The first public lecture is believed to have been given on Tuesday, April 24 at the Waldorf Hotel, before Mrs. Arthur Smith's "Conversation Circle."[2] He gave his second public lecture on May 2 at 19 West Thirty-eighth Street, the residence of Miss Mary A. Phillips. Miss Phillips subsequently became one of his best friends and helped his work in every possible way. Her address was Swamiji's headquarters for his work in New York. Of the many people who attended his first two lectures, the following persons were noteworthy, as they supported his work when the Vedanta Society was started later on: Miss Mary A. Phillips; Miss Emma Thursby, the celebrated singer; Mrs. Arthur Smith; Mr. Leon Landsberg, who later became Swamiji's right-hand man and one of Swamiji's first monastic disciples in the West; and Dr. and Mrs. Egbert Guernsey. Leon Landsberg was on the staff of the *New York Tribune*.

Dr. Guernsey, nearly seventy-one years old at that time, was one of New York's chief physicians. He was successful in his combined practice of homeopathic and orthodox medicine. He was a prodigious contributor to his generation as a writer, and an editor of various periodicals. In addition, he founded the *Brooklyn Daily Times*, the *New York Medical News Times* (of which he was also editor in chief), several important New York medical institutions, and the prestigious Union League Club, which exists today. It has been written and is no doubt true, that he was ... "a man of broad culture and broader experience; a man who had devoted the greater part of his active life to the alleviation of sorrow and suffering; ... a man who had acquired a universal tenderness and breadth of kindly philosophy; a man who, day and night, was at the beck and call of Anguish; ... in brief, a man who so nearly lived up to the example of the Great Master that it seems strange I am writing of him as a doctor of medicine and not of divinity."[3]

The Guernseys' parental affection and high esteem for the Prophet can be known from Dr. Guernsey's letter to Mrs. Bull, describing his impressions of Swami Vivekananda: "Swami who by his kindness of heart, great intelligence, purity and nobility of character has endeared himself to me almost like a son... The Swami from time to time has formed a part of my family for several months. Always welcome, we have all of us derived both profit and pleasure from the rich stores of a mind full of thought in which he seemed to have been able in his investigations of spiritual matters to have eliminated the discordant elements for the true and harmonious."[4]

Although in New York Swamiji spoke many times before clubs and in private homes, information is unavailable about these talks. In the letter to Mrs. Hale from New York on April 2, 1894, Swamiji wrote: "Awaiting further developments. This Thursday [April 5] they (Dr. and Mrs. Guernsey) will invite a number of the brainy people of the Union League club and other places of which the doctor is a member and see what comes out of it. Parlour lectures are a great feature in this city and more can be made by each such lecture than even platform talks in other cities."[5]

DR. GUERNSEY'S "DINNER PARTY OF CREEDS"

Dr. Guernsey was very hospitable and would introduce celebrities to New York society at his very large and handsome house on Fifth Avenue. Swamiji was a respected guest in his house and enjoyed the same freedom that he felt in Mrs. Hale's house in Chicago and in the house of Mrs. John J. Bagley (the wife of the Governor of Michigan) in Detroit. Dr. Guernsey once arranged a dinner party at which each guest, representing his or her religious creed, sat at the table. Dr. Guernsey represented the thoughts of Robert Ingersoll, the well-known agnostic and orator who was absent from the city at that time. His Grace the Cardinal was interested, but did not come nor did he appoint any substitute from his clergy, and so Dr. Guernsey had to ask Miss Gibbons, his patient, to represent the Catholic point of view. Although there was a tacit understanding to be polite in spite of their religious differences with Swami, as dinner progressed, the Evangelical brethren soon began to show intolerance and consequent bitterness, and there was no longer the cordiality.[6] From the reminiscences of Mrs. Constance Towne—Miss Constance Gibbons at that time—we get a picture of this "dinner party of creeds" at the home of Dr. Guernsey. She writes: "A more broad-minded and tolerant man surely could not have been found anywhere in India to carry out the mission of founding Vedanta Centers in America."[7]

THE GREENACRE CONFERENCE OF 1894: A SIGNIFICANT EVENT

SWAMI VIVEKANANDA'S PRESENCE AT THE PARLIAMENT INSPIRES THE CREATION OF THE MONSALVAT SCHOOL

Sarah Farmer had been unable to attend the Parliament of World Religions, but still, had been able to meet Swamiji in

Chicago. She invited him to attend the Greenacre Conference in the Monsalvat School for the Comparative Study of Religion at Eliot, Maine. Swamiji probably went there on July 27.

Sarah Farmer was deeply impressed and said of him:

... To know Vivekananda was a renewed consecration; to have him under one's roof was to feel empowered to go forth to the children of men and to help them all to a realization of their birthright as sons of God. What Greenacre owes to him cannot be put into words ... This great soul came into our midst and did more than any other to give the work its true tone, for he lived every day the truths which his lips proclaimed.[8]

It is known that the Greenacre conferences, whose purpose was to implement the practice of the harmony of religions

"... were a success and attracted the cream of intellectual society: Edward Everett Hale, Frank B. Sanborn, Professors William James, Lanman, and others. The first summer featured Swami Vivekananda and Anagarika Dharmapala, who were the most charismatic speakers of the Chicago Parliament. Vivekananda, in Indian ashrama style, held his classes under a huge pine tree which was known many years after as the Swami Pine ... [the *Portsmouth Daily Chronicle*, 1 August 1894] reported that: "the rare opportunity that is afforded at Greenacre Inn is being recognized and the numbers are increasing daily. On Sunday it became necessary to put cots in the parlors and halls. Many of the outside cottages are filled also." ...[9]

The *Portsmouth Daily Chronicle* additionally reported that:

Vivekananda, the Hind[u] monk from India is also a centre of much interest. Each morning he meets a company of

men and women under a large pine in the woods, and sitting
cross-legged, discourses to them of the things of the soul.
This gentle, loving-hearted son of the East, by his simplicity
and earnest devotion has won to himself some very warm
friends. He is generous in the extreme, giving freely to any
one from his stores of wisdom. On Friday he is to deliver
an address in the large tent, his subject being 'The Reality
of God.' ... He came to this country to speak at the
Parliament of Religions at Chicago and was greeted with
crowds wherever he spoke. His red robe and yellow turban
make him a picturesque figure wherever he goes.[10]

Dr. Lewis G. Janes, had started the Monsalvat School for
the Comparative Study of Religion at Greenacre in 1896. Sarah
Farmer, inspired by Swamiji, dedicated many acres of her inherited estate to its establishment and was the co-founder. A school
brochure dated "3 July-31 August 1902" carried this statement:

The initial steps toward the founding of the Monsalvat
School were taken in 1894, when the Swami Vivekananda
of India was invited to conduct a class in Vedanta Philosophy
under the pines at Greenacre, Eliot, Me [Maine]. His
exposition of the Gospel of Jesus Christ from the standpoint
of an Oriental will never be forgotten by any one privileged
to be a member of his class.
  In time, the Monsalvat School of Comparative Religion
at Greenacre became even more renowned than Greenacre
itself. Leading figures in the field of comparative religion
conducted the school's summer-long lecture programs.
Vivekananda himself came to give the course on Hinduism,
[Anagarika] Dharmapala, the main Buddhist speaker at the
Parliament of Religions, did the same for Buddhism ...
Moslems, Catholics, Zoroastrians, Jews and people who were
recognized scholars in the various fields of Christian
theology lectured. The students were from Harvard and
other Ivy League colleges—young people who delighted

in the unusual intellectual fare. They tented at Greenacre throughout the summer.[11]

One philanthropist, a Mrs. Pratt of Kenilworth, was captivated by Swamiji at Greenacre and offered him $500 for his future work, but he declined her offer.[12] In this context, it may be mentioned that sometime in the middle of May 1894, Swamiji, having addressed a women's club at Lawrence, was invited to visit another wealthy woman, of Swampscott; he declined her offer as well.

It may be said that while Swamiji did not entirely approve of the Greenacre Conference, his association with it was a foreshadowing of what was to come—the beginning of a new method of work.

SWAMIJI TEACHES VEDANTA IN A SPIRITUAL ATMOSPHERE AT GREENACRE AND THOUSAND ISLAND PARK

The Greenacre Conference offered Swami Vivekananda a chance to experience the mood of the contemplative itinerant monk in India, as he was not bound by any responsibilities— he lived in "the wide, unpaved vistas of open country and days in which his mind was free to plunge into profound contemplation or to lift in ecstasy," says Burke.[13]

In this gathering of several hundred men and women— freethinking intellectuals—Swamiji would give talks "on an average [of] seven or eight hours a day" for about two weeks. Here he enjoyed the full freedom of a Hindu monk, and this period foreshadows the beginnings of his new method of teaching in the West.[14] Sitting under the tree now labeled "Swami's Pine", surrounded by the devotees also seated on the grass, he would teach every morning. The Great Prophet of our age experienced such an exalted mood under the "spreading Lysekloster pines" that the spiritual atmosphere attracted hundreds for many years long after he was gone from Maine.

Swamiji again experienced this mood at Thousand Island Park in upstate New York the following summer.[15] Here, according to Burke, "he taught for the first time in America the philosophy of Advaita Vedanta to a group of eager listeners."[16]

SWAMIJI MAKES TWO VALUABLE AND LIFE-LONG FRIENDS

At Greenacre Swamiji again met Dr. Lewis G. Janes, president of the Brooklyn Ethical Association and an old acquaintance from New York.[17] They grew very close to each other. At this time Dr. Janes invited Swamiji to deliver a lecture on the Hindu religion at the Brooklyn Ethical Association. This lecture was to make a very deep impact on the public.

At Greenacre, Swami Vivekananda also met some of his friends from New York, as well as Mrs. Ole Bull for the first time.[18] Swamiji's meeting with her was a providential happening, culminating in a lifelong mother-son relationship. Swamiji wrote her a letter on September 19, addressing her as "Dear Mother Sara."[19] She proved to be a real mother, giving her whole-hearted support as well as financial aid to the cause of Vedanta.

At the Greenacre Conference, a few were inspired by the high quality of Swamiji's philosophy and became his faithful friends. Mrs. Bull and Dr. Janes remained Swamiji's true friends throughout their lives and cooperated with him. After Swamiji's demise, they wholeheartedly supported his followers in spreading the message of Vedanta in America.

THE CAMBRIDGE CONFERENCES

THE PARLIAMENT GENERATES SEMINAL INTELLECTUAL INTEREST IN VEDANTA

Between the day of his departure from Greenacre on August 12, 1894 and his arrival in New York at the end of the

first week of November, Swamiji visited many places. He stayed
with Mrs. Bull at her residence in Cambridge from October 2
to October 10. She was a well-known figure in Cambridge
and her residence was a famous meeting place for intellectual
society and for leaders of great causes. She was the main
sponsor for the Cambridge Seminars in Comparative Religion.

The seminars were the direct outcome of the interest in
non-Western world philosophy and religion that was generated
by the Chicago Parliament of Religions. The brilliant
thinkers—William James and Josiah Royce and Charles
Rockwell Lanman, chairman of Harvard's Sanskrit Department (who was later made an honorary member of the Vedanta
Society of New York)—all had spoken there on various
occasions. The great personalities of Gertrude Stein and the
social worker Jane Addams were noted auditors of these
seminars. Swami Vivekananda had been invited for extended
visits there on several occasions.[20]

WILLIAM JAMES RECOGNIZES THE PRACTICAL VALUE OF
VEDANTA AS TAUGHT BY SWAMI VIVEKANANDA

In Cambridge, Mrs. Bull introduced Swamiji and his
Vedanta philosophy to the celebrities. There were no regular
classes—only one or two informal talks. It is quite likely that
Swamiji and Professor William James became close friends on
that visit. Professor James was to send a letter to Mrs. Bull six
years later, remarking on Swamiji's oratorical power, and wrote
that he was "an honour to humanity."[21] In *Swami Vivekananda
and William James: Asian Psychology at Harvard in the 1890's*, Dr.
Eugene Taylor wrote about the value Professor James
discovered in Swami Vivekananda's teachings:

[James] saw in Vivekananda's inner science a vast
unexplored dimension for the understanding of personality
and character formation. We know from subsequent

references he made to Vivekananda's system that James saw great value in the Hindu practice of systematic, daily rounds of concentrated relaxation. These, James felt, could be of great use in preparing American children for learning in the classroom. James also observed in the methods of Vivekananda's yoga a form of spiritual discipline that could be used by anyone to penetrate into untrapped reservoirs of energy and power for physical as well as mental tasks, and also in the treatment of certain neurasthenic conditions... A language of inner experience, a rigorous psychology of character formation, and practical application to real-life problems were but a few of the advantages that James saw in Vivekananda that were being ignored by the German-trained brass instrument psychologists then taking control of the academic psychology departments in America.[22]

American Mysticism also reported in one of its issues that:

In the *Varieties*, William James illustrated his comments on Vedanta with quotations from the published addresses of Swami Vivekananda. This was appropriate, for Vivekananda had gained international fame in the nineties as India's Vedanta emissary to the West...
Vivekananda has exerted a lasting influence upon mystical thought in America. From his lectures and organizational work of the nineties stems the present-day Vedanta movement in the United States with its ten centers in Boston, New York, Los Angeles, and other cities, and its affiliation with the Ramakrishna Order, which has over a hundred centers in India and the rest of Asia, and one each in England, France, and Argentina.[23]

In the concluding chapter of *Varieties of Religious Experience*, James quotes Swami Vivekananda to illustrate the mysticism of Vedanta:

If this room is full of darkness for thousands of years, and you come in and begin to weep and wail, "Oh, the darkness," will the darkness vanish? Bring the light in, strike a match, and light comes in a moment. So what good will it do you to think all your lives, "Oh, I have done evil, I have made many mistakes"? It requires no ghost to tell us that. Bring in the light, and the evil goes in a moment. Strengthen the real nature, build up yourselves, the effulgent, the resplendent, the ever pure, call that up in everyone whom you see. I wish that every one of us had come to such a state that even when we see the vilest of human beings we can see the God within, and instead of condemning, say, "Rise, thou effulgent One, rise thou who art always pure, rise thou birthless and deathless, rise almighty, and manifest your nature." ... This is the highest prayer that the Advaita teaches. This is the one prayer: remembering our nature... Why does man go out to look for God? ... It is your own heart beating, and you did not know, you were mistaking it for something external. He, nearest of the near, my own self, the reality of my own life, my body and my soul. I am Thee and Thou art Me. That is your own nature. Assert it. Manifest it. Not to become pure, you are pure already. You are not to be perfect, you are that already. Every good thought which you think or act upon is simply tearing the veil, as it were, and the purity, the Infinity, the God behind, manifests itself—the eternal Subject of everything, the eternal Witness in this universe, your own Self. Knowledge is, as it were, a lower step, a degradation. We are It already; how to know It? (Swami Vivekananda: Addresses, No. XII, "Practical Vedanta", part iv, 172, 174 [London, 1897]; and Lectures, "The Real and the Apparent Man", 24 [abridged]).[24]

It was perhaps at this time that Swamiji "demonstrated ... the mystery of divine communion for the noted philosopher by plunging, in his presence, into Samadhi."[25] In his *Varieties of Religious Experience*, William James wrote of the "condition termed *samadhi*." He quoted directly from Swamiji's *Raja Yoga*, that:

> ... the mind itself has a higher state of existence, beyond reason, a superconscious state, and that when the mind gets to that higher state, then this knowledge beyond reasoning comes... All the different steps in yoga are intended to bring us scientifically to the superconscious state or Samadhi... Just as unconscious work is beneath consciousness, so there is another work which is above consciousness, and which, also, is not accompanied with the feeling of egoism... There is no feeling of *I*, and yet the mind works, desireless, free from restlessness, objectless, bodiless. Then the Truth shines in its full effulgence, and we know ourselves—for Samadhi lies potential in us all—for what we truly are, free, immortal, omnipotent, loosed from the finite, and its contrasts of good and evil altogether, and identical with the Atman or Universal Soul.[26]

SWAMI VIVEKANANDA'S "IDEA OF DOING GOOD"

Throughout this period of public addresses, Swamiji expressed his deep-seated feelings of disgust on many occasions. He literally cried like his Master to have a few earnest seekers. He wanted to teach "a select—a very select— few" rather than lecture before a multitude: "My idea of doing good is this: to evolve out a few giants, and not to strew pearls before swine, and so lose time, health, and energy."[27] On October 27 he had written to Alasinga Perumal, "I think I have worked enough, now I want rest and to teach a little to those that have come to me from my Gurudeva."[28]

The Art Institute of Chicago

Professor John Henry Wright

Mary Tappan Wright

Sara Bull

Dr. Lewis G. Janes

Betty Leggett, 1896

Francis H. Leggett, 1896

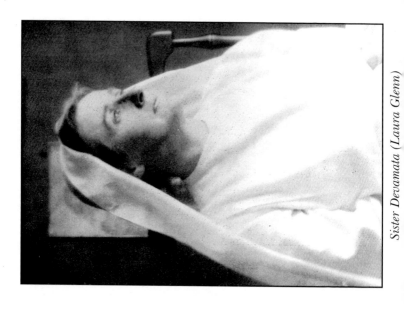

J.J. Goodwin, an English disciple of Vivekananda

Sister Devamata (Laura Glenn)

SWAMIJI'S LECTURE TOUR PREPARES THE WAY
FOR HIS TEACHINGS

Leon Landsberg, one of Swami Vivekananda's later disciples, wrote about this period of hard work in America to the *Brahmavadin*:

> Before even starting this great mission [of the teaching of Vedanta in the West], it was necessary to first perform the Herculean labor of cleansing this Augean stable of imposture, superstition and bigotry, a task sufficient to discourage the bravest heart, to dispirit the most powerful will. But the Swami was not the man to be deterred by difficulties. Poor and friendless, with no other support than God and his love for mankind, he set patiently to work, determined not to give up until the message he had to deliver would reach the hearts of truth-seeking men and women.[29]

It may be mentioned here that Swami Vivekananda was a prophet, divinely ordained, and without any detailed plan of his own. In his so-called "unplanned" lecture tours, where he mingled with the people throughout America, there was a divine plan unfurling to enlighten their hearts and minds of prejudice and ignorance about Hindus and the Hindu religion. He broadcast his ideas unstintingly and scattered them everywhere he could, enduring innumerable hardships. The way was being cleared for the inner transformation of the West through the Vedanta teachings. Burke convincingly states that only then could he settle down in New York to establish a center: "One might well say that during the first sixteen months of his American visit he lit the fire of spirituality in innumerable hearts, and then, during the next sixteen months, left a legacy of spiritual and philosophical knowledge by which that fire might be fed for centuries to come."[30]

Hence, Burke rightly concludes, the activities of Swami Vivekananda make the period of 1893-1894 the most important one in his world mission. His presence and talks all over America were vital and indispensable to his role of a divine prophet in creating a true receptivity to the Vedanta teachings. His presence and sojourn in America can only be correctly understood in this light.[31]

THE NUCLEUS OF A VEDANTA SOCIETY IS
FORMED IN NEW YORK

After visiting Baltimore and Washington, Swamiji returned to New York unexpectedly on November 7 or 8 and remained there for the rest of the month. In that fateful November of 1894 Swamiji organized the nucleus of a Vedanta Society in New York. The Society was not really organized properly, as its aims and objectives were not spelled out clearly. The Vedanta Society was informal and unregistered at this point.[32] Still, this was of historic significance indeed. On November 30 Swamiji wrote to Alasinga, "I have started (an organization) already in New York and the Vice President will soon write to you."[33] According to Burke, "Toward the end of 1894 he was also becoming keenly aware of America's need for the religion of India."[34] The purpose was to create a center from which the philosophy of Vedanta would be disseminated to the world, apart from collecting funds for the future educational projects of India. Swamiji had worked very hard, sometimes giving twelve to fourteen or more lectures per week to deliver his message. Now, for the same purpose, he wanted to have a permanent center to impart intensive spiritual training to a few genuine seekers who would support the Vedanta Movement.

SWAMIJI'S DEDICATION TO INDIA'S CAUSE AND
HIS EMERGENCE AS A WORLD TEACHER

Swamiji was a monk *par excellence*. The idea of earning money to help the cause of India, however noble and desirable, was repugnant to every grain of truth within him. Swami Vivekananda had written to Mrs. Hale from the Guernseys' house on April 10, 1894: "As for lecturing—I have given up raising money. I can not degenerate myself any more. When a certain purpose was in view I could work—with that gone I can not earn for myself."[35] However, subconsciously, the Indian cause was always in his mind. In a letter of June 1894 to Haridas Viharidas Desai, Swamiji had written, "Now lecturing for a year in this country, I could not succeed at all (of course I have no wants for myself) in my plan for raising some funds for setting up my work."[36] He later wrote to Mrs. Bull on February 14, 1895: "Collecting funds even for a good work is not good for a Sannyasin... I had these childish ideas of doing this and doing that. These appear like a hallucination to me now. I am getting out of them... Perhaps these mad desires were necessary to bring me over to this country. And I thank the Lord for the experience."[37] And gradually, the money aspect became completely subdued in light of his world mission. Swamiji had now become keenly and permanently established in the awareness of his world mission. Fully recognizing the new global age with its global interdependence, Swamiji knew that his message of unity and harmony would help to create the new order of a spiritually practical and active humanity.

THE "CYCLONIC HINDU"

Swami Vivekananda was a born World Teacher and always taught the highest spiritual truths everywhere. He taught the fundamental principles of Vedanta: unity of existence, universality of Truth, divinity of life, harmony of religions, and the imperative of realizing God while living. His unbounded love for the people, his simplicity and gentleness, his silent, invisible spiritual force touched the hearts of the people. He created spiritual longing in their hearts by his mere presence, his glance, his touch. He wrote to one of his brother disciples, "There is no end of work here—I am careering all over the country. Wherever the seed of [Sri Ramakrishna's] power will find its way, there it will fructify—'be it today, or in a hundred years'."[38]

A majestic Knower of God, a World Teacher born to conquer the world, Swamiji earned the appellation, "The Cyclonic Hindu." His physical force was very great, but his spiritual force was subtle: his reputation for "gentleness, simplicity, and charm" advanced before him, and remained wherever he had been. His schedule of work and travel throughout 1894 led to his becoming well-informed about Western thought and culture, and the significant differences between East and West. He wanted to translate the "Eternal Religion" of the East for the Western mind in a way that would enable the West to make it its own. He wanted the new age that was emerging to experience and to apply "Practical" Vedanta. He sustained this formidable task in the most resourceful ways.

He again visited Cambridge and stayed with Mrs. Bull from December 5 to December 27, 1894, holding two fully-attended classes daily in her large parlor, and three formal talks, plunging "evidently at once, into the absorbed, uninterrupted delivery of two classes daily, again teaching Vedanta with the same unbroken intensity as at Greenacre."[39] One of those who attended the Cambridge classes was quoted in a later bulletin that had been published for his Brooklyn lectures: "He has helped many students (in Harvard University) in the solution of philosophical problems in which they had become involved in their course of study."

LECTURES AT THE BROOKLYN ETHICAL ASSOCIATION

Having spent Christmas day of 1894 at Mrs. Bull's home, Swamiji came to Brooklyn on December 28 to attend an evening reception arranged in his honor by Mr. Charles M. Higgins at his home. Mr. Higgins, a rich young Brooklyn lawyer and inventor, was also an associate of the Brooklyn Ethical Association. Mr. Higgins brought out a ten-page pamphlet about Swamiji that was circulated "among those interested in the study of Oriental religions."

On December 30 Swamiji delivered his first lecture at the Pouch Mansion, under the auspices of the Ethical Association. The lecture was presided over by Dr. Janes. "The rooms were crowded to suffocation," with about eight hundred of Brooklyn's elite attending. It appears, from Sarah Ellen Waldo's remarks,[40] that after the astounding success of this lecture, there were insistent demands for regular classes in Brooklyn. Swamiji graciously gave his consent and delivered six additional public lectures in Brooklyn between December 30, 1894 and April 8, 1895.[41]

One of these lectures was "Ideals of Womanhood: Hindu, Mohammedan and Christian." The Rama Bai Circle, a women's group led by Mrs. James MacKeen, immediately challenged his statements about Hindu widows and their property inheritance. The women offered their opposing views in a declamation against Swamiji in the Brooklyn press.[42] The pamphlet published earlier by Mr. Higgins became very helpful later on, when Dr. Janes replied to their charges; it enabled him to substantiate his points with factual truth about Swamiji, though the debate remained unresolved.

"I HAVE A MESSAGE TO THE WEST"

In his first lecture in Brooklyn, Swamiji made his now-famous statement: "I have a message to the West as Buddha had a message to the East."[43] This first lecture made a profound impression upon the audience. It also made a deep impact on two reporters: "As my companion and I wended our way homeward, the vast vault of the blue sky was studded with stars, and the blessed fragrance of Christmas still lingered in the streets of the great city. We thought of the old and beautiful legend of the Eastern Magi who followed the star which led them, with their homage of frankincense and myrrh, to the babe lying in the manger at Bethlehem. And he wondered if this Oriental wanderer was not one of the same high caste, who 1900 years later had come to our Western Continent to throw light upon the inner meaning of that pure gospel, which that noble soul had preached and illustrated."[44]

"In the last week of January, 1895," Burke writes, "the Swami "settled in New York in humble quarters to teach intensively and to develop his presentation of a cohesive, detailed, and comprehensive religion and philosophy for the modern West—and through the West for the world."[45]

THE FIRST HOME OF THE VEDANTA SOCIETY

NEW YORK IS CHOSEN FOR THE WORK

On different occasions Swamiji made various remarks about New York. "Here alone in New York I find more men interested in religion than in other cities... New York is a grand and good place... The New York people have a tenacity of purpose unknown in any other city... New York [is] the head, hand, and purse of the country." New York was chosen for its cosmopolitan character, its energetic people, and its liberalism. Burke has described the New York of Swamiji's time:

Although in the 1890s hansom cabs, cable cars, and horse-cars, rather than automobiles, buses and taxicabs, crowded the streets of New York, and although the highest skyscraper was little more than twenty stories, the city was already the metropolis of the western hemisphere, the humming center of New World civilization. People of all races, nationalities, and creeds made it then, as now, a teeming world one could never fully know—a cauldron of human joy, suffering, and striving. Swamiji evidently liked New York, feeling in its people openness to new ideas and energy, which could bring those ideas to fruition. A glimpse of him ... comes to us through the poetess Harriet Monroe, who writes: "Later [after the Parliament of Religions] I knew him quite well, and always I shall remember ... that his vision entrusted to our fresh energies his hope of a more united and glorious world." Indeed, wherever Swamiji saw an expression of man's vitality and creativity, there he saw the vitality and creativity of the Divine Mother. Strength in whatever form spoke to him, as it were, on a deep level where man's energy as expressed in a skyscraper was not different from the divine energy sustaining and moving the universe. It was the same energy and power which he himself embodied.[46]

Swamiji visited Chicago just after his lecture in Brooklyn and returned to New York on January 18, 1895 (date uncertain). He took the initiative in organizing the Vedanta Society with the active cooperation of Leon Landsberg, who shouldered the burden of the practical details, and gave much relief to Swamiji. He was to become Swamiji's future disciple. Landsberg rented two rooms at 54 West Thirty-third Street— not a good neighborhood in those days.

HUMBLE BEGINNINGS AND SOME GENUINE FRIENDS

In order to fulfill his mission and to have independence, Swamiji left the hospitality and comfortable living provided by Dr. Guernsey and moved into the new location on Sunday, January 27, 1895 along with Landsberg. He established his headquarters there. On January 28, he started his classes on Vedanta and Yoga, "beginning the second phase of his Western work, into which he was to pour his heart, mind and soul."

After the demise of Sri Ramakrishna, his disciples had settled down, in a dilapidated "haunted" house infested with snakes and lizards—a place quite unfit for human habitation. That was Baranagore Monastery. The Great Prophet, after the Chicago Parliament, having attained phenomenal success both as orator and teacher by divine right, with tremendous name and fame, and much sought-after as a speaker in every city, also settled down in a poor locality noted for "vice and crime"—obviously due to the lack of money and support. A courageous pastor, Reverend Dr. Charles H. Parkhurst, whom Swamiji had met at Dr. Guernsey's "dinner party of creeds" in 1894, brought effective, though temporary, changes under a brief reform administration in the beginning of 1895. Thus, the locality became for a short period—the period when Swamiji resided in it—a safer, less corrupt place.[47]

Swamiji was sick of public applause and appreciation and cheap celebrity. His new mission was to train a few earnest students by giving them the direction to find the true spirit of mankind. The Society now had its first home. It was here that Swamiji initially met a few of his genuine friends: Miss Josephine MacLeod and her sister Bessie Sturges; Mr. Francis H. Leggett, who later married Miss Sturges; Miss Sarah Ellen Waldo, who later became one of Swami Vivekananda's first Western brahmacharins and disciples; and Leon Landsberg.

SWAMIJI'S SURE REFUGE WHILE FACING THE ODDS

The decent ladies, however, felt a natural abhorrence of this neighborhood and expressed their feelings against it. Swamiji's feeling about their remarks, and his mood and mind can be known from his letter to Mrs. Bull from 54 West Thirty-third Street on April 11, 1895:

> Every one of my friends thought it would end in nothing, this my getting up quarters all by myself, and that

no *ladies would ever come here.* Miss Hamlin especially thought that "she" or "her right sort of people" were *way up* from such things as to go and listen to a man who lives by himself in a poor lodging. But the "right kind" came for all that, day and night, and she too. Lord! How hard it is for man to believe in Thee and Thy mercies! Shiva! Shiva! Where is the right kind and where is the bad, mother? It is all *He!* In the tiger and the lamb, in the saint and sinner all *He!* In Him I have taken my refuge—body, soul and Atman. Will he leave me now after carrying me in His arms all my life? Not a drop will be in the ocean, not a twig in the deepest forest, not a crumb in the house of the god of wealth, if the Lord is not merciful. Streams will be in the desert and the beggar shall have plenty, if He wills it. He seeth the sparrow's fall. Are these but words, mother, or literal, actual life?

Truce to this "right sort of presentation." Thou art my right, Thou my wrong, my Shiva. Lord, since a child I have taken refuge in Thee. Thou wilt be with me in the tropics or at the poles, on the tops of mountains or in the depth of oceans. My stay—my guide in life—my refuge—my friends—my teacher—my God—my real Self, Thou wilt never leave me, *never.* I know it for sure. Sometimes I become weak, being alone and struggling against odds, my God; and I think of human help. Save Thou me for ever from these weaknesses, and may I never, never seek for help from any being but Thee. If a man puts his trust in another good man, he is never betrayed, never forsaken. Wilt Thou forsake me, Father of all good, Thou who knowest that *all* my life I am Thy servant and Thine alone? Wilt Thou give me over to be played upon by others, or dragged down by evil?[48]

Christina Greenstidel, who was initiated by Swami Vivekananda at Thousand Island Park and later known as Sister Christine, also gave her impression of the Society's first home: "The place which was found ... was in a most

undesirable locality, and it was hinted that the right sort of
people, especially ladies, would not come to such a place; but
they came—all sorts and conditions of men and women—to
these squalid rooms. They sat on chairs, and when chairs were
filled, anywhere—on tables, on washstands, on the stairs.
Millionaires were glad to sit on the floor, literally at his feet."[49]

SWAMIJI'S LIFE INSPIRES PEOPLE AND
MAKES A DEEP IMPACT

THE SPIRITUALLY INTENSE LIFE OF
SWAMI VIVEKANANDA

Swamiji, as mentioned, had been inwardly feeling a great
urge to train a band of selected genuine persons by arousing
their inner spiritual hunger and helping them to experience
spiritual enlightenment through the practice of Yoga. He was
also possessed with the idea of enjoying once again the
freedom of a Hindu monk. Both these urges got fulfilled in
New York. Swamiji "lived the austere and spiritually intense
life of the sannyasin," remaining "in a high state of spiritual
consciousness." He would:

recite texts from Sanskrit scriptures, he would repeat the
name of God, or [be] caught up in a mood of divine love ...
while the world slept. He lived both day and night on the
very edge of the Infinite... He literally radiated spirituality... An atmosphere of benediction, of peace, of power
and of inexpressible luminosity was felt by one and all who
came to his classes... One sees him in his New York retreat
... in the morning or the evening quiet, or at dead of night,
meditating. Oftentimes, he was lost in meditation, his
unconsciousness of the external betraying his complete
absorption within. Even while holding a class he would
plunge into profound contemplation. When the Swami

emerged from such states ... he would feel impatient with himself, for he desired that the Teacher should be uppermost in him, rather than the Yogi. In order to avoid repetitions of such occurrences, he instructed one or two how to bring him back by uttering a word or a Name, should he be carried by the force of meditation into Samadhi.[50]

Sister Nivedita records a similar incident in Swamiji's life, which, most likely, she heard from others: "On one occasion, teaching a New York class to meditate, it was found at the end, that he could not be brought back to consciousness, and that one by one, his students stole quietly away. But he was deeply mortified when he knew what had happened, and never risked its repetition. Meditating in private, with one or two, he would give a word, by which he could be recalled."[51] The interested reader may look further in Sister Nivedita's first volume of *Letters* (*Letters of Sister Nivedita*, Collected and Edited by Sankari Prasad Basu [Calcutta: Nababharat Publishers, 1982], 96) for Swamiji's comments to Swami Abhayananda, who witnessed his samadhi in a New York class.

Swamiji was ever established in his true divine Self, yet the secular life was of keen interest to him. He readily absorbed all secular knowledge and gleaned its spiritual significance through his discriminating intellect,. He transformed his experience of a frenetic metropolis by virtue of his extraordinary capacity for intense meditation. In the peaceful dawn or twilight or in the dead of night, he sometimes was lost to the outer world entirely, merged in the thought of the Absolute. His disciples have written that "his friends knew these things and provided for them. If he walked into the house to pay a call and forgot to speak, or if he was found in a room, in silence, no one disturbed him, though he would sometimes rise and render assistance to an intruder, without breaking the train of thought. Thus his interest lay within, and not without. To the scale and range of his thought his conversation was of course, our only clue."[52]

In this connection we should mention the mood in which Swamiji later composed his *Raja Yoga*. Sarah Ellen Waldo wrote: "It was inspiring to see the Swami as he dictated to me the contents of the work. In delivering his commentaries on the Sutras, he would leave me waiting while he entered deep states of meditation or self-contemplation, to emerge therefrom with some luminous interpretations. I had always to keep the pen dipped in ink. He might be absorbed for long periods of time and then suddenly his silence would be broken by some expression of some long deliberate teaching."[53]

The effect of Swamiji's concentrated silence was revealed in many ways. For example, Miss Waldo records that Swamiji seemed to be fascinated by a floor-to-ceiling mirror, before which he stood again and again, "gazing at himself intently":

> In between he walked up and down the room, lost in thought. Miss Waldo's eyes followed him anxiously. "Now the bubble is going to burst," she thought. "He is full of personal vanity." Suddenly he turned to her and said: "Ellen, it is the strangest thing, I cannot remember how I look. I look and look at myself in the glass, but the moment I turn away I forget completely what I look like."[54]

So greatly was his soul expanded.

SWAMIJI: AN "EXCELLENT SPECIMEN OF HIS RACE"

It is interesting to note here, Dr. Edgar C. Beall's description of Swamiji in the *Phrenological Journal of New York*. This article was reproduced in the *Indian Mirror* on October 5, 1895:

> Swami Vivekananda is in many respects an excellent specimen of his race. He is five feet eight and a half inches

in height and weighs one hundred and seventy pounds. His head measures twenty-one and three-fourths inches in circumference by fourteen from ear to ear across the top. He is thus very well proportioned as regards both body and brain. His instincts are too feminine to be compatible with much conjugal sentiment. Indeed, he says himself that he never had the slightest feeling of love for any woman. As he is opposed to war and teaches a religion of unmixed gentleness, we should expect his head to be narrow in the region of the ears at the seat of combativeness and destructiveness, and such is the case. The same deficiency is much marked in the diameters a little farther up at secretiveness and acquisitiveness. He dismisses the whole subject of finance and ownership by saying that he has no property and does not want to be bothered with any. While such sentiment sounds odd to American ears, it must be confessed that his face, at least, shows more marks of contentment than the visages of Russell Sage, Hetty Green, and many others of our multi-millionaires. Firmness and conscientiousness are fully developed. Benevolence is quite conspicuous. Music is well indicated in the width of the temples. The prominent eyes betoken superior memory of words and explain much of the eloquence he has displayed in his lectures. The upper forehead is well developed at causality and in comparison to which is added a fine endowment of suavity and sense of human nature. Summing up the organization, it will be seen that kindness, sympathy, and philosophical intelligence, with ambition to achieve success in the direction of higher educational work are his predominant characteristics. Being a graduate of the Calcutta University, he speaks English almost as perfectly as if he were a native of England. If he does no more than continue the development of that splendid spirit of charity, which was displayed at the World's Fair, his mission among us will certainly prove eminently successful.[55]

SWAMIJI'S MANY CLASSES AND IMMENSE
HAPPINESS DESPITE MANY DIFFICULTIES

He used to hold classes "every morning from eleven till one o'clock and often till later." Here he taught the four Yogas and the Gita. He gave classes in his room, "free as air." Miss Waldo recorded that, "Long before [June], they had outgrown their small beginnings and had removed downstairs to occupy an entire parlour floor and extension."[56]

But in spite of the crowded classes, the collections and donations were too meager to meet the expenses. Miss Waldo wrote that "the rent was paid by voluntary subscriptions and when these were found insufficient the Swami hired a hall and gave secular lectures on India and devoted the proceeds to the maintenance of the classes. He said that Hindu teachers of religion felt it to be their duty to support their classes and the students, too, if they were unable to care for themselves, and the teachers would willingly make any sacrifice they possibly could to assist a needy disciple."[57]

The economic situation did not improve, despite Swamiji's arduous labors in his Vedanta classes, private homes and public places. In May 1895 he wrote in a letter to Mrs. Bull, "The classes are going on; but I am sorry to say, though the attendance is large, it does not even pay enough to cover the rent. I will try this week and then give up."[58] It may be interesting to note that a basket was hung near the door of the classroom to receive money for the work.[59] Swamiji could not change his residence to a better locality mainly due to economic reasons, and he had to work hard in his room, which was, definitely, very uncomfortable. The room was on the second floor and could not have been more than twenty feet wide, with just a few ordinary pieces of furniture. For lack of an extra room, cooking was done in the bedroom with the help of a stove donated by a friend. Perhaps, sometimes, Swamiji would cook meals in a community kitchen. After a class, Swamiji and Landsberg would go to take a light supper at a cheap restaurant.

Notwithstanding these difficulties, Swamiji was immensely happy and began to pour his mind, heart and soul into his new mission. He wrote to Mrs. Bull on February 14: "I am very happy now. Between Mr. Landsberg and me, we cook some rice and lentils or barley and quietly eat it, and write something or read or receive visits from poor people who want to learn something, and thus I feel I am more a Sannyasin now than I ever was in America."[60]

SWAMI TAKES TWO BRIEF, MUCH-NEEDED VACATIONS

Swamiji's health was shattered due to the extraordinary load of work, so in the second week of April 1895 he took ten days' vacation at Ridgely Manor, a graceful estate about eighty miles up the Hudson River from New York. This property of about fifty acres had been acquired in 1892 by Mr. Francis Leggett, who later became the first president of the Vedanta Society of New York. On April 19, during Swamiji's absence, Landsberg moved to a house at 228 West Thirty-ninth Street. Swamiji came back to New York on April 23. Rested and with renewed spirit, he wrote on May 6, 1895 to Alasinga Perumal in India: "I am to create a new order of humanity." He wrote to him again on May 14, 1895: "Now I have got a hold on New York, and I hope to get a permanent body of workers who will carry on the work when I leave the country ... I ought to be able to leave a permanent effect behind me when I go; and with the blessings of the Lord it is going to be very soon... *Men* are more valuable than all the wealth of the world."[61]

He now had to do almost everything by himself to maintain his "household." On June 22, 1895 [date uncertain] Swamiji wrote to Mary Hale, "Landsberg has gone away ... I am living mostly on nuts, fruits and milk." His health was fast deteriorating. He began to feel himself wearing out and "his nerves were racked, his brain tired, his whole body overtaxed. He longed for a brief period of rest and recuperation."[62]

Swamiji left New York for Camp Percy, New Hampshire on June 4 for the much-coveted rest.

THE LECTURES AT THE CORBIN RESIDENCE

During the same lecture season of 1895 and simultaneous to the New York classes, Swami Vivekananda had started a new series of lectures. They were held in February and March at the home of the wealthy Mrs. Austin Corbin and Miss Annie Corbin at 425 Fifth Avenue, where a year later, the mathematician Nikola Tesla and the actress Sarah Bernhardt were destined to meet Swamiji on February 5, 1896. Swami Vivekananda continued to hold classes there in 1896, but in a letter he wrote to Mrs. Bull on March 21, 1895, he was already indicating his intention to discontinue them:

> Those that want to help mankind must take their own pleasure and pain, name and fame, and all sorts of interests, and make a bundle of them and throw them into the sea, and then come to the Lord. That is what all the Masters *said* and *did*. I went to Miss Corbin's last Saturday and told her that I should not be able to come to hold classes anymore. Was it ever in the history of the world that any great work was done by the rich? It is the heart and the brain that do it ever and ever and not the purse. My *idea* and all my life with it—and to *God* for help; to none else! This is the only secret of success.[63]

REMINISCENCES OF SWAMIJI'S INAUGURAL TEACHINGS AND THE PROFOUND INFLUENCE FELT BY MANY

GLIMPSES FROM AN EARLY WORKER AT THE SOCIETY

Some additional glimpses of Swamiji's life in his early days in New York are given below. Miss Waldo was a very well read young woman and one of the earliest workers of the Society. In 1906 she wrote an article in *Prabuddha Bharata* describing the classes in New York during the season of 1895:

At this time the Swami was living very simply in New York; and his earliest classes were held in the small room he occupied, and in the beginning were attended by only three or four persons. They grew with astonishing rapidity, and, as the little room filled to overflowing, became very picturesque. The Swami himself always sat on the floor, and most of his audience likewise. The marble-topped dresser, the arms of the sofa, and even the corner washstand helped to furnish seats for the constantly increasing numbers. The door was left open, and the overflow filled the hall and sat on the stairs. And those first classes! How intensely interesting they were! Who that was privileged to attend them can ever forget them? The Swami so dignified yet so simple, so gravely earnest, so eloquent, and the close ranks of students, forgetting all inconveniences, hanging breathless on his every word! It was a fit beginning for a movement that has since grown to such grand proportions. In this unpretentious way did Swami Vivekananda inaugurate the work of teaching Vedanta philosophy in New York... Some Sunday lectures were also given, and there were "question" classes to help those to whom the teaching was so new and strange that they were desirous to have an opportunity for more extended explanation.[64]

WHAT SWAMIJI SPOKE "WAS TRUTH"

From Miss Josephine MacLeod's reminiscences, we get a further picture:

On the twenty-ninth of January 1895, I went with my sister to 54 West 33rd Street, New York, and heard the Swami

Vivekananda in his sitting room where were assembled fifteen or twenty ladies and two or three gentlemen. The room was crowded. All the armchairs were taken; so I sat on the floor in the front row. Swami stood in the corner. He said something, the particular words of which I do not remember, but instantly to me that was truth, and the second sentence he spoke was truth, and the third sentence was truth. And I listened to him for seven years and whatever he uttered was to me truth. From that moment life had a different import. It was as if he made you realize that you were in eternity. It never altered. It was like the sun that you will never forget once you have seen... His power lay, perhaps, in the courage he gave others. He did not ever seem to be conscious of himself at all.[65]

"I HAVE BECOME ONE OF THEIR OWN TEACHERS"

Miss Laura Glenn (later known as Sister Devamata) was familiar with the basic ideas and ideals of Hinduism. She had read the Gita, *The Light of Asia* by Edwin Arnold, and Max Müller's English version of the Upanishads. This is her impression:

One day, as I was walking up Madison Avenue, I saw in the window of the Hall of the Universal Brotherhood a modest sign saying: Next Sunday at 3 p.m. Swami Vivekananda will speak here on 'What is Vedanta?' and the following Sunday on 'What is yoga?' I reached the hall twenty minutes before the hour. It was already over half full. It was not large, however—a long, narrow room with a single aisle and benches reaching from it to the wall; a low platform holding [a] reading-desk and chair at the far end; and a flight of stairs at the back. The hall was on the second story and these stairs gave the only way of access to it—audience and speaker both had to make use of them. By the time three o'clock arrived,

hall, stairs, windowsills and railings, all were crowded to the
utmost capacity. Many even were standing below, hoping to
catch a faint echo of the words spoken in the hall above.

A sudden hush, a quiet step on the stairs, and Swami
Vivekananda passed in stately erectness up the aisle to the
platform. He began to speak; and memory, time, place,
people, all melted away. Nothing was left but a voice ringing
through the void. It was as if a gate had swung open and I
had passed out on a road leading to limitless attainment.
The end of it was not visible; but the promise of what it
would be shone through the thought and flashed through
the personality of the one who gave it. He stood there – the
prophet of infinitude ... The silence of an empty hall
recalled me to myself.[66]

To make a deep impact on the people, to impart spiritual
ideas and thoughts, which were so alien to the American mind
that was nurtured in an "altogether different culture" was the
task of the prophet. "I have become one of their own teachers,"
Swamiji wrote to an Indian friend in Washington, in October
1894. Burke adds, "But he was also Swamiji, intensely human,
an adored son, and brother to many families in America, an
infinitely compassionate, ever-approachable teacher to
hundreds of his Western followers, a beloved and ever-
sympathetic friend to countless men and women."[67]

"THIS IS THE PHILOSOPHY ... THE IDEA OF GOD"

The influence of his lectures was profoundly felt by many.
The well-known author and poet Ella Wheeler Wilcox first
met Swamiji early in 1895; she wrote about this meeting for
the May 26, 1907 issue of the *New York American*:

Twelve years ago I chanced one evening to hear that a
certain teacher of philosophy from India, a man named

Vivekananda, was to lecture a block from my home in New York.

We went out of curiosity (the man whose name I bear and I), and before we had been ten minutes in the audience, we felt ourselves lifted up into an atmosphere so rarefied, so vital, so wonderful, that we sat spellbound and almost breathless, to the end of the lecture.

When it was over we went out with new courage, new hope, new strength, new faith, to meet life's daily vicissitudes. "This is the philosophy, this is the idea of God, the religion which I have been seeking," said the man. And for months afterwards he went with me to hear Swami Vivekananda explain the old religion and to gather from his wonderful mind jewels of truth and thoughts of helpfulness and strength. It was that terrible winter of financial disasters, when banks failed and stocks went down like broken balloons and businessmen walked through the dark valleys of despair and the whole world seemed topsy-turvy – just such an era as we are again approaching. Sometimes after sleepless nights of worry and anxiety, the man would go with me to hear the Swami lecture, and then he would come out into the winter gloom and walk down the street smiling and say, "It is all right. There is nothing to worry over." And I would go back to my own duties and pleasures with the same uplifted sense of soul and enlarged vision.

When any philosophy, any religion, can do this for human beings in this age of stress and strain, and when, added to that, it intensifies their faith in God and increases their sympathies for their kind and gives them a confident joy in the thought of other lives to come, it is good and great religion.[68]

And, this fateful meeting happened in a very unusual way:

We first heard of these lectures in a somewhat curious way. One evening, just after dinner, the postman brought a letter;

it was from a stranger, addressed to me, and had been three times forwarded. It told of a lecture to be given by Vivekananda, giving the time and the place, and closed, saying: "I feel sure, from what I read of your writings, that you will be interested." The hall where the lecture was to be given was just two blocks from our apartment, and the date was just one hour from the time I received the letter. We had no other engagement for that evening, and my husband proposed going.[69]

SWAMIJI'S STIRRING GOSPEL ATTRACTS SOME GOOD STUDENTS

Swami Vivekananda never spared himself. While imparting a spiritual education of universal character "to create a new order of humanity," he called forth people's inherent divinity and roused them to an awareness of their innate glory and goodness. The West, in its new search for life within, was influenced by Swamiji's sublime and rational thoughts. "What is God?" and "What is the universe?"— these questions will never be asked by the people at large. But the average person can no longer be indifferent to the vital questions—"What am I?" and "Who am I?" Here, Swamiji's stirring gospel of the divinity of man, the dominant theme of his teaching, encouraged his students to open a new portal and receive a new vision of a life of blessedness. Swamiji gave the living bread of life to anguished souls in the West.

His New York classes that had begun January 28, 1895 were over that year on June 1. Although they were a financial failure and physically exhausting—they were held nearly every morning and on several evenings each week—he was very happy to have some good students who "are more valuable than all the wealth of the world."

A BRIEF REST: SWAMIJI AT CAMP PERCY

These students and admirers, some of them persons of
position and wealth, indeed treasured their intimacy with Swami
and his teachings but were also keenly aware of his need for a
rest. Whenever they could, they invited him to spend brief
holidays at their residences, where they knew he would be
allowed to enjoy complete freedom. They also knew that his
divine eloquence would be enhanced thereby, and his human
capacity for joy and ecstasy be revealed and enjoyed by all. For
"he would come down unexpectedly from the mountaintops of
insight to the levels of childlike simplicity in a moment."[70] And
that is how on June 4, 1895, Swamiji left New York to enjoy a
blessed twelve days at Camp Percy, which he felt was "lovely,
quiet and very restful." On more than one occasion in the West,
Swamiji had experienced the beatitude of Divine Consciousness:

At Camp Percy, he was greatly fascinated by the quietude
of the beautiful place and expressed his desire to spend
more time in meditation and the reading of the *Gita* in this
solitary forest. As told in New *Discoveries*: "One morning
before breakfast Swamiji came out from his room with a
Sanskrit *Gita* in his hand. I [Josephine MacLeod] was behind
him. Seeing me, he said, 'Joe, I am going to sit under that
pine (pointing to a nearby pine) and read the *Bhagavad
Gita*. See that the breakfast is sumptuous today.' Half an
hour later I went over to the pine tree and saw Swamiji
sitting there motionless. The *Gita* had fallen from his hand
and the front of his robe was wet with tears. I went nearer
and saw that his breathing had stopped altogether. I
trembled in fear—Swamiji must be dead. I did not shout,
but ran to Francis Leggett and told him, 'Come quick, Swami
Vivekananda has left us.' My sister ran to the spot with
loud cries and my [future] brother-in-law also came with
tears in his eyes. By now seven or eight minutes had passed.
Swamiji was still in the same position. But my brother-in-

law said, 'He is in a trance; I will shake him out of it.' I stopped him, shouting, 'Never do that!' I remembered that Swamiji had said once that when he would be in deep meditation one should not touch him. Another five minutes or so passed, then we saw the signs of breathing. His eyes had been half-closed; now slowly they opened. And then Swamiji, as if soliloquizing, said, 'Who am I, where am I?' Thrice he spoke like that, and then, wide awake, he saw us, was very much embarrassed, stood up, and said, 'I am sorry to have frightened you all. But I have this state of consciousness now and then. I shall not leave my body in your country. Betty, I am hungry, let's hurry'." According to *New Discoveries*, "On the shore of Lake Michigan he had also entered into *samadhi*, but on that occasion it was Sri Ramakrishna who, appearing to him, drew him back 'to the work for which he had come to the world'."[71]

AN EXTENDED REST AND RETREAT: SWAMIJI AT THOUSAND ISLAND PARK

From Camp Percy he went to Thousand Island Park, where he stayed from June 18 to August 7, 1895. Miss Elizabeth Dutcher, a student of Swamiji, had a cottage at Thousand Island Park on the Saint Lawrence River, and invited Swamiji to conduct a retreat as well as to have a rest there. By a singular coincidence, only twelve students followed the Swami at the retreat. Here, he gave initiation to some of his students, both male and female. For the first time, Swami Vivekananda spoke at length about Sri Ramakrishna before this group. Sister Christine was there and wrote of his meditative moods, "There was nothing set or formed about these nights on the upper veranda. He sat in his large chair at the end, near his door. Sometimes he went into a deep meditation. At such times we too meditated or sat in profound silence. Often it lasted for hours and one after the other slipped away."[72]

THE SONG OF THE SANNYASIN AND *INSPIRED TALKS*

The terrible tensions and sleeplessness Swamiji had endured in New York were now given release and he found that he would "sleep at least two hours during the day and sleep through the whole night as a piece of log. This is a reaction...from the sleeplessness of New York."[73] It was here in Thousand Island Park that Swamiji was inspired to compose *The Song of the Sannyasin* one afternoon, immediately following his fervent talk on the joys and freedom in the life of renunciation.[74] The golden fruits of this unique spiritual retreat have been immortalized in the book, *Inspired Talks*. This was a "momentous period in his life in the Western world."

"I BLESS THESE THOUSAND ISLANDS"
SWAMIJI LEAVES FOR NEW YORK

Swamiji's inspired talks and intimate holy companionship ended on August 6, 1895. On the following day he left for New York. Mrs. Mary Funke wrote a letter that describes that last day and the poignant departure:

The last day has been a very wonderful and precious one. This morning there was no class. He asked C. [Christine] and me to take a walk as he wished to be alone with us. (The others had been with him all summer, and he felt we should have a last talk.) We went up a hill about half a mile away. All was woods and solitude. Finally he selected a low-branched tree, and we sat under the low-spreading branches. Instead of the expected talk, he suddenly said, "Now we will meditate. We shall be like Buddha under the Bo Tree." He seemed to turn to bronze, so still was he. Then a thunderstorm came up, and it poured. He never noticed it. I raised my umbrella and protected him as much as possible. Completely absorbed in his meditation, he was oblivious of everything. Soon we heard shouts in the distance. The others had come out after us with raincoats and umbrellas. Swamiji looked around regretfully, for we had to go, and said, "Once more am I in Calcutta in the rains."

He was so tender and sweet all this last day. As the steamer rounded the bend in the river he boyishly and joyously waved his hat to us in farewell and he had departed indeed.[75]

Before departing, Swamiji took leave of Thousand Island Park with the words, "I bless these Thousand Islands."[76] Then, accompanied by Miss Waldo, Swamiji left Thousand Island Park by river steamer and traveled as far as Clayton. They took the train together—Miss Waldo for Albany and Swamiji for New York. He arrived on August 8 and stayed with Miss Mary A. Phillips at 19 West Thirty-eighth Street and conducted classes.

"Miss Mary" belonged to an old and distinguished family of American Colonial ancestry and figured prominently in charitable and intellectual work in the metropolitan area. She had found her "foundational faith" in Vedanta and was therefore an active worker and admirer. When the New York Vedanta Society was founded in November of 1894, she became its first secretary. She had a generous nature and gave away so much of her inherited fortune that she later had to take in boarders.[77]

AN UNFORGETTABLE ENCOUNTER WITH SWAMIJI

It is fairly certain that it was in Miss Phillips' boarding home in August 1895 that the sculptress Malvina Hoffman, who was then a little girl, met Swamiji during his stay there. So unforgettable was he that she wrote many years later about Swamiji in her book, *Heads and Tales*:

India brought back one of my vivid memories of childhood, an exciting evening spent with a relative of my father's who lived in a modest boarding house in West Thirty-eighth Street. In the midst of this group of old-fashioned city boarders was introduced suddenly a newcomer—the oriental philosopher and teacher, Swami Vivekananda. When he entered the dining room there was a hush. His dark, bronzed countenance and hands were in sharp contrast to the voluminous, light folds of his turban and robe. His dark eyes hardly glanced up to notice his neighbors, but there was a sense of tranquility and power about him that made an imperishable impression upon me. He seemed to personify the mystery and religious "aloofness" of all true teachers of Brahma, and combined with this a kindly and gentle attitude of simplicity towards his fellow men.

It was many years later, in 1931, that we visited outside of Calcutta, at Belur, the marble temple which was dedicated to this same man by the thousands of his devoted followers. When I offered the garland of jasmine to be laid on the altar, I recalled, with emotion, that the only time I had seen this holy man, he had revealed to me more of the true spirit of India, without even uttering a word, than I had ever sensed in the many lectures *on* India, or by Indians, which I had attended since.[78]

SWAMIJI LEAVES NEW YORK FOR PARIS AND LONDON

Swamiji left New York for Paris on August 17, 1895. It may be noted that during Swamiji's absence, "weekly classes of the Vedanta Society had been held either by Swami Kripananda (Landsberg) or Swami Abhayananda (Marie Louise),"[79] two of Swamiji's American devotees to whom Swamiji gave the vows of sannyas at Thousand Island Park.[80]

At the invitation of Mr. E. T. Sturdy, a London admirer and Miss Henrietta Müller, Swamiji went to London from Paris. There he sowed the seeds of Vedanta and acquired the friendship of Miss Margaret Noble and Captain and Mrs. John Henry Sevier, all of whom were to become vital to his future work.

SWAMIJI RETURNS TO NEW YORK:
THE SECOND HOME OF THE VEDANTA SOCIETY

Swamiji landed in New York on December 6, "clad in a red and flowing Hindu cloak." It was a very chilly morning, with the temperature six degrees below the freezing point. He was received by Swami Kripananda, who accompanied him to his residence at 228 West Thirty-ninth Street. This lodging house with two large parlor rooms was rented by Swamiji's friends a few days earlier and was his second home in New York. Kripananda had stayed here from April 9 to July 10, 1895. Beginning in November, later that year, he had held classes here on behalf of the Vedanta Society. From Sister Devamata's account, it was "one in a long monotonous row of dingy boarding houses" which, to the Swami himself, was "very dirty and miserable." Both rooms, with no private bath or kitchen, proved very inconvenient. Swamiji and Kripananda now had to share with everyone the community kitchen on the ground floor and the common bathroom above. Swamiji generally did the cooking and Kripananda had to wash many pots and pans, much to his irritation.

SWAMIJI'S DISTINGUISHED INFLUENTIAL
FOLLOWERS AND SUPPORTERS

Swamiji started teaching classes on Mondays, in the evening. In 1895, from December 9 to December 22, he held classes twice daily on four days of the week and a question-and-answer class on Sundays.[81] Kripananda had to take a small room on the top floor of the house in order to accommodate the "crowded preliminary classes" in the two large parlor rooms. Initial attendance varied from 70 to 120. But the quality of the students was quite impressive, as reported by the *New York Herald* on January 11, 1896: "A well-dressed audience of distinguishing appearance." Prominent members of the congregation included Mr. and Mrs. Francis Leggett; Mr. and Mrs. Walter Goodyear; Dr. and Mrs. Egbert Guernsey; Mr. Josiah John Goodwin; Miss Phillips; Miss Ruth Ellis; Dr. L. L. Wight; Emma Thursby and Antoinette Sterling; Mary Mapes Dodge; Kate Douglas Wiggin; Miss Waldo and her intimate friend, Ella Wheeler Wilcox with her husband; and Nikola Tesla. They were all students of Swamiji, and, in all likelihood, attended his classes. Emma Thursby and Antoinette Sterling were famous in the world of music. Mary Mapes Dodge, Kate Douglas Wiggin and Ella Wheeler Wilcox were famous in the literary world. Tesla was the famous scientist. Swamiji certainly had an influential following. Even many of the clergy attended his classes. He received an invitation from John P. Fox, the acting honorary secretary of the Cambridge Conferences, to speak before the Harvard Graduate Philosophical Club, where he lectured twice daily for four days in addition to his public lectures on Sunday afternoon.

SWAMI VIVEKANANDA'S INTELLECTUAL INFLUENCE IS RECOGNIZED

Swami Vivekananda earned such wide acclaim during the 1895-1896 season of lectures and classes that his name was selected for inclusion in the National Encyclopedia of America.[82] The April 11, 1896 issue of *The Brahmavadin* published a letter to the editor from Helen F. Huntington that stated in part:

Swami Vivekananda has made many friends outside the circle of his followers; he has met all phases of society on equal terms of friendship and brotherhood; his classes and lectures have been attended by the most intellectual people and advanced thinkers of our cities; and his influence has already grown into a deep, strong undercurrent of spiritual awakening. No praise or blame has moved him to either approbation or expostulation; neither money nor position has influenced or prejudiced him. Towards demonstrations of undue favouritism, he has invariably maintained a priestly attitude of inattention, checking foolish advances with a dignity impossible to resist, blaming not any but wrongdoers and evil-thinkers, exhorting only to purity and right living. He is altogether such a man as "kings delight to honor."[83]

Huntington wrote again to the editor and *The Brahmavadin* of November 21, 1896 reported from her letter that "It will always be a marvel to us that an oriental could take such a firm hold on us occidentals, trained as we have been by long habit of thought and education to opposing views."

PUBLICATION OF SWAMIJI'S LECTURES:
JOSIAH GOODWIN AND ELLEN WALDO ASSIST SWAMIJI

Swamiji's friends felt the necessity for a qualified stenographer to take notes of Swamiji's lectures and classes. They placed a single advertisement in two local newspapers on December 13, 1895. Mr. Josiah Goodwin, who responded promptly, was immediately hired. From the very beginning, Goodwin worked day and night over the lectures, taking them down stenographically and then typewriting them all in the same day. After a while, the Society decided to publish Swamiji's lectures. These were typed by Goodwin, edited by Miss Waldo, and finally checked by Swamiji. The first pamphlet, "The Ideal of a Universal Religion," was published in January 1896 and marked the beginning of the books on Vedanta philosophy.[84] Gradually, the four Yoga books—*Karma, Bhakti, Raja* and *Jnana*—were published under the auspices of the Vedanta Society, with *Karma-Yoga* and the "The Real and the Apparent Man" being presented to the public on February 23, 1896.[85] The second edition of *Karma-Yoga* was brought out by the Vedanta Society of New York in 1901. *Jnana-Yoga, Part I* was published by the Society in 1902. This was the first Western edition of *Jnana-Yoga*.

MISS WALDO: "A REAL SERVANT OF GOD"

Like Goodwin, Miss Waldo—*Haridasi*, as she was called—proved herself to be a real "servant of God." A few days after classes had started, Swamiji said to Miss Waldo, "The food here seems so unclean, would it be possible for you to cook for me?" She was delighted. Immediately, she approached the landlady and obtained permission to use the kitchen. Sister Devamata described this activity:

> [She] moved about doing everything ... Her service was continuous and untiring. She cooked, edited, cleaned and took dictation, taught and managed, read proofs and saw visitors... She lived at the far end of Brooklyn. The only means of transportation was a jogging horse-car and it required two hours to reach Swamiji's lodging at 39th Street ... The daily journey would have been an arduous one. Undaunted, every morning found her on her way at eight o'clock or earlier; and at nine or ten at night, she was on her way home again. When there came a free day, the journey was reversed. It was Swamiji who took the jogging horse-car, travelled the two hours and cooked the meals. He found genuine rest and relaxation in the freedom and quiet of Miss Waldo's simple home. The kitchen was on the

top floor of the house, in front of it the dining room full of sunshine and potted plants. As the Swami invented new dishes or tried experiments with Western provisions, he ran back and forth from one room to the other like a child at play.[86]

Burke also points out that:

Miss Waldo was deeply devoted to Swamiji. Years later, she expressed the depth of her feeling in a letter to Miss MacLeod, who had shared with her some of his letters: "I brought the dear letters upstairs and read them over again and then put my head down on them and had a good cry over them. My blessed, blessed guru! How was I ever so favored as to be permitted to know him! And not only to know him, but to love him and be accepted by him as his disciple! I always bless the day he came into my life. May I always be faithful to him and to his teachings!"[87]

Shortly before the end of the season, on February 20, Swamiji gave the vows of brahmacharya to Miss Waldo, Mr. Goodwin and Mr. Van Haagen. A week earlier, on February 13, Swamiji gave the vows of sannyas to Dr. Street, who is known to us as Swami Yogananda.

SWAMIJI'S EXPANSIVE DISCOURSES ATTRACT AN INCREASINGLY LARGER AUDIENCE

Apart from conducting classes at the Society, Swamiji also gave many public lectures in Hardman Hall, Mott's Memorial Hall, the People's Church, and Madison Square Garden (with a seating capacity of fifteen hundred) in New York; in the Brooklyn Ethical Association and the Metaphysical Society in Brooklyn; and in Unity Hall in Hartford, Connecticut. Swamis Abhayananda and Kripananda were also holding classes to assist Swamiji in spreading the message of Vedanta. Swamiji, in his letter to Mr. Sturdy on December 16, 1895, had written, "The last month my lectures were in a small hall holding about 600. But 900 will come as a rule, 300 standing, and about 300 going off, not finding room."[88]

SWAMIJI'S IMPACT ON THE GENERAL PUBLIC

In February 1896, Swami Kripananda wrote to the *Brahmavadin*, which printed his letter indicating that Swamiji had a very great impact on the reading public: "The public libraries are running after everything that has reference to India; the books of Max Müller, Colebrook, Deussen, Burnouf, and of all the authors that have ever written in English on Hindu philosophy, find a ready sale; and even the dry and tiresome Schopenhauer, on account of his Vedantic background, is being studied with great eagerness."[89]

"MY MASTER: HIS LIFE AND TEACHINGS" SWAMIJI'S LECTURE LEADS TO THE PUBLICATION OF *RAJA YOGA*

On February 23, 1896, near the time of Sri Rama-krishna's birthday, Swami Vivekananda delivered his final and famous lecture at Madison Square Garden Hall, "My Master: His Life and Teachings." The subject was uniquely chosen for the close of his New York teachings. A lecture on Ramakrishna Paramahamsa was also given in London in the fall of that same year (the exact date and location remain unclear). While Burke claims Swamiji never spoke about his Master in Boston, an account of such a lecture appears in *The Life of Swami Vivekananda*. The two lectures, delivered in New York and London, were subsequently combined under the heading, "My Master," which can be found in the fourth volume of Swami Vivekananda's *Complete Works*.[90] Sister Devamata heard him speak on that occasion and wrote in her reminiscences:

> [Madison Square Concert Hall] was full to the uttermost at that closing lecture—every seat, every foot of standing room was occupied... As he entered the hall from a door at the side of the platform, one sensed a different mood in him. He seemed less confident, as if he approached his task reluctantly... He began his lecture with a long preamble [a not unimportant historical background]; but once in his subject, it swept him. The force of it drove him from one end of the platform to the other. It overflowed in a swift-running stream of eloquence and feeling. The large audience listened in awed stillness and at the close many left the hall without speaking. As for myself, I was transfixed. The transcendental picture drawn overwhelmed me. The call had come and I answered.[91]

Mr. and Mrs. W. H. Starick of Ohio also remembered these lectures with devotion. In 1944 Mr. Starick wrote to Sister Shivani, an American disciple of Swami Abhedananda: "In 1895 I was in New York when I had the good fortune to hear Swami Vivekananda. He was giving the seven lectures at Madison Square Concert Hall, all of which I heard, including *My Master*, to an audience of more than two thousands holding them spellbound for more than two hours. From then on I was bound to Vedanta forever."[92]

Out of these classes and lectures, several books on Vedanta were published, first in pamphlet form and later in book form. Raja-Yoga was published in England in July 1896. Miss Waldo worked very hard to set the manuscript of *Raja-Yoga* in time for publication. Mr. Sturdy, Swamiji's admirer in London, borrowed the manuscript and published it in London, with a good motive. Of course, this created lots of confusion and hard feelings among the members of the Vedanta Society of New York. The American edition was later published with a glossary and other materials added.

THE NEED BECOMES APPARENT:
ONE HEADQUARTERS FOR THE WEST—
IN NEW YORK

There was a distinct lack of cooperation and understanding among the friends of Swamiji, who were spread out in three places: New York, Boston, and London. Burke observed that, "The existing organization—the Vedanta Society of which Miss Mary A. Phillips was secretary, Mr. Walter Goodyear, treasurer, and Miss Waldo, untitled but ever-present worker—was not, in fact, a particularly strong and cohesive group such as could support and promote the young Vedanta Movement. There were no headquarters, no one to take full charge, and little cooperation."[93]

As far as the research shows, the fledgling society appears to have consisted only of officers. According to Burke, Mr. Charles M. Higgins, the Brooklyn lawyer and inventor who displayed much interest in promoting Swamiji's work, may possibly have been the Society's first president (Francis Leggett may subsequently have been made president of the Society, replacing Mr. Higgins). The Society's vice president was Dr. Edward G. Day, of whom very little is known. The secretary, Miss Phillips, as we know, had shown much kindness to Swamiji in her home where he had given his second public lecture in the spring of 1894. The treasurer, Mr. Walter Goodyear, from New Jersey,[94] was an ardent disciple of Swamiji (as was his wife) and a promoter of Swami's teachings. Mr. Goodyear gave the announcements at the meetings. He also got the copyright certificates for the pamphlets, "The Ideal of a Universal Religion"; "The Cosmos"; "The Real and the Apparent Man"; and "The Atman"; and for the book, Karma-Yoga.[95]

MAINTAINING THE PURITY OF THE VEDANTA
MOVEMENT IN THE WEST:
SWAMIJI'S VISION OF AN EFFECTIVE VEDANTA SOCIETY

Swamiji did not want to entangle himself in "horrid money affairs." He had "no aptitude for organization." The existing Society had been "nebulous and largely ineffectual." It had sympathizers but no formal membership. Swamiji did not like the business mentality in a spiritual organization for "in the long run it does harm and sets a bad example."

An Executive Committee Is Formed

In a previous season, before December 1895, Swamiji had delivered paid public lectures to support his classes in the Society. In December 1895 Swamiji took the initiative in setting up an Executive Committee within the Vedanta Society. The committee would take up the secular and business side of the Society. This newly created committee gave Swamiji great relief as he wanted "to step entirely out of the money question—in both public lectures and private classes."

A Publication Committee Is Formed

Later, it was considered expedient to create the new Publication Committee of the Vedanta Society, to take over all the publishing activities of the Executive Committee. Mrs. Bull, who was, in Swamiji's words, "the principal backer" (together with Mr. Leggett), headed the Publication Committee. Henceforth, the Vedanta Society assumed, officially or unofficially, the role of publisher.

On February 23, 1896 Swamiji's first book, Karma-Yoga, was presented to the public. The pamphlet, "The Real and the Apparent Man," which came out on the same day, presented a photograph of Swamiji on its cover; the typefaces on the cover and title page were better chosen than—or at least different from—those of the earlier pamphlets, and their arrangement was more arresting. Both publications included a line indicating they had been published under the auspices of the Vedanta Society. As far as can be inferred, it was during the week *Karma-Yoga* went to press that the Publication Committee was set up to handle it, and to take into its care the publication of Swamiji's pamphlets and future books composed of his New York lectures and classes. Burke informs us that, as far as can be determined, Miss Waldo was officially placed in charge of the editorial work, Mr. Goodwin of the printing, and Mr. and Mrs. Goodyear of the distribution and accounting.[96]

The Vedanta Society, as a whole, now became an entity aware of its unique importance: it was Swamiji's chosen vehicle to keep the message of Vedanta alive in the West after his absence. The Society began to present itself in such a manner, and Swamiji's final lecture at Madison Square Garden Hall was announced in the newspapers as "under the auspices of The Vedanta Society."[97]

THE SOCIETY SETTLES DOWN TO WORK

SWAMIJI SETS THE PRECEDENT— FREEDOM FROM FINANCIAL BURDENS

The age-old tradition of India is that sannyasins give spiritual discourses without charge. Swamiji wanted the Vedanta Society in the West to follow the same principle, to maintain the purity of its character. "Thus Swamiji's decision to set a precedent of free public lectures had a twofold purpose: it would release his successors from the burden of earning money and it would compel the Western societies to stand financially on their own feet," Burke explains.[98]

The financial resources of the Society were not great. Friends of the Society, though not wealthy, spent money for its expenses. It has been said, "There is no doubt that Swamiji lived with utmost frugality, working constantly, giving the best of his life to his Mission in the West." The Society, working behind the scenes, confined itself to the business aspect— renting the hall, printing the pamphlets and making of plans, etc. When, formerly "active and helpful, it had been almost invisible in the radiance of its leader" and "came into being only as Swamiji left New York—much as stars seem to come into being only as the sun leaves the sky."[99]

"MAKE A BLAZE, MAKE A BLAZE"

After remaining "a loosely-woven organization" for some time, the Society emerged as a more effective body and became a vehicle for the "study and propagation of Vedantic literature." According to Burke, Swamiji wrote to Mrs. Bull on April 14, 1896, prior to his departure from New York confirming his appointment of her as caretaker of his work. The mandate given by Swamiji, "I leave everything to your care,"[100] enabled Mrs. Bull to correspond with Swamiji's friends in New York— Miss Phillips, Miss Waldo, Mr. Leggett and Miss MacLeod— in order to make the Society more effective and stable. In one correspondence with Miss Waldo, Mrs. Bull wrote, "I trust the time may come when the good service and the personal devotion felt for the Swami Vivekananda may find a common unity of expression in steadfast loyalty to him and consideration each for the other."[101]

During the last three months of 1896, Miss Waldo rendered commendable services for Swamiji's work in her own way, which was, perhaps, more pleasing to Swamiji than the reorganization along the lines of Mrs. Bull. Swamiji wrote to Mrs. Bull on November 13: "New York has settled down to work."[102]

Swamiji also wrote a very beautiful letter to Miss Waldo on October 8, 1896, from Wimbledon:

Why do you not begin to teach? Begin boldly. Mother will give you all power—thousands will come to you. Plunge in. No clinging to this fellow or that. Wherever Ramakrishna's children boldly come out, He is with them. You know a thousand times more philosophy than the boy Roy. There is nothing in Vedanta which you do not know, and you can argue it out & present it infinitely better than this boy. Plunge in bravely. Have faith you will move the world. Send notices to the class & hold regular talks & lectures. Goodyear & the others will back you right along. *I will be a thousand times more pleased* to see one of you start than any number of Hindus scoring success in America, even be he one of my brethren. "Man wants victory from everywhere but defeat from his own children." I will begin from today sending out powerful thoughts to you all. Make a blaze, make a blaze.[103]

Swamiji urged Miss Waldo earnestly to commence taking classes[104] as he considered her "his ablest and best-prepared student in this country."[105]

SWAMIJI LECTURES IN DETROIT AND BOSTON

Swamiji, accompanied by Mr. Goodwin, went to Detroit on March 3. This was his third visit. He stayed there for two weeks and gave classes. From Detroit he came to Boston, where he gave four lectures before an audience of between four and five hundred people.

A Remarkable Harvard Lecture

On March 25, 1896 Swamiji spoke before the Harvard Graduate Philosophical Club at Harvard University. This is considered to be "one of the most remarkable incidents of his whole American career." Mr. Leggett later published the first edition of Swamiji's Harvard lecture on "Vedanta Philosophy".

An introduction to the booklet was written by Reverend C. C. Everett, the Dean of Divinity at Harvard University.[106] Swami Vivekananda and his teaching had made such a deep impression upon Rev. Everett and upon other Harvard professors that he was offered the chair of Eastern Philosophy at Harvard University (a lifetime post). Part of Dr. Everett's introduction is given here:

> The Swami Vivekananda has created a high degree of interest in himself and his work. There are indeed, few departments of study more attractive than the Hindoo thought. It is a rare pleasure to see a form of belief that to most seems so far away and unreal as the Vedanta system, represented by an actually living and extremely intelligent believer. This system is not to be regarded merely as a curiosity, as a speculative vagary. Hegel said that Spinozism is the necessary beginning of all philosophizing. This can be said even more emphatically of the Vedanta system. We occidentals busy ourselves with the manifold. We can, however, have no understanding of the manifold, if we have no sense of the One in which the manifold exists. The reality of the One is the truth which the East may well teach us; and we owe a debt of gratitude to Vivekananda that he has taught this lesson so effectively.[107]

SWAMIJI LEAVES FOR ENGLAND

Swamiji returned to New York on April 11, 1896 after visiting Chicago and left New York again on April 15 for his second visit to England. From his last known residence at 6 West Forty-third Street, he wrote a short letter of farewell to his dear Hale sisters, conveying his "everlasting memory of love, gratitude and blessings."

In a letter sent by the New York students to Swamiji's brother disciples in India it was written that, "the Swami

Vivekananda sailed for England on the 15th of April. In his farewell address to his friends and pupils in New York, he spoke highly of the Americans, and the freedom of their institutions, which made them peculiarly accessible to the Vedanta Philosophy."[108] "After all," Swamiji would write to Mary Hale upon his arrival in England, "those years there have been some of the best I have yet seen."[109]

REMINISCENCES OF SWAMIJI'S FIRST SOJOURN IN NEW YORK

Thus ended his first visit to America, where he had spent less than two-and-a-half years. About Swamiji's strenuous December days we get this report from Kripananda: "The Swami works very hard lecturing twice a day, and then spending the rest of the time in hard study over the Sanskrit books ... not allowing himself half an hour a day for going outdoors. He eats very little—vegetable food ... Certainly anyone else would have made himself sick." On the same day Kripananda wrote this report, Swamiji was writing to his Madras disciple, "Sometimes I have to deliver two or three lectures a day—and thus I make my way against all odds— hard work; any weaker man would die." He had not "slept even one night soundly in New York," he wrote later to Mrs. Bull on February 6, 1896.[110]

Burke reflects on that period:

It is not possible to estimate the amount of energy Swamiji expended during this season, for one cannot judge his work by ordinary standards. Yet even by those standards, even in terms of physical and intellectual energy, his output was prodigious. At a conservative estimate, he held throughout this season (from December 9 through February 25) seventy classes (including those at Miss Corbin's) and delivered ten public lectures. And this in addition to interviews, initiations, extensive correspondence, the writing of articles, the translating of scriptures, the editing of lectures for publication, and the organizing of his work into some sort of shape that would contain and perpetuate his message. He had given of himself to the point of exhaustion during those three months—and there remained far more to do.[111]

The secretary of the Vedanta Society, Miss Phillips, wrote a letter that was addressed to "Our Indian Brethren." It read:

Dear Friends:

The Western Aryans send cordial greeting to the Aryans of India.

We, in New York, who have been so fortunate as to hear the Vedanta Philosophy taught by the Swami Vivekananda, are desirous of expressing to you in some small measure our grateful recognition of his services to us.

He came, a stranger, unheralded, but, by the force of his magnetic eloquence, and the purity of his personal character, he commanded the attention and interest of thousands, and attracted their minds to the study of a subject almost entirely unknown to them. Here, in New York, where he taught and lectured for two seasons, the impression he produced is so deep that we hope and trust it will extend until the Vedanta Philosophy shall take permanent root among us, and its comprehensive and tolerant teachings shall find lodgment in hearts, and expression in the lives of large numbers of our people. We who came into more immediate contact with him, are deeply grateful for the noble work he did among us, for the unselfish and self-sacrificing efforts he made on our behalf; and we will try to the best of our ability to establish on a lasting basis the study of the Vedanta Philosophy and to promote the growth of knowledge concerning it.

We wish to extend to you, his fellow-countrymen, our heartfelt sympathy in your present afflictions, with an earnest hope that a way may be found to lighten them.

May the Swami Vivekananda's work among his own people be blessed a thousandfold, and meet with the fullest measure of success. Should he return to us in the years to come, he will receive a most cordial welcome. He has made us feel that we are all of one kin, and all expressions of that One Existence which is the background of the Universe.[112]

Through his books, the liberal-minded thinking people will be inspired, no doubt.

2

SWAMIJI'S SECOND TRIP TO AMERICA

"A LION AMONGST MEN"—THE EMINENCE
AND POWER OF SWAMIJI

Swamiji again came to America on August 28, 1899. Mrs. Coulston, the acting secretary of the New York Vedanta Society and others were present at the dock. Swamiji went straight to Ridgely Manor, where he spent his longest vacation in America: it was "the great summer" of ten weeks' duration, from August 28 until November 7. It may be remembered that Swamiji visited Ridgely Manor twice in 1895: one short visit in April and one during the Christmas season of the same year. He came to the Vedanta Society on November 7. It was now located at 146 East Fifty-fifth Street, between Lexington and Third Avenues. He stayed there less than two weeks. Swamiji refrained from giving any public lectures but he was always found attending the classes and meetings of the Society. He also gave short talks there and replied to the questions put to him.

SOME REMINISCENCES OF SWAMI VIVEKANANDA

SWAMI ATULANANDA'S FIRST IMPRESSION

A formal reception was given to Swamiji on November 10, which was attended by many students and former friends of the Swami. Here we give the reminiscences of Gurudas (Swami Atulananda), who saw Swamiji at the reception for the first time:

Let me record only one of my impressions of the evening. I do so because it came to me with such great force... Swamiji was so simple in his behaviour—so like one of the crowd—that he did not impress me too much when I first saw him. There was nothing about his ways that would mark him as the lion of New York society, as so often he had been. Simple in dress and behavior, he was just like one of us. He did not put himself aside on a pedestal as is so often the case with lionized personages. He walked about the room, sat on the floor, laughed, joked, chatted—nothing formal. Of course, I had noticed his magnificent, brilliant eyes, his beautiful features and majestic bearing, for these were parts of him that no circumstances could hide. But when I saw him for a few minutes, standing on a platform surrounded by others, it flashed into my mind: "What a giant, what strength, what manliness, what a personality! Everyone near him looks so insignificant in comparison." It came to me almost as a shock and seemed to startle me. What was it that gave Swamiji this distinction? Was it his height? No, there were gentlemen there taller than he was. Was it his build? No, there were near him some very fine specimens of American manhood. It seemed to be more in the expression of the face than anything else. Was it his purity? What was it? I could not analyze it. I remembered what had been said of Lord Buddha—"A lion amongst men." I felt that Swamiji had unlimited power, that he could move heaven and earth if he willed it. This was my strongest and lasting impression of him... But I am grateful that I have seen him and that during those two weeks he had sometimes been very kind to me. And even now as I read and reread the Swami's lectures, that picture of wonderful strength and purity comes before my mental vision. And in those printed lines there still seems to vibrate something of that great spirit that came to enlighten the Western world.[1]

The Life of Swami Vivekananda further informs us that:

[Although] the Swami's power was indeed immeasurable and awe-inspiring, he had no wish to use it to influence others; on the contrary, he avoided doing so. It was at one of his class talks during this period in New York that, becoming aware of his power over his listeners, he instantly stopped and left the room. There was no more lecturing that night, and everyone went away greatly disappointed. When a friend later asked him why he had broken off his lecture just when his audience was becoming absorbed in it, he replied, he had felt that the minds of his listeners were becoming like soft clay in his hands; he had the power to give them any shape he wished. To do so, however, was against his philosophy; he wanted everyone to grow according to his or her own natural bent. So he had stopped.[2]

When Miss MacLeod asked Swamiji about it, Swamiji replied, "I felt such an inflow of strength and power that had I continued, it would have spoiled my message. All these people would have become my disciples. I don't want disciples. I want everyone to get free by their own efforts."[3] Miss MacLeod at one time said, "The thing that held me in Swamiji was his unlimitedness. I never could touch bottom—or top—or sides. The amazing size of him!"[4]

"THE STIMULUS THAT URGED US FORWARD"

We are tempted to relate an incident highlighting the spiritual eminence and yogic power of Swamiji. This testimony verifies the spiritual stature of the teacher who embarked upon a global mission through the Vedanta Society of New York. During the winter season of 1895-1896, Swamiji's work was being carried on undividedly by Sister Devamata (Laura Glenn at that time) and other friends. Swamiji's message had become the foundation for all their daily activity, "the stimulus that urged us onward." For, as Burke relates:

> To be stirred to one's depths was not always a comfortable experience. Even Laura Glenn, who attended all his New York classes through two seasons, felt so shy in his presence that she never came "in close personal touch with him. There seemed," she wrote, "to be an intangible barrier." Some people reacted with more than shyness. In the *Life* an unidentified disciple is quoted as having said, "It would be impossible for me to describe the overwhelming force of Swamiji's presence. He could rivet attention upon himself: and when he spoke in all seriousness and intensity—though it seems well nigh incredible—there were some among his hearers who were literally exhausted. The subtlety of his thought and arguments swept them off their feet. In one case, I know of a man who was forced to rest in bed for three days as the result of a nervous shock received by a discussion with the Swami. His personality was at once awe-inspiring and sublime. He had the faculty of literally annihilating one if he so chose."[5]

The great power of Divinity that dwelled in Swamiji and that poured from him attracted all created beings, even the animals. He delivered his message to the entire humanity with all-consuming love, with simplicity, and without prejudice.

A "TENDERNESS" AND A "FLOW OF BENEDICTION"

Another sweet memory of Gurudas (Swami Atulananda) is of the time when he went to the Society, holding a large portrait of Jesus in his hand:

> The Swami asked me what I had there. I told him that it was a picture of Christ talking to the rich young man. "Oh, let me see it," he said eagerly. I handed him the picture. And never shall I forget the tenderness in his look when he held the picture and looked at it. At last he returned it to me, with the simple words: "How great was Jesus!" And I could not help thinking that there was something in common between these two souls.[6]

> The doctrine of sin and eternal hell-fire is one of the doctrines on which Orthodox preachers love to harp. Man is born in sin, his nature is sinful. It is only through the grace of God that man can be saved.[7]

It may be of interest to know Swamiji's art of articulating Truth through jovial remarks. In *The Life of Swami Vivekananda* we find that:

> [At the Swami's question classes] everyone was invited to ask any question he wished. So one evening, an old church-lady asked him why he never spoke of sin. There came a look of surprise on Swamiji's face. "But, Madam," he said, "blessed are my sins. Through sin, I have learned virtue. It is my sins, as much as my virtues, that have made me what I am today. And now I am the preacher of virtue. Why do you dwell on the weak side of man's nature? Don't you know that the greatest blackguard often has some virtue that is wanting in the saint? There is only one power, and that power manifests both as good and as evil. God and the devil are the same river with the water flowing in opposite directions."

The lady was horrified, but others understood. And then the Swami began to speak of the divinity that resides in every man; how the soul is perfect, eternal and immortal; the Atman resides in every being...

... Here was hope, here was strength, every man can become divine, by realizing his own divinity. Do you see what an immense consolation Swamiji's teaching was to those that had searched, but had not yet found; those who had knocked, but unto whom it had not yet been opened? To them, Swamiji came as a Saviour. He came to the door of their own hearts and knocked. And blessed are they who opened the door to receive the flow of benediction that came with his presence.[8]

A STRANGE FOREBODING AND PHYSICAL STRESS DO NOT SPOIL SWAMIJI'S SATISFACTION IN THE NEW YORK WORK

Swamiji was wholly immersed in each one of his many activities, his entire being in the service of his mission, but he was not spared a strange foreboding of his life on the mortal plane. In *The Life of Swami Vivekananda* we read that, "One day [in 1899, while in the New York Center] he said to Swami Abhedananda, 'Well, Brother, my days are numbered. I shall live only for three or four years at the most'." The Swami sought to reassure him, appealing to him to rest and recover, and reminded him of all the work yet to be done. The account continues: "But the Swami replied significantly: 'You do not understand me, brother. I feel that I am growing very big. My self is expanding so much that at times I feel as if this body could not contain me any more. I am about to burst. Surely, this cage of flesh and blood cannot hold me for many days more'."[9]

The stress and cold of the East Coast was taking a toll on Swamiji's physical condition. He stayed a little over a week with the Leggetts at 21 West Thirty-fourth Street, and then moved in for a while with the Guernseys, now at 108 West

Fifty-ninth Street. Dr. Guernsey and Dr. Helmer—an osteopath who had treated him once before at Ridgely, again treated him, but the inclement New York weather continued to take its toll on him. There was also an additional sorrow he was forced to bear, when he received two bitter shocks: an unexpected encounter with Swami Kripananda who had betrayed him in April, 1895, and a letter of recrimination and lack of support from Mr. Sturdy. Swamiji always best knew himself, and he wrote from New York to a disciple, "On the whole, I don't think there is any cause for anxiety about my body. This sort of nervous body is just the instrument to play great music at times and at times to moan in darkness."[10]

THE DOOR OF NEW YORK OPENS TO SWAMIJI: "THE VEDANTA SOCIETY HAS A HOUSE OF ITS OWN"

Swamiji came to New York from Chicago on June 7, 1900. During a reception on June 10, he said joyfully, "I have knocked at the door of New York three times: it never opened. But now I am very happy to see that the Society has a house of its own."[11] Swamiji expressed his satisfaction at being able to live in the Vedanta Society's own house at 102 East Fifty-eighth Street, just off Park Avenue. It was actually a rented house in a good neighborhood. There was only one bed in the Vedanta Society and that was given to Swamiji. Swami Abhedananda slept on the floor, as did Swami Turiyananda, who was helping Swami Abhedananda by conducting the children's class.

SISTER NIVEDITA'S IMPRESSIONS

Nivedita was staying in New York at that time and attended most of Swamiji's classes. On June 10 Swamiji lectured on Vedanta Philosophy. This was the first of his lectures she had attended since 1895 and 1896 in London, when, "half-awed, half-skeptical, and more deeply stirred than she had known at the time, she had heard him speak":

> Then as we sat and waited for him to come in, a great trembling came over me, for I realized that this was, simple as it seemed, one of the test-moments of my life. Since last I had done this thing, how much had come and gone! My own life—where was it? Lost—thrown away like a cast-off garment that I might kneel at the feet of this man. Would it prove a mistake; an illusion; or was it a triumph of choice; a few minutes would tell.
>
> And then he came; his very entrance and his silence as he stood and waited to begin were like some great hymn. A whole worship in themselves.
>
> At last he spoke—his face broke into fun, and he asked what was to be his subject. Someone suggested the Vedanta philosophy and he began...
>
> ...The splendid sentences rolled on and on, and we, lifted into the Eternities, thought of our common selves as of babies stretching out their hands for the moon or the sun—thinking them a baby's toys. The wonderful voice went on...
>
> At last—the whole dying down and away in the thought—"*I* could not see *you* or speak to you for a moment—I who stand here seeing and talking—if this Infinite Unity were broken for a moment—if one little atom could be crushed and moved out of its place.... Hari Om Tat Sat!"
>
> And for me—I had found the infinitely deep things that life holds for us. To sit there and listen was all that it had ever been. Yet there was no struggle of intellectual unrest now—no tremor of novelty.
>
> This man who stood there held my life in the hollow of his hand—and as he once in a while looked my way, I read in his glance what I too felt in my own heart, complete faith and abiding comprehension of purpose—better than any feeling....[12]

It was perhaps on this occasion that Sister Nivedita observed that while "teaching a New York class to meditate, it was found at the end, that he could not be brought back to consciousness, and one by one, his students stole quietly away.

Nivedita also spoke at the Society, on "The Ideals of Hindu Women" and on "The Ancient Arts of India."[13] She left on June 28 for Paris. During June, Swamiji gave three Sunday lectures and four Saturday classes on the Gita. His last class at the Vedanta Society was on July 1, 1900.

SWAMIJI'S TEACHINGS HAVE A MARVELOUS EFFECT

Some Vedanta students in America now became aware of the great need for a place apart from the worldly life for those wishing to renounce and to practice the spiritual life more intensely. The mendicant monk of the East was not an accepted tradition in the West, where one joined a monastery or convent as a rule. Swamiji had long foreseen this need for a retreat or ashrama, and had spoken of it often, since the inception of his American work. As early as July 26, 1894, Swamiji was writing to the Hale sisters about this: "Miss Phillips has a beautiful place somewhere in N.Y. State, mountains, lake, river, forest altogether—what more? I am going to make a Himalayas there and start a monastery as sure as I am living—I am not going to leave this country without throwing one more apple of discord into this already roaring, fighting, kicking, mad whirlpool of American religion."[14] While Swamiji was in New York, the momentous fulfillment occurred through the generous instrumentation of Miss Minnie C. Boock, a student of Swami Abhedananda. On June 25, 1900, Miss Boock deeded her homestead in California to Swamiji. It had been issued to her eight years before by President Harrison and contained "one hundred and fifty-nine acres and eighty-nine hundredths of an acre" according to the official plat of the survey.[15]

SWAMI TURIYANANDA IS CHOSEN TO
HEAD THE ASHRAMA

A Swami had to be chosen to head this new project of the ashrama. Swami Turiyananda, who had come to America together with Swami Vivekananda on August 16, 1899, was carrying on Vedanta teachings together with Swami Abhedananda. On Sunday, May 6, 1900, Swami Turiyananda gave the first talk that Swami Abhedananda heard, at 102 East Fifty-eighth Street; Swami Abhedananda was very happy. Swami Turiyananda used to stay at Mrs. Wheeler's residence in Montclair, New Jersey, twenty miles from New York City. From New Jersey, he traveled the twenty miles to give classes at The Vedanta Society of New York on Saturday and Sunday, when Swami Abhedananda was outside the city. Normally, Swami Turiyananda conducted classes for children by telling them stories from the *Hitopadesha* and other books. Some time later, he participated fully in the New York Vedanta Society's work and took charge one entire summer when Swami Abhedananda was abroad.

Gurudas (Swami Atulananda) wrote of Swami Turiyananda's ability to inspire the students. Once, when Gurudas was out walking with the Swami in New York City, the Swami boldly proclaimed, "Be a lion! Be a lion! Break the cage and be free!" The Swami always exhorted his listeners to assert their divine nature, and when he was asked if he suffered exhaustion, Gurudas recorded Swami Turiyananda's reply: "You see, I have lived this life from my youth; it has become part and parcel of me. And Divine Mother keeps the supply filled up. Her store can never be exhausted. Whatever goes out, She at once fills up again." And again, about his love for Vedanta: "Vedanta is not an easy, comfortable religion. Truth is never cheap. So long as we are satisfied with glass beads, we won't search for diamonds. It is hard work to delve into the earth, remove the stones and rocks, and go to great depths to find the precious stone. Vedanta is the jewel among religions."[16]

During this time, Swami Vivekananda preached in California and founded the Vedanta Society of Northern California in San Francisco. The students there requested a resident monk and a more quiet, retreat-like atmosphere for a life of renunciation. Now that Miss Boock had offered her property the way was made clear. When he returned to New York in June 1900 via Chicago, Swamiji had already promised the students he would send them a resident Swami. He had already assigned Swami Turiyananda to be the resident monk in California, but now Swami Vivekananda asked him to establish and take up the project of the new retreat.

Burke describes their discussion. "[Swamiji said] 'It is the will of the Divine Mother that you should take charge of the work there.' But Swami Turiyananda smiled and said to Swamiji: 'Mother's will? Rather say it is *your* will. Certainly you have not heard the Mother communicate Her will to you in this matter.' But Swamiji grew grave. 'Yes, Brother, he said. If your nerves become very fine, then you will be able to hear Mother's words directly'."[17] *The Life of Swami Vivekananda* continues the narrative: "Go and establish the Ashrama in California ... Hoist the flag of Vedanta there. From this moment destroy even the memory of India! Above all, live the life, and Mother will see to the rest!"[18] Swami Turiyananda then cheerfully agreed to take charge, as he accepted that the will of the Divine Mother was being expressed through Swamiji. Swami Turiyananda's overwhelming devotion to the Divine Mother was his radiant characteristic, for Mother's Name was ever upon his lips. Swami Turiyananda was bold and straightforward, an inexhaustible teacher and a living example of Practical Vedanta.

On July 3, 1900, Swami Turiyananda left New York for California for his new assignment, accompanied by Miss Boock. A few weeks after arriving in Los Angeles on July 8, Swami Turiyananda went to San Francisco. He settled down in August to the hard task of developing the ashrama, which he named Shanti Ashrama. He did not leave it until January

10, 1901, to visit San Francisco for some medical treatment. He gave many lectures there and in neighboring cities during that February and March. Then he returned to Shanti Ashrama for a period of five months.

SWAMI TURIYANANDA'S LAST DAYS AT SHANTI ASHRAMA

Gurudas (Swami Atulananda) wrote about Swami Turiyananda's final days in Shanti Ashrama:

One evening, just after dusk, when I entered the little cabin we shared together, the Swami told me of a vision he had had. The Divine Mother had come to him and had asked him to remain in the ashrama. But he had refused. Then She told him that if he stayed in the ashrama the work would grow rapidly, and many beautiful buildings would be erected. Still he had refused. At last She showed him the place full of disciples. "Let me go to Swamiji first," he had said. And the Mother with grave countenance vanished from his sight. The vision had left him unhappy and disturbed in mind. "I have done wrong," he said with a sigh, "but it cannot be helped now." Turiyananda had fully surrendered himself to the Divine Mother, yet he refused Her command. Why? Nobody knows. It will always remain a mystery. Before his departure, Turiyananda called Gurudas to his cabin and gave him his final instructions: "I leave you in full charge. I have told you everything. You have seen how I have lived here. Now try to do the same... Depend on Mother for everything. Trust in Her, and She will guide you. One thing remember: Never boss anyone. Look upon all alike, treat all alike. No favourites. Hear all, and be just."[19]

After he became Swami Atulananda, Gurudas Maharaj again gave his heartfelt and candid testimony of Swami

Turiyananda. His article, "Moments with the Swami Turiyananda in America," was published in the September 1927 issue of *Prabuddha Bharata*: "Swami Turiyananda was not great in the popular sense, he was not a man of world-renown. His influence was local, confined to small circles. But if we apply the same standard to a smaller radius, his influence on individuals instead of on the masses, one would not hesitate one moment to call him a man of rare worth. He himself once said to me, "If I can influence a few students to love the Divine Mother and to live a pure life, I shall consider my work a success."

Swami Turiyananda left Shanti Ashrama for the last time in late May of 1902, for San Francisco. On June 6, he sailed to India, for his health had broken down. Of the two years and nine months he had spent in the United States, eighteen months had been dedicated to Shanti Ashrama.

THE LAST DAYS AND ACTIVITIES OF
SWAMIJI IN AMERICA:
THE FOCUS AND DEPTH OF POWER

Swamiji remained in New York till Tuesday, July 3, 1900, when he left for Detroit, to stay for a brief period with Sister Christine (Christina Greenstidel) and her family. He rested here with this poor yet generous family, and held only one or two informal gatherings to benefit his close disciples and friends. Swamiji returned to New York on July 10. From that day till July 26—the day he sailed for Paris—Swamiji lived at the Vedanta Society. Mrs. Crane, the caretaker of things, Ellen Waldo, and Sister Christine were also with Swamiji at the Vedanta Society.

We would like to further inform our readers of some activities of Swamiji. In June Swami Vivekananda spoke at the Vedanta Society in his usual way, which drew his audience, though small in number, like a powerful magnet. Swamiji definitely was aware of the impact of his lectures and classes, which went into "depths theretofore unguessed." Some twenty years later Swami Turiyananda, who had been present during that time at the Society, said to a group of devotees at Benares: "Swamiji used to tell us, 'Do you think I only lecture? I know I give them something solid, and they know they receive something solid'." Swami Turiyananda continued, "In New York Swamiji was lecturing to a class. Oh, the tremendous effect of it! K. [Swami Abhedananda] said that while listening to the lecture, he felt as if some force was drawing the Kundalini up, as at the time of meditation. After the lecture was finished (it took an hour) K. announced that he would hold a question class. Most of the audience had gone after Swamiji's lecture. Swamiji rebuked—saying, 'A question class after this! Do you want to spoil the effect of my lecture?' Just see! Oh, what a Power Shri Ramakrishna left for the world in Swamiji! Hasn't he changed the very thought-current of the world?"[20]

THE ETERNAL POWER OF SWAMIJI

One Sunday morning in June 1900, Mrs. Lillian Montgomery was in Swamiji's audience. According to Burke, Swamiji's vast and penetrating capacity of power and meditation left an indelible impression upon Mrs. Montgomery:

Thereafter, she attended every lecture and class that Swamiji gave during that brief period—a period of her life that changed her world. The words with which she sought to describe Swamiji's indescribably immense and powerful personality are to be found in a letter she wrote more than half a century later (in 1954) at the request of the then head of the New York Vedanta Society, Swami Pavitrananda, and also in a taped talk that she gave the following year before a gathering of the members of the same Society. She said in part:

"Power seemed to emanate from him. I was fascinated; he looked like a living Buddha; he looked entirely different from any personality I had ever seen... It seemed to me that there was an ocean of consciousness back of Swami Vivekananda, and in some way it focused and flowed through his words.

"I heard him say, 'Blessed are the pure in heart for they shall see God.' I had heard those words all my life, but as Vivekananda was speaking, the purity of that personality was so great, it just seemed to me that Divinity was reflected in him, and [I had a new conception of the quotation]. It was as though his mind was a limpid lake that was reflecting divine light, and ... every word he spoke was a revelation. Other people that I have heard from the pulpit—and I had heard about the best—speak from a standpoint of faith. But I began to realize that this man was speaking from something that he was *living*—that every word he uttered came from a state of realization, such a realization that the ordinary person cannot imagine. At one time, as I listened, I thought that he was so established in the realization that the soul was eternal that he could stand before a cannon without fear, and I seemed to sense that if his form vanished that the light that was shining through it would stay there forever, that it would never disappear. It was a strange sensation at the time. But there was a purity, and an intense power, such a power as I think we have never seen—that I had never seen, and I don't expect I will ever see it again. It seemed to pour from an infinite source, and it was perfectly calm, perfectly reposed.

"Swami Vivekananda's sense of 'I' had expanded to something that was vast and deep and very very pure and very very powerful. It just penetrated within you and aroused something that was never there before. Some place he has said that you never see anything outside that isn't within. And I think perhaps his great power was that he perceived the divinity in all forms, and he perceived it with such a degree that he awakened it in his listeners as he was speaking...

"He was the only person I have ever seen in whom there seemed to be no limit to his personality. It was just as if this outer form was tuned to a realization that was all power and purity and beauty. There was a beauty that just flowed through every word that he spoke—every phrase, and as I say, every word that he spoke took on a different meaning, you had a different conception of the words, and as he spoke, just veil after veil fell from your eyes, because you sensed the vastness of his realization; it was a sort of tremendous joy... There is no one that has appeared at the Metropolitan or on any stage that has that wonderful voice, or that has that wonderful magnetism. He just seemed to be a center of spiritual thought (?) and that emanated from him, and still he was always calm. But every line of his body followed his thought; it was just as if his outer form were floating on a great light... It was something that was very very perceptible and very very tangible that he brought into the whole room... It was the intensity of the emotion of his heart that brought into manifestation the brilliance of his mind. But they weren't separated. We think of the intellect as something rather cold, but in Swami Vivekananda—you felt that all the energy of his body, all of his emotions had been concentrated and turned towards this one vision. That's why there was a complete whole, there was a complete fulfillment. I couldn't imagine that Swami Vivekananda had cast out anything; I don't think that any part of his body he thought was unholy or anything like that, but it seemed to me that he had transmuted all the elements of his body into a much finer element. It was almost transparent—but still it was full of power and force; there was no weakness there. And all the time he was speaking it was that warmth of heart that was clothing the brilliance of the mind; so that with his whole personality you felt that all his energy, *all* his emotions were directed by this vision of his mind; nothing could have gone astray...

"He was filled with such ease, and all you saw was this tremendous beauty, and it was spoken with such childlike simplicity that it just seemed that that was the natural state—that's what we all ought to be doing, just the same as Swami Vivekananda...

"I had the feeling that there was something that penetrated right through the very depth of my being. As I say, the whole world changed as Swami was speaking, because every word he spoke he spoke with his great realization. He lived every word that he spoke...

"I'll tell you, and you just sat there and your whole vision changed, and you saw such a wonderful world; you saw a world just palpitating with light, and you were part of it, and it was all harmony and beauty, and no false notes or anything like that. And as you left you just trod on air; you lived in the presence even after you left him... It stays with you, that's it, you see. You feel that that power is always there, that you can never lose it."[21]

SWAMIJI'S LAST ACTIVITIES IN NEW YORK

These intimate, unpublicized talks of Swamiji in that sweltering June heat were attended mostly by close devotees. About thirty people came to the Saturday morning class, and at the Sunday morning lectures the attendance almost always exceeded one hundred.

Swami Abhedananda's diary reveals some glimpses into this period. The situation was very trying for those devoted to Swamiji's work: the Sunday collections were woefully small, averaging about fifteen dollars for the hundred who attended. But this seemed a goodly amount, as compared to the Sunday collection of the Unitarian Church in Oakland, which averaged only thirty dollars from fifteen hundred who attended.[22]

And again from Swami Abhedananda's diary we have a glimpse of a few simple activities of Swamiji that June:

> We see him ... spending the rainy afternoon of June 14 with Swami Turiyananda and a Dr. Kate Stanton at Coney Island... Again on June 19, we find him riding with Swami Abhedananda on the Third Avenue El to the Bronx Zoo... And on a Sunday afternoon, after lecturing in the morning on "Mother Worship," he and the two Swamis drove in an open hansom through Central Park accompanied—or perhaps trailed—by Miss Waldo, Mrs. Crane, the Society's housekeeper, Sister Nivedita, and a Mr. Thomson. Again, one sees Swamiji and Swami Abhedananda on the balmy, moonlit evening of June 10 walking home (perhaps across Central Park and down Fifth Avenue) from the house of Miss Phillips (then at 208 West Seventy-second Street), where they had been guests at dinner. And we learn that on the evening of June 22, Swamiji again had dinner at Miss Phillips's and later stayed there for a few days, to Nivedita's great joy, for at the time she was also a guest at this quiet and congenial boardinghouse.[23]

The house at 208 West Seventy-second Street was originally built as one of a row of four private houses in 1893 and still stands today, with the exterior architecture of light stone, elaborately carved and tooled, intact except for the removal of the stoops.[24] In 1900 it was rented to Mary A. Phillips for three hundred dollars a month. She also operated it as a boarding house, in conjunction with 210 West Seventy-second Street. Census records of 1900 and 1905 show that Miss Phillips was born in New Jersey and was unmarried. She was in her fifties at the time.[25]

Replying to the remark that it was painful that more were not taking advantage of Swamiji's sublime teachings, Swamiji said to Henry Van Haagen, "I could have thousands more at my lectures if I wanted them. It is the sincere student who will help to make this work a success and not merely the large audiences. If I succeed in my whole life to help one man to reach freedom, I shall feel that my labours have not been in vain, but quite successful."[26]

THE SEAL OF THE RAMAKRISHNA ORDER IS
CREATED AND ITS SIGNIFICANCE EXPLAINED

One July morning at breakfast table, Swamiji designed the emblem that was to become the seal of the Ramakrishna Order. We quote from Sister Devamata's memoirs indicating the circumstances under which it was designed:

> The design which has become the symbol of the Ramakrishna Mission everywhere came into being in the same casual way as did *The Song of the Sannyasin*. It took shape in 1900 during Swami Vivekananda's later visit to America. At that time the Vedanta Society of New York was definitely established and occupied a modest house on Fifty-eighth Street. Mrs. Crane, the housekeeper, told me that the Swami was sitting at the breakfast table one morning when the printer arrived. He said he was making a circular for the Society and wished to have an emblem to go on it, could the Swami suggest something? Swamiji took the envelope from a letter he had just received, tore it open and on the clean inner surface drew the waves, the swan, the lotus, and the sun circled by a serpent—the four Yogas wrapped about by eternity, it seemed. He threw the bit of paper with the design on it across the table and said, "Draw it to scale." Henry Van Haagen, the printer, was an able draughtsman as well as printer. He converted the rough sketch into a finished drawing.[27]

It may be remembered that Van Haagen had taken the vows of brahmacharya from Swamiji earlier.

We like to quote Swamiji, who interpreted the design to Miss MacLeod: "... 'The Sun = Knowledge,' Swamiji explained to Miss MacLeod, shortly after creating the design. 'The stormy water = Work. The lotus = Love. The serpent = Yoga. The swan = the Self. The Motto = May the Swan (the Supreme Self) send us that. It is the mind-lake'."[28]

The significance of the design was again explained by Swamiji at Belur Math in 1901 to the artist, Ranada P. Das Gupta: "The wavy waters in the picture are symbolic of Karma; the lotus, of Bhakti; and the rising-sun, of Jnana. The encircling serpent is indicative of Yoga and the awakened Kundalini Shakti, while the swan in the picture stands for the *Paramatman* (Supreme Self). Therefore the idea of the picture is that by the union of Karma, Jnana, Bhakti, and Yoga, the vision of the *Paramatman* is obtained."[29]

SWAMIJI'S SOJOURNS IN NEW YORK: A CONCLUSION

It remains unclear why Swamiji remained in New York a little over two weeks after returning from Detroit that summer of 1900, "in rest and retirement in the circle of his close followers."[30] He also attended to the publication of his books and had complete confidence that his work would flourish in New York. Nivedita was already gone. On July 12 Swami Abhedananda had left for his vacation in the Adirondacks with his disciple, Dr. Herschell Parker, and would return by September.[31] On July 24, 1900, Swamiji wrote to Swami Abhedananda of his imminent departure: "You need not feel the least anxiety about the N. Y. work, it will go as a marriage bull next season." He felt he had "straightened out" business in the West, and on Thursday, July 26, 1900, Swamiji left New York by the French steamer, *La Champagne*.[32]

After Swamiji had left, one of Swami's friends wrote, "He has broadened in his sympathies and expanded in his knowledge during the four years of his absence from America. While the season is now over for lectures and classes, Swamiji's old friends are basking in the sunshine of his presence. His health is now excellent, and he is his dear old self once more, with yet a mingling of a newer, nobler self that makes us adore him more than ever... He has to be a world-worker, and so no rest can be for him until that work is done."[33]

Swamiji spent nearly thirty-nine months in America. During his two visits, he deeply sowed the seeds of his immortal message, which worked silently, creating a new current of thought in the mind of the nation. Swamiji opened a new horizon, expanded religious consciousness, and deepened our world vision. "The 'spiritual jolt' which Swami Vivekananda gave to the West early in this century," said Burke, "is now proving its impact."

This began with Sri Ramakrishna and was fulfilled in Swamiji, as Burke reminds us:

> The real thing is *the Religion* taught by Sri Rama-krishna.... The one religion in all its aspects had already been formulated and for thousands of years had been called Vedanta. Swamiji could not ignore this fact.... First, he had, as we have seen, attempted throughout his lecture tour to define the harmony of religions in the truest sense and had concluded that it consisted in the recognition of the unity of religions, or, rather, in the recognition of *religion*, which is always one and the same. Now, had he not given religion a name [Vedanta], its concept would have remained vague, and the dangers of such vagueness are apparent. There would, for instance, be little likelihood of the essentials of religion remaining clearly defined and unadulterated if it were left for each creed to interpret them according to its particular inclinations. Compromise would be an inevitable result, and shortly the fundamentals of religion would be again lost in various dogmas. Moreover, not every religion or creed is possessed, or wants to be

possessed, of *all* the fundamentals of religion; in fact, every
religion, other than Hinduism, would be hard put to it to
discover room for them within its tenets.[34]

...as he toured through the United States, meeting
thousands of people, visiting uncounted towns and cities,
Swamiji sowed the seeds of spirituality in another and
deeper sense. On a level that defies the tools of research
but that we nonetheless know exists, he played the role of
World Teacher and Prophet, silently setting in motion a
new current of thought in the collective mind of the nation—
a current, the beneficent effects of which will become visible
on the surface of human affairs only slowly, but the reality
of which we cannot doubt, for the spiritual stature of Swami
Vivekananda was such that he could not live among men
without altering, enriching, and illumining the very texture
of world thought. Indeed, to ignite men's minds not for a
brief, passing moment but on deep, subliminal levels and,
consequently, for long sweeps of time is surely the primary
function and meaning of that marvelous phenomenon,
divine prophethood, that miracle by which humanity has
many times been set aglow in its long history and which
has thereby many times lifted that history out of its otherwise
violent, humdrum, and more or less predictable course.[35]

PART TWO

SWAMI VIVEKANANDA'S WORK FLOURISHES UNDER THE LEADERSHIP OF THE SWAMIS

3

SWAMI SARADANANDA: 1897

THE SWAMI'S BEGINNINGS IN NEW YORK, GREENACRE, AND CAMBRIDGE

In response to a letter from Swamiji, Swami Saradananda had left India to go to London in March 1896 and had arrived there on April 1, 1896. In addition to gaining experience in public lecturing (at Swamiji's instruction he was to teach Gita classes in London) he was also instructed by Swamiji to collect information about the life of Sri Ramakrishna for Professor Max Müller. When material was collected, Swamiji only changed a few words in it and Professor Müller incorporated that manuscript without any alterations in his book, *Ramakrishna, His Life and Sayings.*[1] Swami Saradananda stayed in London as Mr. Sturdy's guest.

Towards the end of June, at the request of Swamiji, Swami Saradananda and Mr. Goodwin came to the New York Vedanta Society. The Swami was well received by its students, and began to conduct classes at the Society. He accepted an invitation to speak at the Greenacre Conference of Comparative Religion on July 7, 1896. This first public speech in the West was reported by Mr. Goodwin in a letter dated July 23, 1896 to the *Brahmavadin:*

The Swami Saradananda began his work on July 7th, with a lecture in which he gave a general presentation of the Vedanta, with the particulars of which I need not deal, excepting to add that he not only received a thoroughly sympathetic hearing for this, his first lecture in the West, but impressed people with the feeling that both from his manner, and the matter of his address, he had much to give them. The following day he began a series of classes on alternate weekdays in *Raja-Yoga*, to many who are systematically earnestly pursuing this method. From the theoretical instruction in *Raja-Yoga*, he next took up the subject of *Karma-Yoga*, in which he is now engaged, and this will be followed by *Bhakti-Yoga*, but the private instruction in *Raja-Yoga* will continue throughout the conference, which will last altogether for two months.[2]

John P. Fox wrote to Mrs. Bull, "I like Swami Saradananda very much. He is exceedingly kind and thoughtful of other people, very quiet and reserved usually, though not without humor. From his clearness in answering questions and readiness to help, I think he will succeed as a teacher, though he has done no such work as yet, [in London] at least."[3] Equally enthusiastic, Mr. Goodwin also wrote to Mrs. Bull, "He will, I have not the least doubt, succeed in endearing himself to his class."[4]

After his success during nearly three months at Greenacre, Swami Saradananda continued to stay in Cambridge in Mrs. Bull's home, where he met Professor William James and other Harvard professors. Mrs. Bull liked to compare Swamiji to the brilliant scorching sun and Saradananda to the cool, refreshing moon. On October 8, 1896, Swamiji wrote to Mrs. Bull, enquiring about Swami Saradananda and suggesting that the New York work was paramount in importance. On October 24, Swami Saradananda delivered his first lecture in New York before the Brooklyn Ethical Association, for which Dr. Janes had made preparations more than a month earlier.

SWAMI ABHEDANANDA'S JOURNEY BEGINS:
FROM INDIA TO NEW YORK VIA LONDON

At the call of Swami Vivekananda, Swami Abhedananda left India for London in the middle of August 1896 and arrived in London at the end of September. By mischance, he did not find Swami Vivekananda and Mr. Sturdy at the dock as arranged, and proceeded to Wimbledon, to the very door of Miss Henrietta Müller's house, where Swami Vivekananda was staying. His first talk in London on October 27, 1896 was on *Panchadasi*—a well-known treatise on Vedanta—and was heard by Swamiji, who "was highly pleased and said, 'Even if I perish on this plane, my message will be sounded through these dear lips and the world will hear it'."[5] While in London, Swami Abhedananda made a deep impression on Max Müller and Paul Deussen.

In the first week of January 1897, Swami Saradananda began teaching classes in New York City, as Swamiji wanted, in his room at 509 Fifth Avenue above Forty-second Street, then in New Century Hall on the ground floor. The Swami lectured at Sunday services, held weekday classes on the Gita and the Upanishads, and gave interviews. In all, he regularly offered six lectures a week in New Century Hall. The landlord of the building was a very responsive and generous man; he cordially allowed the overflowing classes to be accommodated on the ground floor, free of charge. Although Swami Vivekananda worried about the Swami's well being under the strain of so much work, still, for all of 1897, the Swami "moved, unperturbed, between New York, Greenacre, and Cambridge."[6]

"THE MASTER CHOOSES HIS OWN MEN AND WOMEN"

While Swami Saradananda was staying in Boston, Swami Abhedananda came to New York on August 6, 1897, after nearly a year in London. On October 24, 1897 Swami Saradananda went to stay at the Wheeler residence in

Montclair. Mrs. Wheeler was one of Swami Saradananda's most devoted students and her husband, a Christian Scientist, was sympathetic to Vedanta. One day the Swami, who appreciated Mrs. Wheeler's sattvic qualities, showed her his Master's photograph. With great elation and joy she revealed to him that before she was married, in her youth, she had had a vision of a Hindu face which she now saw was Ramakrishna. "It was Sri Ramakrishna, but I did not know it until now. I was so impressed and charmed by the vision at the time, that I remembered the face very distinctly. I have been going about here and there ever since I have had the vision—whenever I heard that a Hindu had come to America—but I was always disappointed not to find the same face. At last I see that it was Ramakrishna."[7] Swami Saradananda later recalled, "The Master chooses his own men and women. We are mere instruments in his hands. It is a privilege to work under his banner. In America He had already prepared the ground for me; I was not alone. He brought to me men and women of exalted character who helped me in our work and bore great love for our Master."

Swami Saradananda held classes in Montclair until the end of October when he went to Cambridge and remained with Mrs. Bull. Dr. Janes, the director of the Cambridge Conference, appreciated the Swami's work and wrote to the editor of *Brahmavadin*:

The many friends of the Swami Saradananda in Cambridge and vicinity cannot permit him to return to India without expressing through your columns their hearty appreciation of the excellent educational work which he accomplished in this country, and the fine accompaniment of personal character and influence which greatly strengthened the effect of the work wherever it was conducted. On every hand, the friends of the Swami express a sense of personal loss in his departure, and hope that he may sometime return to America where his work is so heartily appreciated.

In Cambridge, the classes in the Vedanta philosophy, constituting a single feature in the broad field of comparative study outlined for the Cambridge Conferences, attracted large and intelligent audiences, in part made up of professors and students of the Harvard University. The Swami's exposition of the principles of the Advaita doctrine, in just comparison with other views which are held in India, was admirably lucid and clear. His replies to questions were always ready and satisfactory. His great fairness of mind and soundness of judgment enabled him to present the doctrine in a manner which at once convinced all of his sincerity, while it disarmed the factious opposition which is sometimes stirred up by a more dogmatic and assertive manner. In Boston, Waltham and Worcester, Mass., the Swami Saradananda conducted courses of lectures which were largely attended and which everywhere manifested a sustained interest in his subject.[8]

4

SWAMI ABHEDANANDA: 1897-1910

SWAMI ABHEDANANDA'S DYNAMISM

Swami Abhedananda left London on July 31, 1897 and arrived penniless in New York on August 6, 1897, as the guest of Miss Mary Phillips, the secretary. Although Mr. Van Haagen and others were sent to receive him at the seaport, the Swami again was unlucky and was unable to find anyone there to receive him; he hired a hansom cab and rode to Miss Phillips' address at 19 West Thirty-first Street. Miss Phillips was very surprised to see him arriving alone and the others arriving later—much disheartened for having missed the Swami. In his typical way, Swami Abhedananda quickly set off to view New York City and its environs. Mr. Van Haagen accompanied him. The city's tallest skyscraper, the Woolworth Building, was only fifty-six stories high. On another day, he called on the Leggetts and found Miss MacLeod there. After spending two weeks in America in this way, on August 25 he was given a reception at Miss Phillip's boardinghouse on behalf of the Vedanta Society of New York. Most of Swami Vivekananda's students and admirers were present on that occasion, including Mr. Walter Goodyear, Miss Waldo, and others. After his reception, Swami Abhedananda traveled to many other places

along the East Coast delivering lectures—to Philadelphia,
Washington, Virginia, and New Paltz, New York.

SWAMI ABHEDANANDA AND SWAMI SARADANANDA
MEET IN NEW YORK AND SHARE VIEWS

On the evening of September 27, 1897, Swami Saradananda came to New York from Boston to meet Swami
Abhedananda. They spent the next day together, happy to
see each other again and to share their views on Swamiji's
work in the West. The two Swamis were beloved Gurubhais
who had lived together in India and faithfully served Sri
Ramakrishna. Swami Saradananda shared his own opinions
with Swami Abhedananda about the work in the United States.
The Americans wanted to know the general principles of
Vedanta, and the practical side of Swami Vivekananda's Raja
Yoga teachings. Swami Abhedananda wrote in his diary, "From
that time I made up my mind to make Swamiji's *Raja Yoga* as
the text book in my Raja Yoga classes in New York, which I
did later on."[1]

The two Swamis were also strict vegetarians. Before
returning to Boston, Swami Saradananda encouraged Swami
Abhedananda to set an example by remaining a vegetarian in
order to succeed in his mission. Swami Saradananda returned
to Boston on September 28.[2] Some time later during 1898,
Swami Abhedananda became sick due to his extreme austerity.
Dr. Janes was well aware of the fact and told him, "That would
not do for you here—'When in Rome do as the Romans do.'
You have a mission in your life. You must take nourishing
food, otherwise you will be sick." Therefore, Swami
Abhedananda wrote a letter to Holy Mother, seeking her
advice. In her letter to Swami Abhedananda in March 1899,
she wrote giving him permission to take non-vegetarian food.
Holy Mother did not approve of his austerity and advised him
to take fish. On the evening of March 14, 1899 an auspicious

gift was given to the Swami that must have strengthened and consoled him: Miss MacLeod brought him a photograph of Holy Mother Sarada Devi, and gave him a copy. It had been taken at Sister Nivedita's request in India.

SWAMI ABHEDANANDA BEGINS TO LECTURE IN NEW YORK

After his return to New York City from his East Coast travels, Swami Abhedananda established himself and started giving lectures in Mott's Memorial Hall, which was engaged by Miss Mary Phillips on September 29, 1897. The first lecture he gave on "What is Vedanta?" was presided over by Mr. Edward Emerson, a close relation of Ralph Waldo Emerson. Forty people attended. Gurudas (Swami Atulananda), the only Western monk who came in the early days to the Vedanta Society of New York and who subsequently became one of the venerable monks of the Order, attended one of his lectures. He heard Swami Abhedananda sometime in the summer of 1898 and gave his first impression of him:

> Punctually at three o'clock, a Swami entered the hall. He was dressed in a robe and turban of an orange color. He went straight to the platform and without a moment's delay began to deliver his lecture. He opened with a shloka in Sanskrit: "*Dva suparna sayuja sakhaya samanam,*" etc. This he gave also in English: "Two birds of beautiful plumage, perch on the selfsame tree: one of the two eats the luscious fruit; silent, its mate looks on." And then he began to explain the deep significance of this beautiful simile from the Upanishads. The discourse was lucid, convincing, and impressive. There was not much flourish, nor much eloquence, and hardly any gesticulation. It was a straightforward, well-reasoned-out exposition of the Vedanta philosophy, delivered in a calm, dignified manner. He had

his subject well in hand. And his voice was clear and sonorous.

Young, tall, straight, good-looking, the Swami had his appearance in his favor.[3]

SWAMI ABHEDANANDA'S PRODIGIOUS WORK IN TEACHING VEDANTA TO THE WEST

On October 2 the Swami initiated the classes on Vivekananda's *Raja Yoga* every Wednesday and Saturday at Mott's Memorial Hall. This was followed by his delivery of eighty-six lectures at the Hall.[4] On Mondays he lectured and gave classes at Montclair, New Jersey. Swami Abhedananda tried to bring Swamiji's foreign publication of *Raja Yoga* from London to use in his classes. This proved too costly, so Miss Phillips and the American students published a New York edition, for which Swami Abhedananda added a glossary of Sanskrit words. Swami Abhedananda used this text for all his Raja Yoga classes.[5]

Swami Abhedananda and Swami Saradananda again met at Mrs. Wheeler's residence in Montclair on October 11. For the first time, Swami Abhedananda heard Swami Saradananda speak there two days later on the subject of "Concentration," and was very impressed by his beautiful delivery. On the same day, October 13, the two Swamis visited Thomas Alva Edison and were given a tour of his laboratory. Mr. Edison's single-minded concentration and dedication impressed them. Swami Abhedananda spoke with Edison on the Hindu philosophy, in which the inventor was deeply interested.

During this period, the Vedanta Society had temporarily moved several times, seeking a better neighborhood environment. On Sunday, October 27, the Swami gave a lecture on "Concentration" to one hundred twenty-eight people at Mott's Memorial Hall.[6] Within a few more weeks, the Society had moved from 117 Lexington Avenue to a new address at 170 Lexington Avenue.

From November 29, Swami Abhedananda began to take only milk and fruits when he conducted the Raja Yoga lectures.

On December 18, 1897 Swami Abhedananda lectured on Vedanta Philosophy at the Twentieth Century Club in Brooklyn, where he met Dr. Fridtjof Nansen, the North Pole explorer and statesman, who also gave a talk on his adventures. After his talk, the Swami spoke at length with Dr. Nansen about Indian and Hindu philosophy, for which the explorer had great sympathy.

SWAMI ABHEDANANDA'S LECTURES
INCREASE HIS AUDIENCE

THE SWAMI'S FRIENDSHIP WITH
WELL-KNOWN SUPPORTERS

Published accounts of his lectures and his dynamic personality began to appear in several of New York's prestigious journals and newspapers. Educated audiences for Swami Abhedananda's lectures were growing in number, with representative personalities from the arts, science, and religion attending. Mr. and Mrs. Leggett and Miss MacLeod now began to attend the lectures frequently and were very impressed. On January 3, 1898, the Leggetts invited Swami Abhedananda to their home, where he was introduced to Emma Thursby and other students and supporters. On January 10, at 10:30 P.M., Swami Saradananda came to the Vedanta Society of New York at 170 Lexington Avenue. Swami Abhedananda met Mrs. Ole Bull for the first time, and she invited both Swamis to dinner. On January 12, Swami Saradananda was leaving New York for India, accompanied by Mrs. Ole Bull and Miss MacLeod. Swami Abhedananda bid farewell to Swami Saradananda at the Leggetts' house, and left to give a lecture on "Duty" at Mott's Memorial Hall at 8 P.M. that evening.[7]

REVEREND DR. R. HEBER NEWTON
SUPPORTS THE SWAMI'S WORK

Swami Abhedananda had once lectured on "The Religious Ideals of the Hindus" at the Liberal Congress of Religions in Boston, where the Rev. Dr. R. Heber Newton, Dean of Divinity of All Souls Episcopal Church in New York, had also given an address. On January 25, 1898, Swami Abhedananda was invited to dinner by the Rev. Dr. Newton. He brought along a letter of introduction from the Rev. Mr. Reginald Hugh Haweis, who used to attend the Swami's London lectures. The Rev. Dr. Newton was a liberal Christian reformer deeply interested in the universal principles of Vedanta and Sri Ramakrishna. He had previously met the leader of Brahmo Samaj, Rev. Protap Chunder Mazumdar, whose *Oriental Christ* he admired. The Rev. Dr. Newton was known to speak within his own congregation about the spirituality and knowledge of the Hindus, and in an address entitled "The Limits of Religious Fellowship," spoke of Sri Ramakrishna as a Son of God. The *Vedanta Bulletin* reprinted part of this address in recognition of a universal "Renascence" brought about by Sri Ramakrishna's power of goodness.[8]

During his New York discussions with Swami Abhedananda about religion, the Rev. Dr. Newton became even more impressed: he kept his own copies of the lecture notices and distributed them to his own congregation. The Reverend and Mrs. Newton went to the Swami's lectures, and he encouraged his congregation to attend also. His private library, to which the Swami was welcomed, included the Vedas, Puranas, Max Müller's *Sacred Books of the East*, and the scriptures of the world's religions. He became an honorary member of the organized Vedanta Society of New York, with his name appearing on the circulars. The Rev. Dr. Newton introduced the Swami to other preachers and friends and he lectured together with the Swami at the New York City Religious Conferences of Christian Ministers, which the Reverend organized. All these events relieved the minds of the Christians of much of their prejudice and provided support to the Swami's mission.[9]

Swami Abhedananda knew the importance of enlisting the friendship and support of broad-minded religious leaders, because they wielded great influence upon the educated and cultured Christian community. His goal was to "arouse the interest of the good people of the city and to persuade them to help ... in making the Vedanta Society a powerful religious organization in a Christian country ... determined to find ways and means for making a success of the Vedanta work in New York which was started by Swami Vivekananda." On March 7, 1898, again through a letter of introduction from the Rev. Mr. Haweis of London, Swami Abhedananda visited Rev. Dr. Rainsford, and the respected, liberal Episcopal minister, duly impressed with the Swami's universal religious views, promised to support him in his mission.[10]

SWAMI YOGANANDA VISITS THE SWAMI

On March 3, Swami Yogananda, the disciple of Swami Vivekananda formerly known as Dr. Street, visited the Swami. Swami Yogananda's mystic and psychic powers of clairvoyance about events in distant places were well-known in America and admired by Swamiji. On the eve of the Spanish-American War, from America, he perceived through his gift of clairvoyance the actual event of the Spanish attack on the American battleship, *Maine*, in the port of Santiago, Cuba. He also accurately predicted it would cause the future war between the United States and Spain. Swami Abhedananda enlightened him on the Indian Yogic view of psychic powers, after which Swami Yogananda attended the Swami's classes and public lectures.[11]

DR. ELMER GATES FINDS THE SWAMI'S TEACHING OF RAJA YOGA PERTINENT TO HIS OWN SCIENTIFIC RESEARCH

On April 6, 1898 Mr. Leggett introduced Swami Abhedananda to the well-known scientist and psychologist, Dr. Elmer Gates. Dr. Gates found Abhedananda's knowledge and understanding of Raja Yoga to be so rational and scientific and pertinent to his research on the relationship between the physical and mental sciences, that he invited him to his laboratory and home in Chevy Chase, where the Swami also gave a few talks. Here, the Swami's desire to meet the president of the United States was fulfilled, and he met President William McKinley in the White House on May 19. Despite the Cuban War crisis, the president was kind enough to enquire about the Vedanta work and about the political situation in India. A few days earlier on May 16, the Swami also met John G. Brady, the governor of Alaska.[12]

DR. LEWIS G. JANES A STRONG SUPPORTER OF THE VEDANTA MOVEMENT

On May 25, 1898 Swami Abhedananda went to Boston and met Dr. Lewis G. Janes, who took him to Mrs. Ole Bull's house, where he was staying. On the evening of May 27, the Swami was introduced by Dr. Janes as the guest speaker on "Transcendentalism" at the annual festival of the Free Religious Association at the Parker Memorial Building in Boston. It may be recalled that Dr. Janes was the director of the Cambridge Conferences and was Swamiji's good friend and a strong supporter of the Vedanta Movement—"an eminent scholar and lecturer of science, ethics and religion." He invited Swami Abhedananda to speak before the Cambridge Conference in Maine and generously extended his influence to the Swami, who received many invitations to lecture on the East Coast.

SWAMI ABHEDANANDA'S PIONEERING WORK:
THE VEDANTA SOCIETY OF NEW YORK TAKES SHAPE

Swami Abhedananda began his real pioneering work for the Vedanta Society after the successful season of lectures from October 1897 to May 6, 1898.

On October 29, 1898, the Vedanta Society was formally registered and incorporated under the laws of the State of New York. Swami Abhedananda now began to persuade the reluctant Mr. Leggett—who felt a scholar should be chosen for the post—to become its first president. Undaunted, Swami Abhedananda used his organizational skills to place the Vedanta Society of New York on a solid self-supporting foundation. When the Executive Committee met on November 22 at Mr. Leggett's house, the Swami formally proposed the name of Mr. Leggett for president of the Vedanta Society of New York. He was unanimously elected. Mrs. Mary B. Coulston became the secretary and Mr. Walter Goodyear became the treasurer. Six trustees were appointed, all from New York: Mr. Francis H. Leggett, Mrs. Bessie MacLeod Leggett, Mrs. Mary B. Coulston, Mr. Walter Goodyear, Mrs. Frances B. Goodyear, and Mr. George H. Thomson.

Mr. Leggett was a wealthy and influential man and it became easier for Swami Abhedananda to lease halls in good localities for his lectures—with the rent paid in advance. The Assembly Hall at the United Charities Building at 109 East Twenty-second Street was engaged at Mr. Leggett's own risk for that season's first lecture on November 2. During this season, the Swami lectured for five months in New York and New England.[13]

From the Swami's diary we know that Miss Phillips was still the acting secretary of the Vedanta Society in January 1899—due to Mrs. Coulston's illness and hospitalization, that prevented her from carrying out her obligations that month. When Mrs. Coulston returned to her secretarial duties, she also served as acting treasurer in February 1899, keeping

Swami Vivekananda, New York, 1895

Swami Turiyananda, San Francisco, ca. 1900

Swami Abhedananda in America

Swami Trigunatita

accounts of the subscriptions and voluntary contributions gathered in a basket after the Swami's lectures. All the expenses of the Swami's lectures, room and board, and personal expenses had to be paid from these two accounts, which proved insufficient.

SWAMI ABHEDANANDA'S APOSTOLIC ZEAL AND AUSTERE LIFE

After the lecture season, Swami Abhedananda had to endure his share of hardships, but this did not alter his punctuality and life of dedication. With missionary zeal, he gave up his room at the boarding house for the sake of economy and lectured from place to place. He took his meals upon the invitation of his students and often had to eat in restaurants.[14] In other cities, he had to depend upon the hospitality of acquaintances and carried his belongings wherever he went. He had no personal funds beyond the money donated at his lectures. The severe blizzard of February 13, 1899 in New York brought cold temperatures of forty degrees below zero and nearly sixty-mile-an-hour winds. The water pipes froze and he could not bathe. Undaunted, he waded through the knee-deep snow to arrive punctually for his scheduled lecture, impressing the five students who came.[15]

The hardships of that winter were mitigated when the Swami went to Mr. Leggett's house on the evening of March 5 and saw Miss MacLeod. She had recently returned from India—greatly impressed and with much news. The Swami was filled with joy to learn that Swami Vivekananda had established a permanent Math at Belur for the Ramakrishna Order of sannyasins.[16]

In order for Swami Abhedananda to have more intimate contact with the students, and the students amongst themselves, the Swami arranged weekly informal get-togethers sometime in February 1899. Five such meetings took place in March.[17]

10

SRI RAMAKRISHNA'S ANNUAL BIRTHDAY CELEBRATIONS AT THE NEW YORK VEDANTA SOCIETY

REMINISCENCES OF SISTER DEVAMATA

During one of the early anniversary celebrations of Sri Ramakrishna at the Vedanta Society, Sister Devamata, noted for her spiritual perception, wrote:

In the early spring I returned to New York and soon after became a member of the Vedanta Society, being put in charge of the Publishing Department. At that time books came out in rapid succession; my hours were very full and I was in frequent consultation with the head of the work. One late afternoon he called me to his private study to talk over a new publication. As I entered the room, my eyes fell upon a photograph hanging over the mantel. I stood still, transfixed. It was the figure I had seen in Boston. I walked quickly across to the fireplace and asked almost abruptly, "Of whom is this a picture?" The head of the work replied quietly: "It is my Master, Sri Ramakrishna."

A year passed. The anniversary of Sri Ramakrishna's birthday came. It was observed very austerely at the New York Society. Of the fifty or sixty members who attended the celebration, scarcely one tasted food or drank water from before sunset on the previous evening until after sunset on the evening of the birthday. This was done, not to mortify the flesh, but to give greater freedom to the spirit. All day we sat on the floor of the classroom without mat or cushion, meditating, praying, or listening to the reading of sacred books. There were brief recesses, but a hush of holy silence was upon every heart and there was little conversation— that little being in low undertones.

The atmosphere was charged with fervour. The last hour of prayer had come. We had been told that whatever we asked for in this culminating moment of the day would be granted.

I could think of nothing for which to ask. No desire entered my thought, or rather only one—to see Sri Ramakrishna once again. The stillness in the room was breathless. Something impelled me to open my eyes and there on the platform amid the masses of flowers, which had been brought in as offering, stood the living Presence.[18]

Sister Devamata was extremely reluctant to reveal her mystical experiences, but she changed her mind and put them into writing for the sake of posterity. She was an American nun who lived in India from 1908 to 1910 and received intimate spiritual guidance from Swami Ramakrishnananda, the founder-president of the Ramakrishna Math in Madras. She wrote two books, *Sri Ramakrishna and His Disciples* and *Days in an Indian Monastery*, chronicling the early days in South India of the Ramakrishna-Vivekananda Movement, and contributed many articles to *Vedanta Kesari*.

A NEW YORK CORRESPONDENT'S REPORT
OF THE BIRTHDAY SERVICE OF 1902

On March 13, 1902 *Prabuddha Bharata's* New York correspondent wrote of the annual celebration of Sri Ramakrishna's birthday:

The annual celebration of our Master Sri Ramakrishna promises to accomplish a double mission, in that it must not only deepen and expand the spiritual life of every one who takes part in it, but even more must with every year level and break down all barriers between the East and the West. The very fact that at the same moment in the four quarters of the globe on that feast day his followers are kneeling at his shrine, sending out thoughts of grateful worship towards him, and of affectionate good will towards one another, is enough to knit and strengthen tenfold with each recurring anniversary the bonds of fellowship which have established in recent years through the work of Vedanta. It is especially meet, therefore, that at this sacred season greetings should go from us to you, and that you should learn something of the way in which we, the most distant of all the disciples, observed the festival.

Since it was not possible for us to hold a continuous service throughout the twenty-four hours, as is customary with you, we began our celebration on Tuesday evening with a lecture by Swami Abhedananda on the life of the Master. Although it was intended to be a simple, informal recital of the chief events of that holy life as the Swami had known them, either through the Master's words or through his daily contact with him, the strong emotion which stirred him as he told of them once again, infused such fire and vividness into the narrative that more than once the audience were moved to tears; and the impression left was so profound that all came with hearts still better prepared for the more solemn portion of the celebration on Wednesday morning.

Although there was less effort made to gather in a large number than to bring together those who having the habit of meditation might really profit by the service, when the doors of the meditation room were thrown open at eleven o'clock, the Swami found the library crowded with earnest worshippers who had brought with them not only lavish offerings of fruits and flowers but in many instances, also generous contributions to Ramakrishna's work in India. An altar had been erected on the platform under the star, where the Swami's chair usually stands, and on this was placed the picture of the Master, wreathed in flowers while all about were massed baskets of fruit, bunches of cut flowers or pots of blooming plants. When the incense had been lighted, the Swami took his place on a tiger-skin to the left of the altar, those who preferred to do so, sat on the floor around him, while the majority occupied the chairs behind. The service lasted for an hour and a half and consisted of meditation, chanting, and occasional inspiring words from the Swami, in which loving reference was also made to Sarada Devi, the devoted wife of Ramakrishna.

At the close of the final meditation the fruit was passed, and all those who did not care, like the Swami, to prolong their fast until evening, partook of it. The Swami then gave a flower to each one present and with this the celebration ended.[19]

SRI RAMAKRISHNA'S BIRTHDAY SERVICE OF 1905

On March 8, 1905—despite heavy storm conditions and a transportation strike—the service and meditations for Bhagavan Sri Ramakrishna attracted an unusually large attendance. The service began at 11 A.M. with a series of meditations by Swami Abhedananda. After an intermission at 12:30 P.M., Swami Abhedananda chanted some of the Holy Master's favorite hymns. At 3:30 P.M. Swami Nirmalananda held a meditation, followed by a moving talk on the childhood and hamlet life of Sri Ramakrishna, another meditation, and an hour-long silence in prayer. The evening service at 7:30 P.M. included devotional exercises and readings from *The Gospel of Sri Ramakrishna*. The offerings were more generous than in any of the previous years. And the *Bulletin* reported: "It is customary at the time of the birthday celebration of Bhagavan Sri Ramakrishna to send an offering to the Math at Belur for the relief of the poor of India. This year through the generosity of different students and friends the offering amounted to $71.50. $10.00 were also sent to the Poor Men's Relief Association, and $30.00 to the Vivekananda Memorial Fund."[20]

LENGTHIER SERVICES OF DEEP DEVOTION

It is interesting to know that in those days, even lengthy services were accepted by the devotees. Swami Trigunatita-

nanda held services continuously for eighteen hours on Sri
Ramakrishna's birthday and Christ's birthday.[21] As Burke has
written, "Even [after the death of Swami Trigunatitananda on
January 10, 1915] on Sri Ramakrishna's birthday, February
21, 1915, the students conducted a fifteen-hour service. Mr.
Petersen gave the three lectures, and in between there was
reading and singing. 'Quite a number stayed all through the
long service,' the Monastery Notes read, 'and such was the
atmosphere of spirituality and devotion awakened by the
tangible presence of that *great* soul, our great teacher, that all
remarked how quickly the day passed and all felt greatly
profited spiritually by the grace of God and the Swami
Trigunatita'."[22]

SWAMI ABHEDANANDA'S OFFERING TO
SRI RAMAKRISHNA
THE NECTAR OF SRI RAMAKRISHNA'S LAUDATIONS

On March 6, 1906, when the Vedanta Society was in its
home at 62 West Seventy-first Street, Swami Abhedananda
observed Sri Ramakrishna's birthday celebration. As part of
the celebration, he offered his own composition, *The Nectar of
Sri Ramakrishna's Laudations*, a lofty Sanskrit hymn of nineteen
verses. This hymn was sent to Udbodhan for publication in
India. The entire hymn with its English translation may be
seen in Swami Prajnanananda's book, *The Philosophical Ideas
of Swami Abhedananda*.[23]

SWAMI ABHEDANANDA INITIATES
SIX BRAHMACHARINS FOR THE WORK

On the auspicious evening of Easter Sunday, April 2, 1899,
Swami Abhedananda initiated six brahmacharins in a simple,
harmonious, and impressive ceremony. This took place at Miss

Lindquist's home, in the room normally used for the meditation meetings, and was attended only by some brahmacharins of Swami Vivekananda and others who understood and sympathized with the occasion.[24] Sri Ramakrishna's picture and humble offerings of fruits and flowers were placed on a small altar covered with *gerua* cloth. The altar fire was burning and incense was offered. The Swami sat close beside the fire and the students meditated and prostrated.[25] The Swami read *slokas* from the Hindu scriptures and chanted his own Sanskrit verses praising and adoring Sri Ramakrishna. Swami Abhedananda inspired the new brahmacharins by speaking to them at length about their new life of dedication to self-mastery, chastity, universal divinity and love, non-harmfulness, truth, and self-sacrifice for the service of God in all. And one by one they approached the sacred fire to repeat these vows. The Swami touched their foreheads with sacred ash, offered each the ochre cloth and, sprinkling holy water upon them, gave to each a name: *Satyakama* (Miss Lindquist), *Gurudasa* (Mr. Heijblom), *Muktikama* (Miss Mulford), *Shantikama* (Dr. Kate Stanton), *Sevaputa* (Mrs. Coulston) and *Premakama* (Miss Kohlsaat).[26] Gurudasa later became Swami Atulananda, after he received sannyas from Swami Abhedananda at Belur Math on February 18, 1923.

THE VEDANTA SOCIETY OF NEW YORK EXPANDS UNDER SWAMI ABHEDANANADA'S LEADERSHIP

THE SOCIETY PUBLISHES THE SWAMI'S FIRST BOOK: *REINCARNATION*

The summer of 1899 found Swami Abhedananda lecturing and visiting throughout New England, meeting men of influence, including professors from Cornell, Iowa, Yale, and other universities. At the Greenacre School for the

Comparative Study of Religion, Swami met the famous writer, Ralph Waldo Trine, who attended his lectures there. On another occasion, Mr. Trine and his wife saw Swami Abhedananda at Greenacre and the Swami presented his book, *Reincarnation*, which was very popular. It contained the three lectures, "What is Reincarnation?" "Which is Scientific— Resurrection or Reincarnation?" and "Evolution and Reincarnation." Earlier in 1899, on March 28, an American gentleman, Mr. Vanderbilt, had printed it for free and donated two thousand copies of the book for the Swami's distribution. This was Swami Abhedananda's first book, printed under the auspices of the Vedanta Society of New York. Once, he gave a talk on reincarnation before an audience of eight hundred.[27]

PROGRESS AT THE SOCIETY

In August 1899 Swamiji returned to America after an absence of almost three-and-a-half years. Swami Abhedananda joined Swamiji and Swami Turiyananda at Ridgely Manor on September 8, arriving from the Greenacre School for the Comparative Study of Religion, where he had been lecturing. He stayed there for ten days, and reported on the progress of the Vedanta work in America and especially in New York, where the Society had recently moved to its first permanent quarters at 146 East Fifty-fifth Street. Through generous subscriptions, a headquarters for the office and library of the Vedanta Society was established here in October 1899, giving a new driving force to the work. The library featured rare and excellent books on the metaphysics, philosophy, and religion of India. Swami Abhedananda formally opened the "Vedanta Society Rooms" on October 15, 1899 and held regular classes there beginning October 22. The rooms were open daily for classes, the sale of literature, and the general business of the Society. From October until April 1, Swami Abhedananda spoke each Sunday in Tuxedo Hall, which was used for the Sunday services.

THE BROAD SCOPE OF SWAMI ABHEDANANDA'S
WORK FROM NEW YORK

When Swami Vivekananda arrived in New York on Tuesday, November 7, 1899, Swami Abhedananda greeted him. A letter to the *Brahmavadin* in September 1899 stated: "In New York, the most difficult city in the United States in which to reach the spiritual nature of people, Swami Abhedananda has made a profound impression. Two years of patient, persistent, loving service has established Vedanta in a consecrated body of earnest students who are devoted to the continuance of the work."[28]

But interest and admiration for the work was not limited to students of Vedanta. The October 1988 issue of the popular and respected *Arena* had two articles. The *Brahmavadin* reported them both. One article, "The Swamis in America" by the Vedanta student Miss Anna J. Ingersoll, acknowledged the vigorous and important work being done by the Vedanta Society "since 1894, sustaining a teacher and giving a course of eighty lectures during the winter months [and] now recognized as a growingly important factor in the thought-movement of the day." The other article, "An Interpretation of Vedanta" by Boston's Horatio W. Dresser—another interested observer of the work of Vedanta—treated Vedanta as "a noble and needed philosophy."[29]

YOUNG MEN'S YOGA ASSOCIATION AND
A CHILDREN'S CLASS

On January 25, 1900 Swami Abhedananda started the Young Men's Yoga Association in New York, with a view to teach the principles of Yoga to the young boys. A children's class was also established in January 1900, to train the young minds in higher thinking through India's well-known repository of parables and stories. Swami Turiyananda aided

Swami Abhedananda in this aspect of the work. The class was reviewed in the *New York Herald* of March 4, 1900 and was later reprinted in *Prabuddha Bharata* in May 1900:

"New York's Juvenile Vedantists:
Little Ones Who Are Learning Brahminism"

Not the least among the extraordinary things of these times is the realization that India, the land of the heathen and benighted, according to popular impressions among our people, is sending missionaries of the Hindoo religion into the very core and heart of our Western civilization. Here in New York a few picturesque monks of the Brahmin faith have banded together a society for the propaganda of their religion and philosophy, which is taking such deep root and spreading so rapidly that children in this city are being reared and trained in the faith of Brahma, and are sent every week to sit at the feet of the Eastern Mahatma to learn wisdom and grace.

Every Saturday afternoon a class of young boys and girls gathers together in the rooms of the Vedanta Society in East Fifty-fifth Street, to speak an hour or so with the Swami Abhedananda and drink in the teachings of the Hindoo philosophy, which is expounded to them in the most fascinating way. The young people come in with beaming, expectant faces, and draw their chairs around the handsome Oriental figure of the Swami, who sits in the circle wearing a robe of rich red, and holding in his hand an ancient Sanskrit book—the *Hitopadesha*, or book of 'good counsels.' This book is one of the oldest pieces of literature in the world. It dates back to the thirteenth century B.C. and is the source of all our fables of animals, our tales and fairy stories.

The life and teachings of Jesus enter largely into the text of the Vedanta philosophy, and never a lesson goes by but that some saying of Jesus Christ's or some incident of his life is used to illustrate a moral lesson or point a principle.

The Swami selects a story every Saturday afternoon from the *Hitopadesha* and tells it to the children. The stories are all about kings and queens and animals who converse freely together upon subjects of astounding range for young minds, but the children sit in rapt attention eager for every word. Woven into the glittering fabric of wonder and imagination are all the doctrines of the Vedas—such ideas as reincarnation, *Karma* and *Yoga*, with bits of wit, wisdom and good advice, which will linger, doubtless, in these young minds during all their lives.

The Swami ends the story, and then follows a little talk about it, and each child is asked to repeat the story in his own way and to tell the moral lessons and reflections which it has given him. It is wonderful to see how much of the real meaning of the tales makes its way into their heads and how eager they are for more.

A philosophy which calms and embraces all religions is a little wide for the minds of most grown folk, but these young ones seem to take to it with avidity.

One little boy in the class is so earnest and devout that he sacrifices the whole of his weekly holiday to glean the wisdom dispensed by the Swami, and early Saturday morning he makes his way from Brooklyn and comes to the rooms of the Vedanta Society, where he is allowed to listen to the class of grown up students who are studying the Upanishads with Swami Abhedananda.

When the children's class was first formed the Mammas and Aunts of the little ones were allowed to come in with the children, but it soon became evident that the older folk were too eager to take part in the lessons and absorb the attention of the Swami, so that the little ones had no chance. Now all grown folks are excluded, and the Swami and the children have things all their own way.[30]

Understandably, the Christmas tree of the children's class of 1900, illuminated with fifty candlesticks, was impressive and very gratifying to all.[31]

THE FIRM ROOT OF VEDANTA IN NEW YORK

When Swami Vivekananda arrived in New York from Ridgely on the evening of November 7, he made his first appearance in the new quarters of the New York Vedanta Society on the same day. He presided over the meeting that evening and opened it to questions and answers, much pleased that his work had taken firm root under Swami Abhedananda's strong leadership. The followers of the Vedanta Movement and the general public now recognized it as "a growingly important factor in the thought-movement of the day."[32]

Under the directorship of Swami Abhedananda, the work of the Vedanta Society of New York had developed and expanded, and the dynamic Swami needed to have more personal freedom in his work. A misunderstanding arose between Swami Abhedananda and Mr. Leggett. Mr. Leggett resigned as president in the spring of 1900 and was replaced by one of Swami Abhedananda's disciples—the unanimously elected Dr. Herschell C. Parker, professor of physics at Columbia University. Miss J. Faure became the secretary, and Mr. Walter Goodyear, the treasurer. The by-laws were also changed, allowing the Swami-in-charge to have some amount of control of the activities of the Society.[33]

MEMBERSHIP ROLL ATTRACTS EMINENT SUPPORTERS

The Society's funds had increased through a membership roll officially opened by the trustees in March 1900; the dues were $12 annually or $250 for a life membership. Non-members were charged 25¢ for the classes on Tuesday evenings. The Society, previously at 146 East Fifty-fifth Street, was now able to move to 102 East Fifty-eighth Street. The entire house was rented for its new headquarters. The Rev. Dr. R. Heber Newton, Dean of Divinity of All Souls Episcopal Church in New York, and Professor Charles R. Lanman, professor of Sanskrit at Harvard, were among the Society's honorary members. Other significant individuals who now supported or were sympathetic to Vedanta were Professor Seth Low, president of Columbia University; Professor A. V. W. Jackson of Columbia University; Professors Thomas R. Price and E. Engalsmann of the College of the City of New York; and Professors Richard Botthiel, N. M. Butler, N. A. McLouth, E. G. Sihler, Calvin Thomas, and A. Cohn of New York University.[34]

THE SWAMI'S "UNSHAKABILITY OF SOUL" AND POWER OF REASON EARN THE RESPECT OF HARVARD PROFESSORS

Many philosophical discussions also took place between Swami Abhedananda and some eminent professors of Harvard University. The Swami wrote in his diary:

In Mrs. Bull's house, on the 29th of May, I gave a lecture on "One in Many" at the Cambridge Conferences. Dr. Janes presided over the meeting. During the lecture I raised Professor James's objections to Monism and showed by logical reasoning how irrational and false those arguments were... At the end of the meeting, Professor James shook hands with me and praised highly my rational and simple explanation of Monism and invited me to dinner in his house the next evening... I went to Professor James's house with Dr. Janes. There were along with us at the same table Professor Seller, Professor Royce and Professor Lanman. After the dinner was over, Professor James started arguing against Monism... I myself began to refute his arguments by giving further reasonings. This discussion went on for nearly four hours... Professor Royce, Professor Seller and Professor Lanman and Dr. Janes took my side. Afterwards, Professor James was compelled to say that my arguments in favor of the Oneness of the cosmic reality were indeed irrefutable.[35]

The interested reader may refer to *Vedanta Kesari*, October 1939, pp.236-238, for a detailed report of their discussion.

Seven years later, Professor James was to write "The Powers of Men," an article published in the November issue of *American Magazine*, in order to contribute his estimate of the value of *Yoga*: "The most venerable ascetic system, and the one whose results have the most voluminous experimental corroboration is undoubtedly the Yoga system in Hindustan. From time immemorial, by Hatha Yoga, Raja Yoga, Karma Yoga, or whatever code of practice it might be, Hindu aspirants to perfection have trained themselves, month in and month out, for years. The results claimed, and certainly in many cases accorded by impartial judges, is strength of character, personal power, unshakability of soul."[36]

MEMORIAL SERVICES FOR SWAMIJI IN NEW YORK

THE FIRST MEMORIAL SERVICE: 1902

On July 4, 1902, Swamiji attained Mahasamadhi. The Vedanta Society of New York could not hold a memorial service in his honor immediately due to the normal restrictions imposed by the summer vacation that had already begun. Therefore, a memorial service took place on the afternoon of October 26. Swami Abhedananda gave an intense and stirring address. Extracts of letters from Swamiji's brother Swamis were read. Dr. Parker, the president, Mr. Walter Goodyear, the treasurer and Swamiji's intimate friend, Dr. Street (Swami

Yogananda), Swamiji's disciple, Miss Josephine MacLeod and
Mrs. Ole Bull all spoke of Swamiji, of his irretrievable loss to
humanity, and of the noble work of Vedanta. Mrs. Bull gave
an impassioned speech, appealing for earnest, grateful workers
who sincerely valued India's ageless spiritual teachings that
needed no addition or reform. She spoke of India's need for
social reconstruction through the practical application of the
eternal teachings. Thus, many in the audience were convinced
to share in the work.[37] Miss Sarah Farmer, the founder of the
School for the Comparative Study of Religion at Greenacre,
could not attend due to the severe illness of a near relative,
but sent a deeply heartfelt letter of praise and gratitude.[38]

In 1902 a resolution was passed by The Vedanta Society
of New York to hold a public memorial tribute to the world
mission of Swami Vivekananda that would be given by well-
known speakers. Due to the passing away of many of those
who could offer such testimony, the forum was modified to a
public lecture about Swamiji and his works. It may be
interesting to the reader to know about the feelings of the
devotees in San Francisco during their observance of Swami
Vivekananda's memorial service:

> As he loved and revered his Master, so we will love and cherish
> his sacred memory. He was one of the greatest souls that has
> visited the earth for many centuries. An incarnation of his
> Master, of Krishna, Buddha, Christ and all other great souls.
> He came fitted to fill the needs of the times as they are now.
> His was a twin soul to that of his Master, who represented
> the whole philosophy of all religions be they ancient or
> modern. Vivekananda has shaken the whole world with his
> sublime thoughts, and they will echo down through the halls
> of time until time shall be no more. To him all people and
> all creeds were one. He had the patience of Christ and the
> generosity of the sun that shines and the air of heaven. To
> him a child could talk, a beggar, a prince, a slave or harlot.
> He said: "They are all of one family, I can see myself in all of

them and they in me. The world is one family, and its parent an Infinite Ocean of Reality, Brahman."[39]

A MEMORABLE DEVOTIONAL SERVICE: 1903

On March 8, 1903, one week after the Society's celebration of Sri Ramakrishna's birth anniversary, Swami Abhedananda spoke about his appreciation of Swami Vivekananda at Carnegie Lyceum Hall. His speech was memorable and devotional:

The message of truth requires neither the protection of the sword nor the support of gunpowder for its propagation. The preachers of truth are very few, but their powers are felt by those who happen to come within the atmosphere of their divine personality. Such a preacher of truth occasionally appears like a gigantic comet above the horizon, dazzling the eyes and filling the hearts of ordinary mortals with wonder and admiration, and silently passes away into the invisible and unknown realms of the universe. The late Swami Vivekananda was one of those great comets who appeared in the spiritual firmament, once perhaps after several centuries. A well-known writer of this city wrote the other day, "The passing of Swami Vivekananda was like the flashing of a mighty star upon our wondering eyes. For in truth no greater, wiser, truer, holier soul has ever dwelt among us than this marvellous man who has recently gone into spirit life."

No country has ever produced such a many-sided character harmoniously combined in one form as we have seen in the late Swami Vivekananda…. Poverty, self-abnegation, self-renunciation, and disinterested love for humanity were the ornaments of this exemplary character…. I had the honour of living with this great Swami in India, in England, and in this country (U.S.A.). I lived and travelled with this great spiritual brother of mine, saw him day after day and night after night and watched his character for nearly twenty years, and I stand here to assure you that I have not found another like him in these three continents and that no one can take the place of this wonderful personage. As a man, his character was pure and spotless; as a philosopher, he was the greatest of all Eastern and Western philosophers. In him I found the ideal of *Karma-Yoga, Bhakti-Yoga, Raja-Yoga* and *Jnana-Yoga*; he was like the living example of Vedanta in all its different branches....

Many have asked me why so great and good a man must die. I have said: Why should he not die? His task was finished. One ordinary human body was not enough, nor twenty, nor a hundred for such tremendous energy. Such an intense intellect and spirituality would soon dissolve the granite foundation stones.

Vivekananda is not dead, he is with us, now and forever. He is the Senior Brother to the whole world.[40]

THE SOCIETY'S COMBINED TWELFTH ANNIVERSARY AND MEMORIAL SERVICE FOR SWAMIJI: 1906

On January 17, 1906 Swami Vivekananda's Memorial Services and the twelfth anniversary of the New York Vedanta Society were observed together. The meditation was at 3:00 P.M. Swami Nirmalananda gave a talk that included glimpses of Swamiji's life, not yet known to the listeners. More than one hundred people attended the evening service with Swami Abhedananda and the guest of honor, Mr. Ramanathan, the solicitor general of Ceylon, who was visiting America at the time. Swami Abhedananda spoke of Swamiji as modern India's saint and ideal. He stressed Swamiji's vision of the mutual benefit of a reciprocal relationship between the materialistic West and the spiritual life of the East. He also spoke about the role the Vedanta Society of New York played in that vision:

"Today after twelve years of earnest effort we have succeeded in making the Society stand as a recognized center where Eastern and Western thought meet. Blessed are they who are helping in this noble work begun by the great patriot saint Swami Vivekananda!" The secretary, Mrs. Emily Palmer Cape, Miss Sarah Ellen Waldo, Mr. Walter Goodyear and Miss Laura Glenn gave short talks. Mr. Ramanathan was the final speaker and compared the simple life of the East and the complex Western way of life. He ended with highest praise for Swamiji's character and work and a description of Swamiji's overwhelming reception at Colombo on his journey home from America.[41]

THE SOCIETY'S COMBINED THIRTEENTH ANNIVERSARY AND BIRTHDAY SERVICE FOR SWAMIJI: 1907

In 1907 Swami Vivekananda's birthday celebration was observed together with the Society's thirteenth anniversary. Swami Abhedananda conducted a morning meditation. Swami Paramananda, whom Swami Abhedananda brought from India, spoke of Swamiji's character as the true testimony of his teachings. In the afternoon Swami Bodhananda, the head of the Pittsburgh Center who was assisting Swami Abhedananda at that time, read and explained the meaning of passages from the Upanishads which Swamiji specifically appreciated and loved. Swami Abhedananda opened the 8:00 P.M. service with a brief meditation and gave an address which included the entire scope of Swamiji's life and work—the inspiring influence of his writings, the institutions founded by him or in his name, and the spread of his message through dedicated, inspired workers.

Swami Abhedananda gave the greatest emphasis in his lecture to Swamiji's fulfillment of Sri Ramakrishna's mission to link East and West, and the proof of that mission's success: a reciprocal mutual understanding and implementation between India and America of educational and civic goals.

The Swami acknowledged the crucial role of the Vedanta Society on behalf of the Indian students arriving in America. The secretary, Mrs. Cape, also elaborated upon the crucial role of the Vedanta Society:

> The celebration of this day has a deeper meaning ... We have reached in the growth of the development of our Vedanta work in America a great "Mile-post." If the large-hearted, broad-minded, beautiful-souled man who brought the first fire of Vedanta to America were able to speak today to us, it would be one great theme he would flood our very innermost hearts with: Love, a cry of Divine Love; for no noble lasting work can ever be completed without the deep inspiring, sincere, self-forgetful Love. Our Society has come to a mile-post, and never perhaps, in its history has the power to decide, the power to be strong, and to be self-forgetful, and to remember the Master's work more than any other cry of our souls been before us greater than it is today. Every heart in America who loved Vivekananda, who has watched the work of his brother workers, should rise with one great accord and, forgetting all minor differences and petty disagreements, rise with one magnificent force, and lay our hearts on the altar of Love. Such a true, sincere, selfless uniting of all those who want earnestly the power of the Vedanta teaching to be a great marching onwards— burying all foolish pride, egoism, discussion, and criticism— and once more, each and all, work shoulder to shoulder for Truth, being conscious only of "that great love Divine" which must be the basis of our work.[42]

The Society's vice president, Mr. Stansbury Hagar, and others also gave short addresses. Mr. Nelson Smith said that Swamiji's universal vision saw the infinite intelligence behind it and directing it, "Everything we have we owe to him." Miss Glenn said that Swamiji's lifelong and silent strenuous activity was his abiding characteristic and the true strength behind his message to the world, which he gave towards the end. Swami Bodhananda, Swamiji's disciple, gave the last address: "If we wish to celebrate his birthday, let us take a vow on this solemn occasion to follow in the path he has laid out. This is the most permanent monument we can make to his memory."[43]

SWAMI PARAMANANDA CONDUCTS A BIRTHDAY MEMORIAL SERVICE FOR SWAMIJI: 1908

On January 25, 1908 Swami Paramananda conducted a uniquely solemn and simple service for Swami Vivekananda's birthday memorial service. Students recited Swamiji's *Song of the Sannyasin*. Swami Paramananda spoke about Swamiji's life and teachings in a very humble and stirring way. The *Vedanta Monthly Bulletin* reported that, "After all were silently seated, Swami Paramananda came slowly into the room, clad in the salmon-pink robe of the Sannyasin, and prostrating himself before the dais, as though he would salute the feet of his beloved Master, he knelt silently for a few minutes, then, raising his head, he chanted in Sanskrit, in a low voice of great sweetness, a little song ... It was, indeed, not the worship of a personality, but communion with a spirit which is universal, which will strengthen and inspire us to live as he did—for the service and elevation of our common humanity." The solemnity and beauty of this devotional service is fully described in the *Vedanta Monthly Bulletin* of February 1908.[44]

THE SOCIETY MEETS THE UNIVERSAL DEMAND FOR VEDANTA LITERATURE:

THE VEDANTA MONTHLY BULLETIN

From 1900 to 1906 the demand for Vedantic literature had increased fourfold, and from 1904 to 1906 the book and

pamphlet orders from customers doubled. The demand was
so great that the library remained open for most of the summer,
with two hundred twenty-two volumes borrowed for home
reading alone. In April 1905 the Society, now at 62 West
Seventy-first Street, began to publish its own journal, the
Vedanta Monthly Bulletin. Its purpose was described in its first
issue:

> The BULLETIN sets out on its mission with a double
> purpose: To make known the universal message of Vedanta
> to those who have not yet heard it; and to draw the
> individual and scattered units of the work into closer union
> and cooperation. This must result in a greater solidarity
> and fellowship, and add power and strength to the entire
> movement. We, therefore, earnestly appeal to all to further
> this new effort to spread the lofty truths of Vedanta.[45]

A report from the *Vedanta Monthly Bulletin* of May 1905
shows its relevant instrumentality for the Vedanta Movement:

> The strong resemblance between the philosophy of Vedanta
> and the philosophy of Plato was brought out by Professor
> Edward Howard Griggs in a lecture delivered before the
> Society. Professor Griggs himself admitted that Plato's belief
> in the conquest of the senses as the only means of attaining
> true knowledge was pre-eminently oriental and non-Greek,
> but he did not call attention to the many other points in
> which the two philosophies meet. Plato's figure of the men
> chained in the cave is an allegorical presentation of the
> Vedanta doctrine of *Maya*, while his other figure of the
> chariot is a favorite one with Vedic writers. How far this
> resemblance is coincident and how far derivative is a
> question of dispute among scholars, but one instance, at
> least, of direct communication between Greece and India
> at that time is accepted as authentic. A Hindu philosopher,
> we are told, came to Athens and had a discussion with

Socrates, during which, in reply to Socrates' statement that his philosophy consisted in inquiries about the life of man, the Indian philosopher asked the famous question: "How can one understand things human without first understanding things divine?" It is search for the divine essence behind all phenomena which relates Plato so closely to the Indian teaching and which makes a student of the Platonic philosophy a natural follower of the more ancient system of Vedanta.[46]

PUBLICATION INCREASES AT THE SOCIETY
ALONG WITH REQUESTS FOR NEW CENTERS

In 1905 the books that were sold numbered 7,563 and demands for Vedanta books were coming from Texas, Alaska, Hawaii, the Philippines, Austria, Italy, France, Holland, the West Indies, Vancouver, Mexico, Scotland, and other places.

In 1906 the number of books and pamphlets being published reached 50,000[47] (the bulk of the books were authored by Swami Vivekananda and Swami Abhedananda), and 7,750 books and pamphlets were sold—of these, over three hundred were given for free. The *Vedanta Monthly Bulletin*, for example, had a circulation of over 3000 copies, of which 300 were sent for free to libraries and student organizations.[48]

Within the five years following the publication of Swami Abhedananda's first book, *Reincarnation*, in 1899, several other books written by the Swami were published, including the *Sayings of Ramakrishna, Spiritual Unfoldment, Philosophy of Work, How To Be a Yogi, Self-Knowledge,* and *India and Her People.*

Swami Abhedananda was also receiving calls with requests for Vedanta centers as far distant from New York as Mexico, South Dakota and Canada, as well as areas closer to New York.[49] Hundreds of free leaflets were finding their way to many parts of America and abroad. In October 1905 the *Vedanta Monthly Bulletin* reported that:

From Texas to the northern-most borders of Canada, from the Atlantic to the Pacific, there is not a state or province from which the Society has not received orders for its literature or inquiries concerning its teachings; and within the last five years 39,836 books and pamphlets on Vedanta have gone into circulation from its headquarters. The other day came a letter from Bohol, Tagbilaran, Philippine Islands, asking about the conditions of Society membership; and in the same week a large order of books was shipped to Alaska. Such is the vast area which the work now covers.[50]

By 1906 books and pamphlets were being mailed throughout the United States, Alaska and Hawaii, the Philippine Islands, Canada, Mexico, Europe and the West Indies. People who were unknown to the Society as members were still inspired to form centers of Vedanta literature, by the circulation and sale of books amongst themselves. The Publication Committee of the New York Vedanta Society reported that:

We are trying in every way possible to utilize these new channels to enlarge our field of influence. Our method of work indeed is not unlike that of modern warfare. The men who stand and train their guns on some distant point on the horizon know little of where the shell will strike or what havoc it will cause. So, as we from this one small centre send out these messages of Vedanta into space, we can never know whom or how many they will reach, but of one thing we may be certain—that wherever they fall, they will surely destroy some error and clear the way for the onward march of Truth.[51]

The published teachings of Vedanta inspired in diverse ways. *The Sayings of Ramakrishna*, compiled by Swami Abhedananda, was first published by The Vedanta Society of

New York in 1903. The Preface to the first edition stated, "An attempt has also been made for the first time to classify and arrange in logical sequence the Sayings which were published in *Brahmavadin* and *Prabuddha Bharata* (Awakened India), as well as in *Ramakrishna, His Life and Sayings*, by Professor Max Müller, all having been carefully compared with the original and revised." In 1907 a third edition of *The Sayings of Ramakrishna* was published.[52] In 1909 Tolstoi had already culled one hundred sayings of Sri Ramakrishna and it is reported that he wanted to add to his collection from Swami Abhedananda's books.

Thanks to the various lectures and journeys of the Swami, Vedanta book sales and library collections everywhere flourished, and included the great public libraries of New York, Boston, St. Louis, the State Library at Albany, and a circulating library in Paris, France.[53] In such ways, the message of Vedanta reached far and wide, illuminating and encouraging many.

VEDANTA'S BROAD APPEAL AND EFFECTS OF SWAMI ABHEDANANDA'S LECTURES

SWAMI ABHEDANANDA TRAVELS IN THE U.S. AND EUROPE

In 1901 Swami Abhedananda's lectures were sometimes drawing as many as six hundred people. A broad sociocultural spectrum of Americans and people abroad proved to have a serious interest in Vedantic teachings. In June 1901 the Swami left New York City to visit Buffalo, Cleveland, and Chicago. By August 1 he was in San Francisco, and briefly visited Shanti Ashrama. In September he lectured at the University of California at Berkeley and then went to Los Angeles. He returned to New York on October 7, 1901, after traveling across the country and visiting Thousand Island Park. He continued to lecture and give classes, and traveled to cities on the East Coast during the summer recess of 1902. On August 7 he left to tour Europe, including England, Scotland, France and Switzerland. He returned to New York in early October. In 1902 the *Pacific Vedantin* related the New York lectures to a "Great Movement ... The best minds are taking profound interest in it."

In the summer recess of 1903, with the New York Vedanta Society enjoying financial security and increased membership, Swami Abhedananda traveled again to Europe— to Italy, Switzerland, and Belgium and returned to New York on October 6.

SWAMI NIRMALANANDA ASSISTS IN THE WORK WHILE SWAMI ABHEDANANDA TRAVELS AND LECTURES

On November 12, 1903 Swami Nirmalananda arrived in New York, sent by the Ramakrishna Order. The Vedanta Movement had grown considerably and he was to help the Swami by teaching classes.

The annual business meeting of the Society was held on January 14, 1904 and all the committee reports inspired confidence for the Society's continued success. Swami Abhedananda spoke about Swami Nirmalananda's value and impetus in the Society's work. Various letters to the Society were read, including one from Dr. Hiram Corson Professor Emeritus of English Literature at Cornell University, who requested the honor of becoming an active and honorary member of the Society. His letter extolled the power and teachings of Swami Vivekananda, of whom he considered the Society to be the representative. With high praise for the Society's publications of books written by Swami Vivekananda and Swami Abhedananda, Dr. Corson wrote an urgent appeal for Swami Abhedananda to immediately honor the students and faculty of Cornell University with a lecture that February. In March, *Prabuddha Bharata* reported the events at the annual meeting and the resignation of the treasurer, Mr. Walter Goodyear, who had been known to the Society from the very beginning.[54] After his resignation at that meeting, Mr. Goodyear no longer appeared at any of the Executive Committee meetings.

On May 4, 1904 the Society moved to 62 West Seventy-first Street (Swami Abhedananda, *Amar Jivankatha*, 321). It now had a large hall that could accommodate up to three hundred people. That same May, Swami Abhedananda arranged for an exhibition of Vedanta literature at the World's Fair, which he attended in St. Louis, Missouri. He returned to New York and left for Europe in June. He visited Holland, Bavaria, France, and England and returned to New York on October 16.

THE NEW YORK VEDANTA SOCIETY OPENS BRANCHES IN BROOKLYN AND WASHINGTON, D.C.

On January 30, 1905 Swami Nirmalananda became the monk-in-charge of a newly inaugurated branch of the Vedanta Society of New York in Brooklyn. The second of two Brooklyn lectures that Swami Abhedananda had given the winter before drew audiences so large that no standing room was left.

On March 27, 1905 Swami Abhedananda went to Washington, D.C. to give a lecture. He returned the next day to New York. On April 18 he returned a second time to Washington, D.C. to give a series of lectures on the Gita.[55] As a result of these lectures and several addresses which he had given there a few years before, the Vedanta Center of Greater Washington, D.C. was opened as a branch of the New York Vedanta Society in Room 610 of the Corcoran Building, with Miss L. W. Browne as its secretary.[56] A committee was also formed.

SWAMI ABHEDANANDA'S LECTURES IN TORONTO:
"A PROMISE OF MUCH THAT IS TO COME"

Swami Abhedananda was invited to speak on February 1 before the Historical Society of the University of Toronto, where he met many distinguished people. Several hundred of Toronto's leading citizens attended, including ministers and professors. Swami's profound ability, his lecture "The Religion of the Hindus," and his brilliant extemporaneous answers to questions so greatly roused their interest, that they requested him to start a center there. Lengthy accounts of that evening and the lecture appeared in many newspapers: "A lecture of remarkable depth and interest ... filled the ... Hall with an audience not to be easily matched for culture and broad thought, met with much attention during his visit of four days in Toronto." The Swami also visited the chancellor and provost at Trinity College and had a significant discussion with Professor Clark of Toronto University. The lieutenant governor held a reception for him. He was honored and respectfully invited to the homes of distinguished hosts. He kept to his customary spare diet, but generously gave of his philosophical brilliance and spiritual expression. Various Christian ministers openly admired and recommended some of his books. One leading citizen later wrote to the Swami, "I have spoken with many but have not heard one discordant note. I feel that your visit with us is merely a promise of much that is to come."[57] He gave many other lectures in and around Toronto, some of which were reported in the *Toronto World* and was interviewed on February 2 by the *Toronto News*.

SWAMI ABHEDANANDA ADDRESSES CLERGYMEN:
"THE RELATION OF SOUL TO GOD"

On March 6, 1905, one week before his two lectures in Washington, D.C. on March 27 and April 18, Swami

Abhedananda was the guest of honor at a meeting of the New York Churchman's Association held at the Hotel Vendôme. His lecture, "The Relation of Soul to God," was attended by nearly forty prominent clergymen from in and around New York City. The question-and-answer period that followed the Swami's inspired lecture included his response to a remark made by one of the attending clergymen who challenged him with the words, "We have heard a profound exposition of the highest form of natural religion, but our religion of course is supernatural or revealed religion." Swami's profound response is worth noting here:

> India is the home of all revealed religion. The idea of revelation first came from there. As to the distinction between natural and supernatural religion, that is purely arbitrary, depending entirely upon one's conception of nature. If that conception be narrow, then everything beyond the limit of that circle is accounted supernatural. Extend the circumference of the circle, however, and what was supernatural now becomes natural. If, therefore, the conception of nature, as in Vedanta, is extended until it includes infinite space, then nothing remains outside and the natural has brought within its field the whole realm of the supernatural. Thus the natural religion of Vedanta includes not only the supernatural religion of Christianity but all sects and creeds.[58]

SWAMI ABHEDANANDA TRAVELS IN THE U.S. AND MEXICO: A CENTER IS ESTABLISHED IN MEXICO CITY

On June 29, 1905 Swami Abhedananda and Professor Parker, the president of the New York Vedanta Society, traveled to Alaska by way of Canada, and to Mexico by way of Oregon, California, and Arizona. They visited Swami Trigunatitananda in San Francisco and Swami Satchidananda in Los Angeles before arriving in Mexico City on September 14, where the Swami gave a lecture series and established a center. After giving a lecture in St. Louis, he returned to New York on October 27.

"GREAT SAVIOURS OF THE WORLD" AND
INDIA AND HER PEOPLE
SWAMI ABHEDANANDA'S LECTURES AND
BOOK REMOVE PREJUDICE

From November 14 to December 19 he lectured before three to four hundred people on "India and Her People" at the prestigious Brooklyn Institute of Arts and Sciences Hall on Tuesdays. These lectures were published in his book, *India and Her People*. The book earned the reputation of being the most authoritative and comprehensive history of India circulating in the West. An audience of serious professionals, critics, and students thus acclaimed Swami Abhedananda's superior scholarship. The Swami was now able to speak about the glory of India and be heard with some interest by those who were uninformed and extremely prejudiced against the teachings about India and the Indian religion. The Swami valiantly and patiently sowed the seeds of unity of religions.

That same fall of 1905 Swami Abhedananda also gave a series of Sunday lectures on "The Great Saviours of the World" at the New York Vedanta Society. In 1905 *Broadway Magazine* of New York published a report that:

> The Sunday morning lectures have an average attendance of about five hundred, drawn from varied ranks of life. The banker, the broker, the man of letters, the artisan, the woman of fashion, and the wage earner. It is noted at the Society House that there is a large demand for Vedanta literature from miners and ranchmen. It seems that living close to nature develops a quality of introspection that leads

to serious speculation. In fact, one cannot tell in what soil the seed will bring forth a sturdy growth. It is related by the librarian that an extension and costly relay of Vedanta literature was ordered for a Fifth Avenue mansion. The messenger was amazed when ushered into the presence of the Danish cook who ordered the books and who announced her earnest desire to join the Society. On another occasion a man in the uniform of a trolley motorman purchased a number of pamphlets not only for himself but for the "boys at the power house!"[59]

THE SOCIETY ENJOYS THE LARGEST MEMBERSHIP SINCE ITS BEGINNING

On January 27, 1906, Swami Nirmalananda returned to India. A spirit of unity and enthusiasm characterized the quarterly business meeting that was held on April 19. The secretary reported that the season had brought more new members to the Society than any other season, and that the Society's membership was the largest since its organization. Professor Franklin W. Hooper, director of the Brooklyn Institute of Arts and Sciences, was elected an honorary member of the Society.[60]

SWAMI ABHEDANANDA TRAVELS TO INDIA, LEAVING SWAMI BODHANANDA TO WORK AT THE SOCIETY

Swami Abhedananda sailed to India on May 16, 1906, leaving the Vedanta Society in the care of Swami Bodhananda, a direct disciple of Swami Vivekananda. Swami Bodhananda had been sent from Bombay on April 15 to assist Swami Abhedananda and took up the work on June 1, 1906.[61] In India, Swami Abhedananda enjoyed many warm receptions and gave many lectures throughout India. He

visited Calcutta for a week. He visited his mother and they
offered worship together at Kalighat. Then he went to Belur
Math. The experience of the Vedanta work in America
demanded an assistant Swami. The Belur Math authorities
readily agreed and decided to send Swami Paramananda back
to America with him. The two Swamis arrived in New York
in November 1906. On January 23, 1907, Swami Abhedananda accompanied Swami Bodhananda to Pittsburgh,
Pennsylvania. Swami Bodhananda was to take charge of the
Vedanta Society there for some years.[62] Swami Abhedananda
kept Swami Paramananda in New York to give classes and
restructured the New York Vedanta Society in a way that would
enable him to lecture freely and to revive the Vedanta
Movement in London.

On March 2, 1907, the Vedanta Society of New York
purchased a four-story house at 135 West Eightieth Street and
rented some of the upper rooms. The house stood between
Amsterdam and Columbus Avenues—a good neighborhood
with easy access to public transportation. The first floor had
two rooms that could be united to provide space for public
lectures. Remaining rooms inappropriate for the Society's pur-
poses were rented as the need arose.[63]

A RETREAT FOR THE EAST COAST
IN THE BERKSHIRES

A retreat at Berkshire Hills was also purchased and
inaugurated by Swami Abhedananda and on June 26 he left
for London, leaving Swami Paramananda in charge. The East
Coast now had a retreat much like the ashrama that the West
Coast was enjoying. Swami Paramananda would conduct
summer school at the ashrama during the summer vacation.
Swami Bodhananda also used to stay there in the summer,
when he was free from the work at Pittsburgh.[64] From an ardent

disciple of Swami Abhedananda, Sister Shivani (Mrs. Mary Le Page), we get an idea of the ashram:

> This Ashram in the Berkshires! Three hundred and seventy acres of rolling pasture lands and hills, a brook and several springs. Two old New England houses needing only renovation and some remodelling; barns, carriage house, sheds, all made to fit the purpose the Swami had in mind. The first year Mr. Le Page built the swimming pool, and what a joy it was to all. There were groves of standing timber, birch, maple, ash, hickory and oak and pine to mention some. A good horse, then followed cows, and fowl, even pigs for marketing. The place within a few years was self-supporting; feed for stock raised on the place. Fruits of many kinds, and a splendid kitchen garden kept the table well supplied for summer guests who came and went the season long. The place was kept very plain, everything simple and the Swami's routines for the workers mainly voluntary and in line with training and aptitudes. There always was to be found among the students some one who had training as carpenter, or knew something of the trades. The place was kept in good repair without hired labour. Always there was hard work to be done, always some addition being made, some project under way, nothing ever finished. Season after season the works went on. If ever Karma Yoga maintained a school for study such was here. Sometimes guests would mingle with the workers and share a load or by their too kind willingness disrupt a project or throw the routine out, and within and of these tangles no effort wasted, no lesson spared. We learned our Yogas on our feet in that Lotus Cottage kitchen where centered all the business of house and farm.[65]

How true it is, as Goethe said, "Talents are nurtured best in solitude, but character in life's tempestuous sea."

THE EXPANDED ROLE OF THE NEW YORK
VEDANTA SOCIETY AS HEADQUARTERS
FOR THE VEDANTA TEACHINGS

Swami Abhedananda's work in establishing new centers in America and abroad was prodigious. Towards the end of 1908 Vedanta Centers were started by one of Swami Abhedananda's students, Sister Avavamia, in Australia and New Zealand. The New York Vedanta Society was now the central flame of Vedanta teachings, with rays reaching far and wide: it united three capitals of the world at that time, Washington, London and Paris, while the West Coast center largely served the local regions. The Vedanta Society of New York became the headquarters that provided inspiration, established new branches, and heralded and distributed the publications of the prolific Swami Abhedananda. The Vedanta Society of New York had become the principle center of Vedanta in the Western world.

THE GOSPEL OF SRI RAMAKRISHNA: THE SWAMI'S BOOK IS PUBLISHED IN NEW YORK AND ABROAD

From the time of his arrival in America and for the benefit of sincere students, Swami Abhedananda's mind had nurtured the desire to print the teachings of his Master, Sri Ramakrishna, who declared that "religion is nothing if it is not realization." The diary of "M", the householder disciple of Sri Ramakrishna who recorded his words verbatim, was published in Calcutta between 1902 and 1903, in two volumes as *Ramakrishna-Kathamrita*. Swami Vivekananda had high appreciation of it. Swami Abhedananda received the manuscript of *Ramakrishna-Kathamrita* and a letter from "M" authorizing him to edit and translate it into English. In 1907 Swami Abhedananda translated it, added many useful notes, and remodeled the original manuscript into fourteen chapters. In December 1907 the Vedanta Society of New York first published Swami Abhedananda's *Gospel of Sri Ramakrishna*. In the Preface to the American edition, he wrote: "The completed work is now offered to the Western world with the sincere hope that the sublime teachings of Sri Ramakrishna may open the spiritual sight of seekers after Truth and bring peace and freedom to all souls struggling for realization." The book enjoyed a wide popularity and tremendous enthusiasm.

The first Spanish translation of Swami Abhedananda's Gospel of Sri Ramakrishna, El Evangelio de Ramakrishna, came from the renowned publishing house of Editorial Kier in Buenos Aires in 1909. A Vedanta Society was formed around the same time in Buenos Aires by admirers interested in the life and teachings of Sri Ramakrishna and Vedanta.[66] By 1915 many other foreign editions of the *Gospel* had been published—in Portuguese from Brazil, and in Danish, Scandinavian, French and Czech in Europe. This *Gospel* of the "child and servant of Sri Ramakrishna" continues to guide the path of the Ramakrishna Movement in the West more than any other book.[67]

For the interested reader, the *Vedanta Monthly Bulletin* of March 1908 printed a lengthy review of *The Gospel of Sri Ramakrishna* that was published in the *New York Herald*. The Bulletin included a small introduction to the review: "That unique document, *The Gospel of Sri Ramakrishna*, wherein are recorded, 'For the first time in the history of the world, the exact words of the Master,' is receiving considerable attention from the secular press. The *New York Herald* of March 8 publishes a picture of *Panchavati*, where Ramakrishna attained Divine Communion with the Mother of the Universe, and this review of the gospel."[68]

THE INSPIRED PORTRAITS OF SRI RAMAKRISHNA
AND HOLY MOTHER

Swami Abhedananda had traveled to London more than several times between 1907 and 1909. During the Swami's stay in London in May 1909, the famous Czechoslovakian artist from Prague, Frank Dvorak, came to see him at the Vedanta Center. Mr. Dvorak had learned about Sri Ramakrishna and Swami Vivekananda from Swami Abhedananda, whom he had met earlier in New York. Mr. Dvorak regarded the Swami as his guru, and the *Gospel* had inspired him. After experiencing a vision of Sri Ramakrishna, Mr. Dvorak had painted the Master's portrait. When Swami Abhedananda chanced to show Mr. Dvorak a photograph of Sri Ramakrishna, the artist presented him with the painting. Abhedananda took it to India. It remains the best available portrait of the Master thus far. With great devotion, Frank Dvorak also painted the portrait of Holy Mother. It was duly published in the Calcutta Dailies in 1928, one year after Frank Dvorak's death.

There are several interesting notes to Frank Dvorak's life. Rabindranath Tagore had visited Mr. Dvorak in his studio in 1921 and again in 1926. When Swami Ranganathananda visited the artist's two sisters, Miss Helene Dvorak and the younger Marie Rijackova in his studio where they resided, he was very cordially welcomed. During his visit he was shown a group photograph taken in 1921 that included Mr. Dvorak, Tagore, and the famous Prague Indologist, Professor Lesny. We also know that he had acquired a ticket to the Parliament of World Religions in 1893, but was unable to attend because he had to fulfill a painting assignment.[69]

SWAMI ABHEDANANDA'S STRONG APPEAL CREATES NEW INTEREST AND BRINGS MANY STUDENTS

While Swami Paramananda was at the New York Society, he was also invited to Mrs. Wheeler's place in New Jersey and to Mrs. Ole Bull's place in Boston. During this period from 1907 to 1908 Swami Paramananda was conducting classes at the Society and conducting summer school at the ashram. On June 26, 1907 Swami Abhedananda went to London. By the second week of July, he was teaching classes there on Yoga and Vedanta. He returned to New York on September 6, 1907. On January 29, 1908 Swami Abhedananda again went to London. On July 1 he established the Vedanta Society in London at 22 Conduit Street. On the same day Swami Abhedananda spoke about the history of Vedanta and its aims. Sister Nivedita also spoke. During her many visits to him in London, Sister Nivedita was able to discuss the difficulties in her work. Swami Abhedananda visited Paris for a few days and returned to New York on August 21, 1908.

In addition to his London trip in 1908, Swami Abhedananda had a heavy schedule of lecture engagements and was creating new interest throughout America towards Vedanta. He met and became intimately acquainted with the famous Unitarian Church preacher, Rev. Dr. J. T. Sanderland. In August 1908 Swami Abhedananda made an extensive tour of Chicago, Denver, and other Western cities. On December 19, 1908 the younger brother of Swami Vivekananda, Mr. Bhupendra Nath Datta, visited the Vedanta Society. Early in January 1909 Swami Abhedananda formed the Indo-American Club with the purpose of giving Indian students an opportunity to have close contact with American friends. This was reported in the *Vedanta Magazine* in 1909.[70]

In January the Swami was conducting lectures at Duryea's Hall, with seating for 500, at Seventy-second Street and Broadway.[71] The *Vedanta Magazine* reported an increase in literature sales during the course of these lectures.[72] The Vedanta Society also sponsored an event at Duryea's Hall that raised substantial funds for victims of a recent earthquake in Italy. The program included Mr. Edwin Markham's recital of his epic poem *Lincoln* and Hindu devotional singing by Mrs. A. Ghosh, who was visiting America.[73] Sister Nivedita and Sister Christine were given a reception at the Society on November 10.

SWAMI TURIYANANDA COMES TO THE SOCIETY

THE TEMPERAMENTS OF SWAMI ABHEDANANDA
AND SWAMI TURIYANANDA

Swami Atulananda, the close disciple of Swami Abhedananda, relates his impressions of the Swami:

> Swami Abhedananda did not mix with his students as freely as some of the other Swamis have done. It is true that he held social meetings where the students could freely talk and mix with him, and he gave one hour each week to meeting personal inquiries. But by nature he was always more or less reserved, and in private life he was not easily accessible. Swami Abhedananda insisted on a certain amount of privacy. This was probably wise and necessary on his part. He gave himself heart and soul to his work, and he needed hours of solitude to prosecute his studies and to prepare his carefully thought-out lectures, free from outside disturbances. But one could always be assured of his ready assistance, his sympathy, and encouragement when one made it a point to approach him.
>
> I rarely visited the Swami in his own rooms, but on many occasions I found it possible to have very close and intimate talks with him, at which time he would give me the most valuable advice.
>
> In years there could not have been much difference between us. The Swami may have been my senior by five or six years at the most. But I regarded him as a wise and loving father—a guide who understood my struggles and difficulties—and I felt that he loved me as a son. I was exceedingly happy to have found a teacher who had realized that for which I was striving. I considered myself greatly blessed to be guided by one of Sri Ramakrishna's direct disciples. And sometimes when shaking hands with the Swami, I thought, "Now I am touching the same hand that has performed service to the great Master."[74]

Swami Atulananda gives further impressions of those early days:

> Such were the early days of the Vedanta movement in New York. Simplicity and earnestness was the predominating note in those days. The Society had rented a house in one of the modest quarters of the city. Here Swami Abhedananda lived, and here he met his students and held his classes. The parlor being rather small, a hall was rented for his Sunday lectures. The audiences gradually increased in number and, one after the other, large[r] halls were necessary.
>
> The Sunday lectures appeared in print and these, together with the different publications on Vedanta, were offered for sale at the hall and at the Vedanta headquarters.
>
> The Swami became popular and his work increased. He was a very busy man, lecturing, holding classes, giving private instructions, and writing books on Vedanta. The Society flourished, and the intellectual world was attracted. The Swami was invited to speak before university assemblies and to address different clubs and societies. What had begun in a private, unostentatious manner, developed into a public movement. The Society was reorganized and the headquarters removed to a better section of the city. Different classes of students enlisted as members, and the Vedanta Society became a busy center.
>
> The change was natural and inevitable. Nothing remains stationary in life; it grows or decays. But the old students did not like the change so much. They preferred the quiet simplicity of the early days. This also was natural. They had experienced the benefit of small, more intimate gatherings at some student's home where everyone knew each other. There was a close bond between these few students and their teacher. And with larger classes and many strangers dropping in, the atmosphere changed. Perhaps it was not quite reasonable to expect that things would

continue exactly on the old footing. Anyhow the Swami felt
that he was called to reach out beyond his little circle, that
his message had to go forth to all quarters, that the success
of his work necessitated his meeting with the intellectual
and well-to-do people of New York, and that Vedanta was
not for the few, but for the many.

It was at this stage of the Vedanta movement that
Swami Turiyananda appeared on the scene... "Fresh from
India" was in itself a recommendation in the sight of the
old students. We do not want a westernized Swami. Business
and lecturing we have enough in America; we want a simple,
meditative man—was their attitude.

Right or wrong, this was the state of affairs. Swami
Abhedananda, always strong and positive, followed his own
counsel. He wanted to spread Vedanta, so he had to follow
his own plan. And he flourished: he became a very fine
speaker, enriched the Vedanta literature with a goodly
number of his productions, was invited to other cities to
lecture, and was loved, admired, and applauded wherever
he went.

And so we had two Swamis of different temperaments,
attracting the different students.

With the coming of Swami Turiyananda the work that
was spreading out became further intensified, for in him
the fire of spirituality was always burning, ready to flame
up at the least occasion. It was my good fortune for several
years to be closely associated with him. What had been
implanted in me by the loving care of Swami Abhedananda, was now protected and nourished by the new
Swami. Swami Abhedananda went ahead, ploughed new
fields, and planted new seeds. Swami Turiyananda took
charge of the growing plants. But be it understood, Swami
Abhedananda kept a loving, watchful eye over his old
students. If he could not give them the time and attention
of former days, he never forgot them or ceased to love
them. And it was perhaps during these very days that I

saw in him the most unmistakable marks of a tender, loving heart.[75]

Swami Turiyananda was not interested in organized public works. He was dedicated to the work of building character on an individual basis. He was of the opinion that spiritual work suffers under the burden of organizations and numerous lectures. He used to say, "Lectures are to reach the public. But the real work can be done only through close personal contact. Both are necessary. And everyone has his own way of working." He knew that to be true to himself would be as useful as Swami Abhedananda's usefulness in reaching vast audiences through lectures. Swami Turiyananda also lectured when Swami Abhedananda was absent, but to smaller audiences and in a briefer way, using his own method. "He talked with fire and enthusiasm, and he would lose himself entirely in his subject, forgetting everything else for the time being. Swami Turiyananda impressed everyone who heard him, and all classes of people felt attracted towards him."[76]

THE POLARITIES INCREASE AT THE SOCIETY

The discussion of the temperament of the two Swamis is given with a view that although their respective groups of students had reactions which were normally expected, the spiritual atmosphere remained unaffected. But during the period of Swami Paramananda, the polarities of the congregation increased and did affect the spiritual rhythm of the Vedanta Society in New York.

Swami Abhedananda's astounding success was due to his hard work, erudite scholarship, captivating oratory, his deep faith in the saving truth of Vedanta, his apostolic fervor in his mission and, above all, his magnetic personality. It should be remembered that he was a great, venerable monk who can be ranked next only to Swami Vivekananda in his eloquence and scholarship. He was the much-wanted person by the enlightened people of two continents: Europe and the U.S.A. He loved and enjoyed scholastic dialogue with the scholars. His deep knowledge about Western philosophy and the Christian religion placed him in the unique position of engaging in interesting, meaningful, and enjoyable dialogue with them. He was also intimate with many leaders of the clergy, and with scholars, professors, and philosophers of the day.

Although his work was prodigious in America and abroad, some New York members were very discontented by his departures for travel. He had remained in Europe for several months in 1907, for eight months in 1908, and for half a year in 1909, establishing Vedanta Centers. But the Society in New York was experiencing a financial strain and lack of funds; in 1908 the *Vedanta Monthly Bulletin* could no longer be published and continued through the August/September issue only. The bulletin was revived from January to December 1909 bearing the title *Vedanta Magazine*.

Swami Abhedananda's long absences from the New York Vedanta Society, his scholastic aloofness from the congregation, his extremely demanding life as a writer and speaker, did not give him ample scope and the necessary aptitude to feel at-one-ment and rapport with the members. He was temperamentally unsuitable as the role model of a teacher of devotional temperament fulfilling the personal needs of the individual student. The loss of membership and the consequent financial deficit caused a heavy financial burden for the Society. Swami Paramananda, the acting head of the Society, was a monk of different character—sweet, loving, and very cordial in his dealing with the members. The congregation felt the contrast and some of them, obviously, switched their allegiance to the such caring and sharing junior Swami, who also touched the hearts of the congregation by his lectures that had overtones of devotion—in contrast to the scholastic lectures of Swami Abhedananda.

THE POLARITIES SURFACE

The New York Vedanta Society's members were thus divided. They were basically comprised of two groups: the earliest group of students who became members under Swami Vivekananda's personal and intimate leadership, and the later group of students who came in response to the more impersonal, scholastic and expansionist approach of Swami Abhedananda. It is of interest here to note that in spite of Swami Abhedananda's offer to resign in favor of Swami Paramananda in 1908, the Society's support and majority vote allowed him to remain.

Swami Paramananda's presence and his intimate rapport with the devotees and Swami Abhedananda's prolonged absences from the Vedanta Society of New York caused an unpleasant situation. After some time, Swami Paramananda left New York for Boston during December 1908 to explore new pastures and to gain independence. The students gave him a farewell reception. It should not be construed that there was any unfriendly relationship between the New York Society and Swami Paramananda. The needs of the two groups were accommodated felicitously by a unique arrangement of classes. The *Vedanta Monthly Bulletin* reported that Sunday lectures were offered in the morning and afternoon by the respective Swamis at different locations, and the Tuesday and Thursday evening lectures were given at the Society's rooms by Swami Paramananda and Swami Abhedananda, respectively.[77] Swami Paramananda often visited the New York Vedanta Society and occasionally gave lectures there.[78]

While Swami Paramananda was working in Boston, the progress of his work was duly published in the *Vedanta Magazine*.[79] His first book, *The Path of Devotion*, was published by the New York Vedanta Society and reviewed in the *Vedanta Monthly Bulletin* in 1908.[80] He authored two other books, *The True Spirit of Religion* and *Vedanta in Practice*, that were mentioned in the *Vedanta Monthly Bulletin* in 1908[81] and the *Vedanta Magazine* in 1909,[82] respectively. On March 7, 1909 he officiated at the birthday celebration of Sri Ramakrishna and gave the address.[83]

In spite of his success, Swami Abhedananda continued to absent himself from the New York Vedanta Society by traveling to Europe the following three years. This foreshadowed unpleasant events in the life of the Society and made it impossible for Swami Abhedananda to carry on the work in the Society.

Writing about this unhappy phase of our history, we quote from Swami Abhedananda's own disciple. In his Bengali book written from the diaries of Swami Abhedananda, Swami Shankarananda writes:

On June 12 (1910) he wrote to Swami Brahmananda that he was returning to India, and so another monk should be sent for the New York work. We saw earlier that the New York Vedanta Society had a home of its own, which had been purchased with money raised by a loan that was being gradually repaid. Owing to Swami Abhedananda's stay in England for most of the time, the membership of the Society decreased, and the income fell, till it became impossible to liquidate the loan, and it was decided to sell the house. Meanwhile, the Society sold off the property of the Vedanta Ashrama (at Berkshire) to Swami Abhedananda, since it was not in a position to clear the debt on it. The Swami purchased it with the money he had realized from the proceeds of his books. He offered a similar proposal for the Society building itself, which the members of the Society turned down. In order to repay the loan, they let out most of the rooms of the Society building; and therefore on May 5, 1910, Abhedananda left New York, never more to live in the Society building.[84]

SWAMI ABHEDANANDA DEPARTS, LEAVING
A LEGACY OF DISTINGUISHED SERVICE

Directed by the Belur Math authorities, Swami Bodhananda now had to close the Pittsburgh center and take charge
of the New York Center in October 1912.[85] Swami Abhedananda went to the Berkshire Retreat and remained there for
most of the period from 1910 to 1919. In 1919 he sold the
retreat and left for New York on December 14. On December
15 Swami Bodhananda and the devotees gave him a farewell
reception. He left for San Francisco, arrived there on December
21, 1919, and remained there for one year. From December
1920 until June 19, 1921 he remained in Los Angeles and
lectured there. On July 27, 1921 he left for India from San
Francisco.

For a quarter of a century, from 1896 to 1921, Swami
Abhedananda's dynamic spiritual personality had appeared
in Europe and America—crossing the Atlantic Ocean
seventeen times to carry the message of Vedanta to the West.
He was popular, hard working, erudite and inquisitive and
established intimate friendships with such personalities as Max
Müller, Paul Deussen and Annie Besant. And, due to his
intimate contacts with members of the clergy, his message
penetrated the congregations of different denominations of
faith.

New York's *Literary Digest* featured an article under its
column "Religion and Social Service" for its readers to ponder:
"The East is sending its emissaries to us... 'Yoga' classes, which
were first made fashionable by the society set, have become in
many cities as popular as Browning and Shakespeare classes.
Placing the Hindu Scriptures above the Bible, many women
today are studying these teachings who were formerly Baptists,
Methodists, Presbyterians, Episcopalians, Catholics, and
Jewesses." It provided the Swami's photo along with the
caption, "One of the most successful and popular preachers
of Vedantism in America."[86] In addition to the *Literary Digest*,

other highly respected New York newspapers carried articles
by journalists acknowledging great appreciation of Swami
Abhedananda's teachings and personality. The *Sun*, the *New
York Tribune*, the *Critic*, the *Times*, the *Intelligence*, and the *Mind*
were among these.[87]

It is interesting to note that the two oldest Vedanta
Societies are found in America—in New York and San
Francisco, and that both were inaugurated by Swami
Vivekananda and thrived under inspired, dynamic Swamis:
Abhedananda and Trigunatitananda, respectively.

5

SWAMI BODHANANDA UNDERTAKES THE LEADERSHIP OF THE VEDANTA SOCIETY OF NEW YORK: 1912-1950

"A MONK WHO DUG DEEP INTO THE SOIL OF ONE PLACE"

Swami Vivekananda once said that his future missionaries would be of two types, "those who moved like wildfire, spreading ... their news, and those who dug deep into the soil of one place, putting down roots and shedding fragrance on those in their shade." Swami Bodhananda was the second type of monk. He did his best to live his spiritual life and thus kept the congregation together. He was a man of deep faith with a singular aspiration. His nature was very austere, simple, and enduring—fitted to grapple with difficulties, and to die for a cause.

During the great economic Depression of the thirties—when many Americans were unwilling to declare their affiliation with a foreign religion—he bravely faced the menace and helped his congregation with constant encouragement and guidance. It is no wonder the Swami inspired others to follow the same principles. Swami Satprakashananda had hoped to cultivate interest in Vedanta by preaching in various cities. Discouraged by the difficulties in the work, he visited Swami Bodhananda in New York and asked the Swami's advice about starting a new center in St. Louis. Swami Bodhananda replied, "Go there and bite the earth!" Swami Satprakasha-nanda, like other second-generation Swamis, followed Swami Bodhananda's advice, settled down in one place, and dug roots deep into the American soil. The development of seventeen official Vedanta Centers and innumerable unofficial ones— eight expansive territories for retreats; two historical monuments—the Vivekananda cottages at Thousand Island Park and Pasadena; seven temples; sixteen monasteries; and two convents—are all the direct result of their singular dedicated labor.

Swami Bodhananda's purity of vision and innate saintliness kindled a sincere enthusiasm in the hearts of the devotees for a holy life. He confined himself to the Vedanta Society and tried to hold the Society through his able personal guidance without being distracted in the least by the apostolic fervor of his reputed predecessors—his was the introspective spiritual life.

A BRIEF SKETCH OF THE STATURE OF SWAMI BODHANANDA

Swami Bodhananda was one of those fortunate few who came to Baranagore Math in its very early days. He took initiation from Holy Mother and got sannyas from Swami Vivekananda in 1898. He was a graduate of Calcutta University. During his stay with Swami Vivekananda at Benares, Swamiji told him, "I ask you to lead the life and work in your own sincere ways and success will be surely yours."[1] Prior to coming to the United States, he was in charge of Bangalore Math. We have seen that he left Bombay on April 15, 1906 and reached New York before June 1906. He started giving classes throughout the summer from June 1906, in the New York Vedanta Society[2] while Swami Abhedananda visited India that year. Swami

Bodhananda's lengthy article, "Synthesis of Hinduism," was published that July in the *Vedanta Monthly Bulletin*.[3]

SWAMI BODHANANDA'S PRIOR WORK
IN THE PITTSBURGH CENTER

It may be remembered that when Swami Abhedananda returned to the New York Vedanta Society in November 1906 with Swami Paramananda, Swami Bodhananda went to Pittsburgh in January 1907 to take charge of the Vedanta Society there for some years. Readers were informed of the activities at the Pittsburgh Center in the *Vedanta Monthly Bulletin* and the *Vedanta Magazine*. In 1907 the *Bulletin* published Swami Bodhananda's Pittsburgh lectures[4] and reported the developments and classes at the Pittsburgh Center.[5] In 1908 the *Bulletin* published a lengthy description of the successful new weekly children's class conducted by the Swami in the home of Dr. Harry Sheppard.[6] In 1909 the *Vedanta Magazine* reported the growing interest in Vedanta and the favorable prospects of the Vedanta Society of Pittsburgh.[7] The *Voice of Freedom* reported in 1909 that the Pittsburgh Center was "progressing favorably" with regular Sunday and weekly lectures.[8]

Swami Bodhananda did not travel very much, but on one occasion, The *Voice of Freedom* reported the three "greatly appreciated lectures" that the Swami gave in San Francisco on August 15, 1909: "Vedanta as a Religion and Philosophy," "The Steps to Self-Knowledge," and "Evolution and Reincarnation."[9]

When Swami Bodhananda first came to the Vedanta Society of New York in 1910, it was located at 135 West Eightieth Street. The *Vedanta Monthly Bulletin* of October 1915 reported the Society's next new residence: "The Vedanta Society of New York, under the charge of Swami Bodhananda, has moved to new quarters at 236 Central Park West. Here the Swami will continue his earnest work, holding the usual Sunday services and biweekly classes. During the mid-summer

Swami Paramanand, Boston, c. 1910.

Swami Bodhananda

Swami Pavitrananda

Joyful Genêt sisters

Rolande Genêt

Jeanne Genêt

the Society suspended its meetings and the Swami spent some time at Greenacre, where he was warmly welcomed by many friends whom he had made there in previous years."[10]

THE SOCIETY ACQUIRES ITS PRESENT QUARTERS

In 1921, in the days when tax exemption status for religious organizations had not yet been introduced, the Vedanta Society of New York acquired its present home at 34 West Seventy-first Street. The Society's brownstone building was purchased by the Society for forty thousand dollars, of which the sum of twenty-two thousand dollars was paid by Miss Mary Morton, a devoted student of Swami Bodhananda. She was the daughter of Levi Parsons Morton, himself the son of a pastor of old New England stock. Mr. Morton was the former vice president (1889 to 1893) under United States President Benjamin Harrison and a former governor of New York State (1895-1896). In addition, he played a unique role in America's history during his appointment from 1881 to 1885 as United States Minister to France: On July 4, 1884 Mr. Morton received the official document of the statue, "Liberty Enlightening the World," from the government of the French Republic. On that day Ferdinand de Lesseps—in the name of the Committee of the Franco-American Union—formally handed over the official document with its illuminated silk badge of France in a gold box to Mr. Morton. This symbolic gesture represented the transfer of Bartholdi's colossal statue to the United States.[11]

Mr. Morton died in 1920. Unfortunately, Miss Morton also died suddenly, leaving Swami Bodhananda with the heavy burden of half the mortgage for the permanent building of the Society. In order to meet the Society's expenses, every room had to be rented—some to students and the downstairs dining room to a Greek journalist for his use as a study. It took many years to pay the mortgage, with interest.

SWAMI BODHANANDA'S PILGRIMAGE TO INDIA

In its December issue, *Prabuddha Bharata* reported Swami Bodhananda's plan for a pilgrimage to India in December 1923. Swami Raghavananda was sent from India. After training him for five or six months, Swami Bodhananda was able to leave him in charge. The *Prabuddha Bharata* report included extracts from a letter written on October 8 by Swami Raghavananda. It described a two-week visit the Swamis made together to Grand Isles, Vermont, when Sister Christine was also visiting there. Their joint work in the Society, including the two lectures given every Sunday at 11 A.M. and 3 P.M., was challenging and successful. The same December issue mentioned a cable the journal received from London. It confirmed the arrival there—en route to India—of Swami Bodhananda and Sister Christine of Nivedita's school in Calcutta. A warm reception awaited them in India.[12] Swami Bodhananda arrived alone in Bombay on December 10, 1923.

Prabuddha Bharata described his arrival and some of his travel plans in India in the January 1924 issue. Sister Christine and others who were to accompany the Swami to India decided in Genoa that they would "like to see the continent before they come to India." Therefore, they arrived later, in the first week of January. The journalist also gave his impression of the Swami: "The whole of yesterday I was with him. He is such a simple and kind man. There is no change in him though he has come after 17 years of stay in America. He is that pure, simple and sincere old-type Indian monk."[13]

During Swami Bodhananda's visit to India, *Prabuddha Bharata* sent a representative to interview him about his life and work at the New York Center. This interview was published in the journal's March 1924 issue. It reported the Swami's perceptive impressions of the culture and economy of the American people, and of their education and public health practices. During his interview, Swami Bodhananda again articulated Swami Vivekananda's observations: the West needs the spiritual teachings of India and India needs the practical skills of the West. Swamiji's deep respect and appreciation for the role of women also reverberated in Swami Bodhananda's words: "I was deeply impressed by the culture and education of the American woman. She is the guiding spirit of the American life."

He was also asked about his duty to preach Vedanta in the West. The Swami again responded with the same uncompromising dedication to the ideals of Vedanta that Swamiji had boldly proclaimed. He stated, "This is the message of Vedanta to the Western world—to show to the West the truth of the Christian teaching, 'Love thy neighbour as thyself,' not by force of external laws but by love as a result of spiritual love from within. To reach this ideal, man must practice Yoga (inner discipline of the mind), and Vedanta sets forth clearly the practical methods by which this control and serenity of the mind can be attained."[14]

Swami Bodhananda returned from India to the Vedanta Society in New York on September 20, 1924. *Prabuddha Bharata* published an article in January 1925, describing his journey home by the Atlantic route and of his warm reception in New York. The Swami visited Switzerland. He spent four weeks in Interlaken and spoke on Vedanta to a small group of sincere students at Berne, before arriving in New York.[15]

SWAMI BODHANANDA VISITS THE WEST COAST

THE SWAMI'S FIRST VISIT

On November 6, 1925—eluding a very severe winter in New York—Swami Bodhananda visited the West Coast. He gave lectures and held classes in Los Angeles during December and January. In April, he was the guest of Swami Prakashananda at the Temple of the Vedanta Society of Northern California in San Francisco. Swami Bodhananda gave four classes and four lectures at the Society. One member who considered herself fortunate to have met Swami Bodhananda wrote to her friend, "He has helped us much in our meditation classes. He radiates great power during meditation." The two Swamis enjoyed the opportunity to reminisce about their early days together in India.

In early May Swami Bodhananda visited Swami Prabhavananda and the newly inaugurated Vedanta Center in Portland, Oregon. He gave three lectures under its auspices and became very endeared to the members of the Society, though his visit was brief. On May 11 Swami Bodhananda went to Seattle, Washington, where he gave two lectures under the auspices of the Theosophical Lodge. After the second lecture he went to spend a few quiet days in the home of a friend in Tacoma, Washington. He gave two lectures at the Universalist Church there. While the Swami was in Tacoma, Swami Prabhavananda was invited to Seattle to give three lectures at the Theosophical Lodge and another Sunday lecture at the Chamber of Commerce Auditorium for the Congress of Religions that was sponsored by the First Unitarian Church of Seattle. On the following Monday, Swami Prabhavananda went to Tacoma and spent a few hours with Swami Bodhananda to bid him farewell.

Swami Bodhananda returned to New York via Chicago by train in late May 1926, with a promise to visit the members in the West again the following year. He realized that there was a desire awakening in people for the Vedantic teachings and that new centers were needed to expound them to the needy people. *Prabuddha Bharata* reported all these activities in its August 1926 issue.[16]

THE SWAMI'S SECOND VISIT

Swami Bodhananda again traveled to southern California in 1927 to spend the winter. While he was there, Swami

Prakashananda, who had succeeded Swami Trigunatitananda as leader of the Vedanta Society of Northern California in San Francisco, passed away on February 13, 1927. *Prabuddha Bharata* reported the funeral service in its June 1927 issue. The tributes for the Swami came from near and far. Swami Prabhavananda immediately traveled from the Portland Center to San Francisco when he heard the news. He had come from India with Swami Prakashananda when he had visited there four years before, and had been with Swami Prakashananda at the Temple until 1925, after which Swami Prabhavananda left to open the Vedanta Center in Portland.

Swami Bodhananda also immediately traveled north from Riverside to participate in the memorial service of his brother monk and lifelong friend. He began the services with a Sanskrit prayer and spoke with cordial reverence for his Guru Bhai about the spiritual significance of death. Swami Prabhavananda then spoke of the ideal that the departed Swami represented in his life and narrated an incident in the life of Swami Vivekananda that Swami Prakashananda loved to relate and which he exemplified: "Swami Turiyananda, when he met Swami Vivekananda after many years, inquired of him, 'What have you realized?' and Vivekananda replied, 'Brother, I do not know anything about your realization, but this I know, that the heart has grown big'." Swami Dayananda also spoke. After the service, the funeral cortège drove to the crematory and Swami intoned the final chant. The members of the San Francisco Center felt it "an indelible privilege and comfort" to have Swami Bodhananda with them "during the first sad days of bereavement."

SWAMI BODHANANDA'S SOUL FORCE

Swami Bodhananda lived quietly and unobtrusively, yet had a profound impact on others. We would like to relate one of many stories illustrating the Swami's soul force. Miss

Dorothy Mercer was a member of the Vedanta Society of Northern California. Before she was born, her parents had heard Swami Vivekananda speak in San Francisco. Her mother had taken lessons from Swami Trigunatitananda, who had gone to San Francisco in 1903, and she regarded him as "the most important light in her moral and spiritual struggle." When she was still a little girl, Miss Mercer accompanied her mother to see Swami Trigunatitananda and greatly enjoyed his presence, and the Vedanta environment, in which he lived and circulated. After Swami Trigunatita was killed by a religious fanatic, Swami Abhedananda came to San Francisco. Miss Mercer now became entirely absorbed in Swami Abhedananda and the Vedanta teachings. But Swami Abhedananda stayed only two-and-a-half years in San Francisco. Therefore, when Swami Bodhananda visited the West Coast, Dorothy Mercer was there to hear him speak. "I do not know to this day," she wrote, "why Swami Bodhananda made an impression on me. He was not fatherly as Swami Trigunatitananda had been, nor had he the commanding presence of Swami Abhedananda, nor did he speak eloquently. He said nothing that I had not heard time and time again. But I was uplifted for quite a period—long enough to face my brother's death with an equanimity which astonished my mother..."[17]

Swami Bodhananda's simple living, his intense spiritual personality and unswerving efforts to teach the message of Vivekananda inspired the American heart.

MONKS COME TO ASSIST SWAMI BODHANANDA IN THE WORK

During his leadership at the Society in New York, Swami Bodhananda received the assistance of four monks: Swami Raghavananda, Swami Jnaneswarananda, Swami Devatmananda, and Swami Nikhilananda.[18] Through their assistance to Swami Bodhananda, the four young Swamis received invaluable training from him before setting out to establish and expand the work in other Centers.

Swami Raghavananda

Swami Raghavananda was sent from India and arrived in June 1923. He assisted Swami Bodhananda while also developing Vedanta work in Philadelphia. He took charge of the New York Center during Swami Bodhananda's pilgrimage to India. The *Vedanta Monthly Bulletin* reported that "Swami Raghavananda ... is gradually winning his way in that great city through his earnest efforts and unflagging zeal," in its January 1927 issue.[19] Due to ill health, Swami Raghavananda was forced to return to India in 1927.

Swami Jnaneswarananda

Swami Jnaneswarananda, a disciple of Swami Brahmananda, came in 1927, at only thirty-four years of age, to help with the work for two years during the difficult days of the Depression. During the Swami's two years under the guidance of Swami Bodhananda, he mastered English very successfully. He was able to communicate remarkably well with Americans, as few Swamis had done before him. His articles and lectures were admired: the *New York Times* printed a notice of the 11 A.M. and 3 P.M. lectures by the two Swamis scheduled for September 23, 1928 at the Vedanta Society.

Wendell Thomas, author of *Hinduism Invades America*, attended Swami Jnaneswarananda's afternoon lecture on "Vedanta in Everyday Life." In his book, Mr. Thomas detailed the substance of the Swami's lecture and its emphasis upon the three levels of conduct for realizing Vedanta. Mr. Thomas' interest in Vedanta prevailed and he made an appointment to meet with Swami Jnaneswarananda. After that meeting, the author's discussion with the Swami left him convinced that he "understood at least this much about the Vedanta Society. It was here in America to make us peaceful and tolerant Christians by means of a meditation free from magic."[20]

During Swami Jnaneswarananda's stay at the Vedanta Society of New York, *Prabuddha Bharata* published a lengthy article in May 1929. It described the sixty-sixth birth anniversary of Swami Vivekananda at the Vedanta Society of New York on January 10 of that year: "At 11 A.M. Swami Bodhananda most feelingly related the story of his own experience with his Master, the great Swami Vivekananda... At 3 P.M. Swami Jnaneswarananda spoke on the life and message of the Swami and flowers were distributed ... as a token of *Ashirvada* or blessings from the great Master, which everyone appreciated."

The "India-America Friendship Dinner" at the Ceylon India Inn that followed the birth anniversary service at 7 P.M. was also described in the article. There was chanting of *Brahmarpanam*. A vegetarian dinner cooked in the Hindu fashion was reverently enjoyed. Swami Jnaneswarananda and Mrs. Kamala Mukherjee performed Hindu vocal and instrumental music. Many distinguished guests were there, including Mr. Hager and Mr. Goodyear, who knew Swami Vivekananda when he was in New York. "Although the function was declared closed at 11 o'clock at night, many of the guests were eager to hear more music and were not willing to go home. So musical recitals had to be continued till 1 o'clock in the morning. There was indeed an atmosphere of pure and serene joy and happiness during the entire programme and all were highly gratified."[21]

Towards the end of 1927, while Swami Jnaneswarananda was still at the Society in New York, Swami Bodhananda received a call from Swami Paramananda. He requested Swami Bodhananda to take care of the young Swami Akhilananda, whose health had deteriorated at the Boston Center. Swami Bodhananda received him and tended to his care. Swami Akhilananda was very much touched by his loving care and from that time he maintained a very intimate and cordial

relationship with the Vedanta Society of New York. Swami
Akhilananda helped the Society in many ways during Swami
Bodhananda's time and also after his passing. It may be
remembered that Swami Sarvagatananda, who succeeded
Swami Akhilananda in the Boston area, also developed an
intimate relationship with the Vedanta Society of New York.

In December 1929, only two months after the Great
Depression began, Swami Jnaneswarananda went to start a
Center in Chicago, which he was able to inaugurate by January
19, 1930. This was a very bold move during the Depression,
but the Swami had a desire to start a Center in the city of
Swami Vivekananda's victorious beginning in America. Swami
Jnaneswarananda was courageous from his youth, when he
was drawn to a life of service. He had been aroused to the
higher consciousness of spiritual love and strength by his
association with Swami Premananda and Swami Turiyananda,
the disciples of Sri Ramakrishna. He had the gift of oratory.
He was also a gifted vocalist and instrumentalist, and was
drawn to religious drama. He remained at the Vivekananda
Vedanta Society in Chicago until his death in 1937.

Swami Devatmananda

Swami Devatmananda came to assist Swami Bodhananda
in 1930 and left in 1932 to take charge of the Portland Center
for Swami Prabhavananda, who had to leave to start a Center
in Hollywood. Swami Devatmananda left the United States
for India, where he passed away in 1954.

Swami Nikhilananda

Swami Nikhilananda, a direct disciple of Holy Mother
who received his sannyas from Swami Saradananda, came to
the Society in 1932 to assist Swami Bodhananda. Swami
Bodhananda had decided to retire from all active service and
continued to remain in the Society. Swami Nikhilananda, who

found his calling as a dynamic speaker and scholarly writer, took charge. He began to conduct all the classes and Sunday services. The November 1932 issue of *Vedanta Darpana* covered these events.[22]

In April 1933 the Society's monthly journal also covered a special service at the Society that commemorated the 98th birth anniversary of Sri Ramakrishna. Swami Bodhananda and Swami Nikhilananda both addressed the congregation. *Vedanta Darpana* described it: "Lighted candles, a profusion of lovely flowers and beautiful garlands plaited by the loving hands of a few devotees for the portraits of the Master and of Holy Mother, made an unforgettable scene. The services were preceded by fifteen minutes of Hindu music and closed with violin selections. Light refreshments were then served to all attending the celebration, and 98 red roses, donated by a devotee, one for each year of the Anniversary, were distributed. Everyone felt the sublime presence of the Master in the sincere devotion and reverence prevailing in the hearts of those assembled."[23]

But after almost one year, Swami Bodhananda had to come out of retirement to assume the leadership of the New York Vedanta Society once again. His close and personal guidance through hard days was still appreciated and needed by many of the Society's members. Swami Nikhilananda founded the Ramakrishna-Vivekananda Center in New York City in 1933, also with a following sympathetic to his intellectual approach.

VEDANTA DARPANA IS PUBLISHED:
SWAMI SHIVANANDA BLESSES THE SOCIETY

Swami Shivananda gave his blessings to the work of the Society. In 1931 the Society had started the new monthly publication, *Vedanta Darpana*, or "Mirror of Vedanta." Each issue of *Vedanta Darpana* featured a first section on prayer,

followed by extracts from the *Gospel of Sri Ramakrishna*, and
Swami Vivekananda's works. There were selections from the
sacred scriptures, reports, and a final section, "Questions and
Answers." The February 1931 inaugural issue published "A
Blessing from Swami Shivananda":

> I hail with joy the project of the Vedanta Society of
> New York of starting a magazine from the coming year. We
> are living in an age of growing unity and harmony ... At
> this juncture Vedanta, which is the synthesis of all
> philosophies and religions, will undoubtedly be a great
> cementing factor ... As such, the new Vedanta monthly will,
> I am sure, be the medium of a healthy exchange of the
> ideals of the Orient and the Occident. May it always present
> the lofty spiritual ideals of India, the discoveries of her
> ancient sages, to the truth-seekers of the West, without
> diluting them to suit the taste of present-day materialism!
> May it ever stand for truth, purity, love and peace—as befits
> a mouthpiece of the great Masters, Sri Ramakrishna and
> Swami Vivekananda! May it vindicate the potential divinity
> of the human soul, which is birthless and deathless, beyond
> the mind and body, the essence of Existence, Knowledge
> and Bliss! May it bring home to all the truth that having
> sincerity and perseverance each one is bound to reach the
> one Goal of the universe—God or *Brahman!*[24]

Vedanta Darpana was published through December 1933,
its last issue.

AN INTERESTING GUEST ATTENDS SRI RAMAKRISHNA'S
BIRTH CENTENARY ON MARCH 15, 1936

The Vedanta Society celebrated the 100th birth anniversary of Sri Ramakrishna on March 1, 1936. The Ceylon-India
Inn was again chosen for the banquet, with Swami Bodhananda

and Swami Akhilananda present. Distinguished and interesting guests attended the banquet. One amongst these was M. Jules Bois. Mr. Bois had the singular privilege of meeting Swami Vivekananda in Paris in 1900. The main event of Swamiji's stay in Paris had been the Congress of the History of Religions, which was held from September 3 through 8, 1900 at the Sorbonne, in connection with the Paris Exposition. The purpose of the Congress was similar to the Chicago Parliament of Religions: to enquire into the historic evolution of the different faiths. Swami Vivekananda had been selected to debate on the origin of the Vedic religion. Scholars who were mostly devoted to this subject attended the Congress.

Swamiji did not speak French. This might have proved a handicap at the Congress, and elsewhere in distinguished circles during his stay in France. Therefore, Swamiji desired to learn French. He found a cordial host and French conversationalist in M. Jules Bois and stayed with him for the most part in Paris—from the first week in September until he left France. To begin with, Swamiji could not speak French nor could Mr. Bois English; however, Swamiji mastered enough French to meet the occasion of the Congress and to speak on highly technical matters before the scholars. The *Indian Mirror* had twice reported the Congress; the second report appeared long after the event, in December 1900, and referred to Swamiji's debate as "very impressive and eloquent in French."[25]

The *Life of Swami Vivekananda* informs us of the relationship between Swami Vivekananda and Mr. Bois: "M. Bois had heard the Swami speak at the Parliament of Religions in Chicago, and had long hoped to meet him. This hope was fulfilled: not only did he meet Swami Vivekananda, but he had him for many weeks as a guest in his quarters, accompanied him to Brittany twice, and was to travel with him on the tour through south Europe."[26] Mr. Bois authored numerous books and was best known for a scholarly work on the origin of satanism and magic. He migrated to America in 1915 and remained there until his death in Manhattan.

In an article in *Prabuddha Bharata*, "Vivekananda in the Near East, 1900—I," Swami Vidyatmananda describes Mr. Bois' participation in the banquet celebrating Sri Ramakrishna's birth centenary and suggests his close relationship with Swami Bodhananda:

> Jules Bois seems to have guarded in his heart some devotion to the guest whom he housed so agreeably on Rue Gazan. In 1925 he contributed an ode *"To a Sage"* on Vivekananda to *Prabuddha Bharata* (March, 97) in which occur the appellations "brother" and "master" and which concludes: "Hail to you! My Thanks!" In 1936 Bois participated in a celebration of Sri Ramakrishna's birth centenary organized by the Vedanta Society of New York. The occasion was a banquet held on March 15 at the Ceylon-India Inn. Swami Bodhananda, a disciple of Swami Vivekananda, and Swami Akhilananda, a disciple of Swami Brahmananda, were present, together with about fifty or sixty guests. A photograph was taken on that occasion, showing Bois seated between the two Swamis. The beard and the mustache are now smaller, the forehead higher due to receding hair, the eyes still enquiring, but kindly. Bois gave a talk about Vivekananda at the banquet, and it is remembered that he spoke feelingly about the Swami. Swami Pavitrananda, the present head of the Vedanta Society, says that he understands that Bois in his later years was very close to Swami Bodhananda.[27]

SWAMI BODHANANDA'S REMINISCENCES OF SWAMI VIVEKANANDA

Swami Bodhananda wrote reminiscences of his youth and the significance of Swami Vivekananda in his life as a monk. *Prabuddha Bharata* published an article by Swami Bodhananda, "How I First Met Swami Vivekananda" in October 1934. It includes some rare glimpses, when monks felt the call to renounce all for God in those early days.[28]

SWAMI BODHANANDA PARTICIPATES IN THE BOSTON CENTER'S CHAPEL DEDICATION

On April 1, 1942 Swami Bodhananda participated in the inauguration of a new home for the Ramakrishna-Vedanta Society at Boston. Swami Bodhananda and Swami Vishwananda of Chicago assisted Swami Akhilananda in the elaborate dedication ceremonies. Swami Bodhananda, Swami Vishwananda, Professor Walter E. Clarke of Harvard University, and Dr. Earle Marlett, dean of the School of Theology at Boston, all spoke. It was reported in *Vedanta Kesari*: "The occasion was one of deep spiritual significance. The new home of the Society, a residence admirably suited to become a temple, is located in an ideal spot for quietness, though not far from the heart of the city. It overlooks the Charles River, as the Monastery in India overlooks the Ganges."[29]

SWAMI BODHANANDA PASSES AWAY

Swami Bodhananda passed away at 79 years of age on Thursday, May 18, 1950. He had received his early training at a young age, as a close direct disciple of Swami Vivekananda. He came to the United States in 1906 and labored from 1912 for nearly forty-four years at the Vedanta Society of New York. With steadfast silence he spread the message of Vedanta. He worked long hours each day, despite his declining health in the last years of his life. The Order lost one of its most distinguished senior members, venerated by all those who came in contact with him. Swami Nikhilananda and Swami Akhilananda attended the memorial service at the Vedanta Society.

Prabuddha Bharata reported in its June 1950 issue that "Swami Bodhananda was a cherubic soul, gentle in spirit and full of the warmth of human kindness ... His deep spiritual personality, his learning and intellectual attainments, and his rich inheritance of religious experience gained through years of Sadhana and his intimate contact with Swamis Vivekananda and Brahmananda and the other direct disciples of Sri Ramakrishna, eminently fitted him for the role of the great pioneer and spiritual teacher that he was."

The July 1950 issue of *Vedanta Kesari* reported the profound sorrow felt by many, for, "By dying in harness in the field of his work ... he has not only proved himself a true follower of Swami Vivekananda but has also left behind him an example worthy of emulation. His remains being embosomed in Yankee soil, America is, so to say, spiritually fertilized all the more and we hope that this laying down of life there by another teacher of Vedanta, like few others before him, will bear fruits in the future, and this will surely be for the good of the world. This is our great consolation."

SWAMI BODHANANDA'S UNIQUE ROLE AT A CRUCIAL TIME IN THE HISTORY OF THE SOCIETY

Swami Bodhananda was the third man to take charge of the Society at a crucial period of its history. Unlike his predecessors, he was neither a scholar nor an orator but he was a hero in the battlefield of life. He did show exceptional courage and dogged determination in the greatest crisis of his life in the Society. He had a living faith in Sri Ramakrishna and his mission. This faith makes life more orderly and simple, yet more complete. His strict and frugal life, meticulous adherence to righteousness, self-confidence, patience, and good will and charity to people irrespective of superficial differences—helped him to hold the congregation.

The Great Depression in the United States occurred from 1929 to 1941. The worst of it was during the first three-and-a-half years. There were food riots, violent labor strikes, widespread migration of the population, and discontent, which made people fearful. With the passage of time this fear gradually changed to alarm, and then to something only slightly less than a premonition of total disaster. Fear hung like a heavy cloud over the national life; panic gathered like a storm, dark and foreboding.

Against the background of national depression and paralyzing fear, Swami Bodhananda's role as a spiritual teacher of Vedanta was to restore confidence and morale in the congregation. He engendered in thinking people a virile attitude of hard work, deep faith in God, and hope for the best.

TWO DEDICATED DEVOTEES

Those who are experienced in the field of the work always know the difficulty of gaining a few dedicated and loyal members—those who will serve the Society in its day-to-day life. This particular point was highlighted in the Society's Business Report of 1905: "The Secretary, Mrs. Cape, reported the accession of an unusual number of new members, but she pointed out eloquently that although the membership list was lengthening, the Society still remained in great need of more workers, of members who would come forward with true love and earnestness and offer to share the burden of labor and responsibility which must be carried on by some one in so great a work as this." The survival of the Society depended upon the model example of Swami Bodhananda's pure monastic life and a few committed members inspired and guided by him in close relationship.

During those days, two young, intelligent, and energetic girls came to the Society. Miss Jeanne and Miss Rolande led a legendary life of dedication. Without minimizing the importance of other devotees, these two devotees are to me something like the pearls of great price. What a magnificent epic of sincerity, loyalty, and dedication to the cause of Vedanta! Their lifelong devotion, self-denial, courage, and their sincere regard for Swami Bodhananda gave him immense satisfaction in his mission, comfort in his personal life, joy to the congregation, and hope to all.

Jeanne and Rolande were born in 1906 and 1907, respectively, in a well-to-do family in Ottawa. Their father passed away while they were still young. Their mother then moved the family to Montreal, where the two sisters were privately tutored and raised. In 1932 the family moved again, this time to New York for better career opportunities. Rolande was gifted in dance and Jeanne pursued a vocation in music. Jeanne and Rolande, however, were destined to lead ideal spiritual lives. They were inexorably led to Sri Ramakrishna and Swami Vivekananda when the book, *Prophets of New India*, by Romain Rolland came into Rolande's hands. They read it in the original French. The two sisters were moved and inspired to discover for themselves the eternal soul of India with a "unifying, pacifying love for all beings." The intuitive experience of Divinity and Truth in Sri Ramakrishna and Swami Vivekananda entered into the two sisters. Their inner transformation momentously and radically was begun.

They came to the Vedanta Society of New York after only one year, in 1933, to hear their first lecture on Vedanta by Swami Bodhananda. The Swami became in due time, their spiritual father, best friend, philosopher and guide. Jeanne and Rolande joined the Sanskrit class and took part in all the activities of the Society. The family moved to the same block, in order to be close to the Society. Rolande was the first to respond wholeheartedly. When Swami Bodhananda was ill, she cooked and brought food for the Swami for several months in 1949. She then came to live in the crude, unfinished basement of the Society. She cheerfully assumed responsibility not only for all his care, but also for the care of the entire household. When Swami Bodhananda passed away in 1950, Rolande remained at the Society, to express her eternal gratitude to the source of the spiritual fulfillment she had found in Vedanta.

Swami Pavitrananda succeeded Swami Bodhananda in 1951. Around 1953, Swami Pavitrananda invited Jeanne and her mother to live in the basement of the Society, to assist Rolande in the work. So that Rolande and *Maman* could freely serve the Society, Jeanne gave her piano away to charity and assumed a full-time position in a large corporation. This proved to be an invaluable experience for her, as she became the secretary of the Society in 1957. After almost thirty years of loyal service, Rolande passed away in full consciousness at the Society in 1960 at the age of fifty-three on Good Friday. In 1962 Jeanne retired from the corporation in order to better serve the Society and to care for her mother. After Swami Pavitrananda and *Maman* passed away in 1977, Jeanne continued to serve nobly and with serene confidence and devotion. With a unique detachment and inner joy she passed away on August 28, 1998. She had looked upon the Society as the embodiment of Swamiji. Her exalted life and work were a loving offering at the feet of the Twin Masters.

The two sisters were rooted in deep faith in the Divine, which allowed them to remain always in the background. They fully understood Swamiji's message of renunciation and sacrifice. They were singularly established in self-forgetfulness, self-denial, endurance, courage, dedication and discrimination. It is my conviction that their spiritual destiny brought these twin providential devotees to the Society that they may be fulfilled in Ramakrishna-Vivekananda.

During his time, Divine Grace came through Swami Bodhananda in the form of a permanent home for the Society and in the form of two unique devotees—Miss Jeanne Genêt and Miss Rolande—who served the Society for almost half a century.

REMINISCENCES OF SWAMI BODHANANDA'S TIME

In 1999, during the period of Navaratri, the worship of Divine Mother, Dr. Stuart Grayson visited the Society to attend the Sunday discourse. I was very pleased to hear Dr. Grayson's reminiscences of Swami Bodhananda's spiritual work from this American student of Vedanta, who is now the pastor of the First Church of Religious Science at Lincoln Center. Dr. Grayson came to Vedanta Society of New York while still a young man of twenty-one and was profoundly influenced by the teachings. Prior to his coming, he was actively involved in a Christian Science church located near the Society at Central Park West. It was not easy for the young man to visit the Vedanta Society regularly. His attendance at the Society was strongly opposed by his family, but he stood firm in his loyalty and devotion to Vedanta. He was very involved in the activities of the Society and continued to be a devotee, notwithstanding the harassment meted out to him. After attending but one service at the Vedanta Society, he completely cut off his connection from his parent church and withdrew his membership.

Dr. Grayson recalled those early days when Swami Bodhananda wrote brief dramas in Sanskrit on episodes from the *Ramayana* and the life of the Buddha. These vignettes depicted the lives of Hanuman, the Buddha, and other Prophets and sages. The content of the dialogue was brief, but the actors and actresses gave lively performances by their skill and artistic expertise. These dramas were performed by Rolande and Jeanne Genêt, Mercedes Mendoza, Dr. Grayson and other devotees, and they had a dramatic effect. The performances took place, at first, in a small studio at Carnegie Hall and, later, at the main auditorium of International House. Dr. Grayson related many of his sweet memories to us of Swami Bodhananda's time, one of which was his cherished recollection of Swami's trip to the celebrated Horn and Hardart's Automat on Seventy-second Street and Broadway, where, for a few nickels, dimes, and quarters placed in the slots adjacent to glass-encased displays of foods and beverages, he could select a simple meal. Dr. Grayson also attended classes and services during Swami Pavitrananda's time and gave personal service to him and the Society. For most of the period between Swami Bodhananda's passing and the arrival of Swami Pavitrananda, Dr. Grayson presided at the Society on Sunday mornings, reading from the book of lectures given by Swami Bodhananda.

In 1947 a group of younger people began to attend the Society's meetings. They became the nucleus of helpers planning a re-design of the Chapel. Among them were Joseph Heil, Lee Russell, Marita Lomquist, Pratap Madhami and Gwen Thomas. Clay Lancaster designed the new altar and helped Daisy Rieger with the redecorating.

ADDITIONAL REMINISCENCES

In March 2000, Donald L. Karr called the Society and mentioned that he had been associated with it in Swami Bodhananda's time. I immediately invited him to have lunch at the Center. He gave his impressions of the old days, and, while remaining a Christian, he still feels very respectful with high regard towards the Swami for his teaching. He lived nearby and came to the Society at the young age of eleven. He walked the few blocks, rang the bell, and was greeted by Swami Bodhananda, who "looked surprised." It was Tuesday afternoon. The year was 1947. The Swami invited him inside. "I asked many questions," Mr. Karr recalls. "The Swami talked with me for an hour and invited me back."

Soon, he became a regular at Tuesday night classes and Sunday morning lectures. The Center," he says, "became a very important part of my life ... he [Swami Bodhananda] was a very great man. He was so good to me. He just opened up his place to me."

Mr. Karr remained in association with the Society until 1951 and recalls taking part in a dramatization of the life of Buddha, performed in Sanskrit, staged by the Genêt sisters. He played the role of Buddha's wicked cousin. Stuart Grayson played Buddha and Rolande Genêt played the part of Mara. Mr. Karr came to the Society one more time, in 1984.

Of his association with the Swami, Mr. Karr says, "I learned a great deal spiritually. He was an enormously good example. I received a tremendous grounding ... he was a stimulating, effective speaker ... who spoke with great depth and conviction ... and preached against the sins of America: racism and greed. He had strong feelings about imperialism, politics, and ethical questions. He was a fiery preacher, very dynamic and outspoken."

One of Swami Bodhanada's sayings has been important to Mr. Karr in his own life: "If you think God is beyond good and evil and make that your excuse, you have an indigestion of Vedanta."

6

SWAMI PAVITRANANDA UNDERTAKES THE LEADERSHIP OF THE VEDANTA SOCIETY OF NEW YORK: 1951-1977

Swami Bodhananda, the disciple of Swami Vivekananda, had served faithfully for over forty years. After his passing, Swami Pavitrananda was sent to the Vedanta Society of New York by the Ramakrishna Order and Mission and arrived in 1951 to serve as its spiritual leader. He was a member of the governing body of the Ramakrishna Mission. When the Swami arrived to fulfill his mission, the membership of the Society hovered around sixty and the annual budget was nine or ten thousand dollars, with special appeals for projects that were considered necessary and significant.

A BRIEF SKETCH OF SWAMI PAVITRANANDA

Swami Pavitrananda entered the Ramakrishna Order at age twenty-six, after receiving his Master's degree in English literature at Calcutta University. He was blessed to receive initiation from Revered Swami Brahmananda and had his sannyas from Swami Shivananda. After taking sannyas, he spent more than twenty years in the Advaita Ashrama in the

Himalayas, working in various capacities. He served as head of this ashrama for eleven years, concurrently serving four of those years as editor of *Prabuddha Bharata* (Awakened India).

Swami Pavitrananda authored several books: *Holy Mother* in 1942, *Common Sense about Yoga* in 1944, and *Modern Man in Search of Religion* in 1947. He also wrote two booklets—*Siva-Mahimnah Stotram (Hymn on the Greatness of Siva)* in 1946 and *Ramakrishna Mission: What It Is* in 1951. All were published by Advaita Ashrama, Mayavati. *Common Sense About Yoga* was translated into German as *"Was Yoga Ist"* and published in Zürich, Switzerland in 1951. The booklet, *This is India*, was published in 1954 by the Vedanta Society of New York.

THE SWAMI SPEAKS WITH CARL JUNG

It is also interesting to note Swami Pavitrananda's candid and engaging conversation with Professor Carl Jung in Calcutta. Swami Pavitrananda's account of the entire conversation was first published in the May 1938 issue of *Voice of India*:

"An Evening with Professor C. G. Jung"

I was alone in a room with Professor Jung—a great psychologist, who was at one time a collaborator with Freud, but who afterwards differed from his school—who is respected all over the world. I thought it was a rare opportunity to have a heart-to-heart talk with him.

"I am sorry," I said, "that I could not attend your lecture. I was away from Calcutta."

"Then you did not see the pictures I showed in my lecture. I will show them to you now," the professor said.

With this he took some slides from his box and began to show them to me one by one. Some pictures (rather symbolic representations) were taken from Tibet, some from India, and some were the photographic representations of images from the unconscious.

"What do you mean by photographs of the unconscious, Professor?" I asked in astonishment. "How could you take photographs of images from the unconscious?"

"When patients come to me, I ask some of them to concentrate their minds on themselves. Then some image comes to their mind, sometimes faintly, sometimes clearly. Hearing from them the description, I ask them to draw the picture." Then the professor began to explain what these symbols meant.

"How do you give such interpretations to these pictures?" I enquired.

He then explained how he arrives at the correctness of the explanation he gives to these symbols.

The subject did not greatly interest me, and I did not wish to enter into a controversy over the matter.

"If you don't mind, Professor," I said, "I will ask you some straightforward questions. I hope you will excuse my frankness. As I read the books which you psychologists and psychoanalysts write, I find them revolting. I feel as if I were entering a dark, unhealthy world, where there is darkness within darkness—a darkness that terrifies one's mind, and paralyzes one's activities for higher pursuits. Why do you speak only of the lower nature of man? Do you think man is simply an animal? Do you mean to say that human nature is so very depraved? Some psychologists try to prove that the only concern of man's life is sex. But man is more than food and raiment; man is even more than food and sex. I was glad to read some years ago in an American magazine—most probably in the *Forum*—an article written by you in which you stated that the dominating factor in man's life is spiritual yearning. I was surprised that you could say that."

He replied, "Yes, I feel that way. But because I say that, I have to pay a very heavy price. People are against me, they criticize me, they write all manner of things against me. I am fighting against great odds—all alone."

"Yes, but by so fighting you will be doing a great service to the whole world," I remarked.

"The fact is," said the professor in an animated tone, "many of the psychoanalysts come into contact with people of gross materialistic minds, whose only concern in life is sense-pleasure, people who are morbid in their natures. What higher things can you expect from the analysis of such minds?"

"That's exactly what I was thinking," I said to Professor Jung. "I realize that the psychoanalysts generally meet with lower types of people and that is why they come to the conclusions which they do. I do admit that there is the animal in man. But is there not also the divine in him? Many psychoanalysts try to prove that the animal in man is the general law of human life. Some time ago an American minister—Fosdick, if I remember rightly—wrote, 'People nowadays talk openly of things which twenty years ago one would not dare whisper in a brothel.' I think I am not wrong when I say that psychoanalysts are responsible for this unfortunate state of affairs. Ramakrishna used to say, 'If you always say that you are a sinner, a sinner you will become. Why not think that there is God within you? Then your hidden divinity will manifest itself.' Some of you say that sex is the sole motive force of human conduct, with the result that people become more and more sex-minded. Well, there is the desire for food. Would you like to say that man is only a glutton and nothing else? Would you like to explain everything in man by his food-consciousness? You repeatedly call a man a sinner, and a sinner he becomes."

"You see," said the professor, "in the West religion has failed and men can no longer think in terms of spirit. Religion has become the garment of hypocrisy and insincerity. As a result everywhere people shudder at the name of religion and they cannot think of spiritual matters. Some say Bolshevism will be the fit substitute for religion, while some, turning to psychology, lose themselves in the dark alleys and blind lanes of the underworld of the human mind."

"Yes," I remarked, "I admit religion has been a failure in many cases as far as its application is concerned. But the ideal is there; why do people not strive after the ideal? In a marching army, many fall, but nevertheless, others return victorious."

"I don't like to talk about ideals," said the professor. "Why do you talk so much of ideals? Why don't you talk about the *way* in which to realize the ideal? People talk to others about ideals but in their own life they do nothing. I myself do not tell my patients, 'You ought to do this or that.' What is the use of telling them that they ought to do this or that when they are unable to follow what I say? I am concerned with the present and not with the future. I don't believe in talking about mere ideals."

"But, as a doctor you have certainly some end in view. You want your patients to have perfect health. Is that not an ideal?" I argued.

Professor Jung replied, "That may be. But I do not think in that way. I am concerned with how to remove their immediate malady. In the world all are eager to teach others, preach to others. Why do they not try to realize their ideals in their own lives instead of preaching them to others? People are out to do good to others, but they do not know how to do good to themselves. The only way to do good to the world is to do good to oneself."

"Yes," I said, "I believe selfishness is ingrained in man's nature. If that be so, let a man become selfish in a proper manner. Let him try to solve the problems of his own life—the problem of life and death—by realizing the Self. People sometimes say that those who leave society for meditative life are 'selfish'."

"But," the professor remarked, "such people will purify the atmosphere if they are sincere and earnest."

"I believe," I continued, "if one single man realizes his Self, he will do more good to the world than all the so-called workers trying to do good to the world. And when a man is earnest about realizing his Self he must withdraw himself from the ordinary preoccupations of life, just as a student before examination foregoes the pleasure of the cinema and football. Swami Vivekananda would say jokingly, 'Is God sleeping that you will have to do good to the world – to help Him in His work? If you want the world to be better, put your whole energy to bettering yourself. That is the only way to do good to the world'."

The professor said, "The reason why people are more eager to preach than to practice is that it is easier. Can you explain why people always go after cheaper things? Why people prefer to go downhill rather than up?"

I remarked, "Yes, it is true, almost all prefer the downward journey. But the trouble is, you make it a general law—that to go down is the nature of man. Why don't you think of those— their number may be very few—who like to go up, who forget all else in their attempt to explore the unexplored peak, who believe in the truth—'It is better to struggle and fail than not to struggle at all'."

There was a sadness in his voice as he asked, "Why do people go after cheaper things, why do they prefer the downward journey—the way to destruction?"

These words reminded me of the Upanishadic saying: "The Self-Existent [God] has made the senses face outward, and so man looks outward and does not see the inner Self. Some wise men, desirous of immortality, turn their eyes inward and behold the inner Atman."

1951 TO 1957: THE EARLY YEARS OF SWAMI PAVITRANANDA'S LEADERSHIP

Swami Pavitrananda's leadership was one of spiritually oriented creativity. During this period, the Swami held a regular schedule of Sunday public lectures and general classes on Tuesday evenings with a question-and-answer period. Friday night classes were held and usually reserved for members.

Library sessions were also held on other evenings, primarily for the benefit of the members. Mrs. Ruth Rieger, the treasurer for some years, noted in an annual report the special privilege of membership, which was the Swami's personal spiritual guidance: "In Vedanta religion is not an organized affair; the Society is not a Church but a group of people, and it is the spiritual growth of each person that is important."

THE SOCIETY'S NEW CHAPEL IS DEDICATED

On March 26, 1952, at 8:30 P.M., a special evening service was dedicated to the newly renovated Chapel at the Vedanta Society. The inspiration of that evening drew from the practical demonstration of the Vedanta philosophy of the harmony of religions. The message from the *Rig-Veda*, TRUTH IS ONE, MEN CALL IT VARIOUSLY was rendered in lucid gold lettering upon a white background on the west Chapel wall. Rendered in gold above the Vedic message were the universally accepted symbols of the five major world religions: the Star and Crescent of Islam, the Wheel of Buddhism, the Sacred Word *OM* of Hinduism, the *Magen David* or Star of Judaism, and the Cross of Christianity.

According to the account in *Vedanta Kesari*, the new Chapel was "most simply and tastefully decorated. Across the south end of the room a beautiful low altar table in gray, hand-decorated in gold with a motif of lotus blossoms, and dominated by the picture of Sri Ramakrishna, stands before a superb wall drapery of gold and silver. The altar and curtain are illuminated by soft directional lights. Flowers, an integral part of the design of the new altar, will be continuously in use in homage to Sri Ramakrishna ... Pictures of the Holy Mother and Swami Vivekananda are hung on opposite walls near the altar ... Recessed light in the ceiling gives a soft diffused light which can be varied to give quiet and meditative effects. The Chapel is entered through an attractive foyer, and from foyer

to altar the beautiful Chapel is permeated with an atmosphere
of serenity, quiet and meditative peace."[1]

Swami Pavitrananda's address was the keynote of the
dedication service. He spoke of the founding of the Society by
Swami Vivekananda, and the bearers of his legacy—the direct
disciples of Sri Ramakrishna and Swamiji. He invoked blessings
upon the Chapel and offered Sanskrit prayers. The harmony
of religions was demonstrated by the participation of five
ministers from various faiths who invoked blessings for the
Chapel from their respective religions. Swami Akhilananda of
the Vedanta Centers of Boston and Providence spoke briefly on
the spiritual impact of Hinduism on the West and offered a
Sanskrit prayer. The Venerable Hosan Seki of the New York
Buddhist Church, who saluted Sri Ramakrishna and offered a
prayer in Japanese and English; Rabbi Samuel Segal of the Mt.
Nebo Temple of New York read from the Old Testament and
offered his invocation, both in Hebrew and English; Reverend
Allen E. Claxton, Minister of the Broadway Temple Methodist
Church of New York, gave his Pranam to Sri Ramakrishna and
offered the Christian prayer after reading from the *Epistles*; and
Mr. Abraham Chowdhury, the representative of Islam, concluded
with a prayer in Arabic and English.

Swami Pavitrananda then invited Mr. John van Druten,
the noted author and playwright, to speak. He gave a talk on
Vedanta of the specific and symbolic significance of the Chapel.
Prabuddha Bharata reported the dedication service in its July
1952 issue at length. John van Druten said in part:

> I would like to ask what this is that we are dedicating
> tonight. The invitation calls it a "Chapel." Others may call it
> a church, or a temple. What do we mean by these words? ...
> Is not the teaching of the Advaita the fact that we ourselves
> are the temple, all of us? ... I heard the Swami [Pavitrananda]
> say ... 'God is the world we see, and the world we do not see.
> God is the whole universe. God is all. God Is.' ... How often
> do we know this? ... That is the mystical experience ... the

final unbandaging of our eyes. It happens just occasionally by the grace of God ... the revelatory experience of universal Godhead in everything we see, so that it is revealed in the very cups and railings as Vivekananda saw it ... When we have seen it, we need no church or chapel ... The church or chapel is everywhere and in everything. But when we do not see it, when it is removed again from our awareness, when we feel the bandages on our eyes once more, then we need that chapel as a memorial, a mark of that unbandaging if we have ever felt it, a symbol that we believe in it and long for it, if we have it not ... There are pictures on the walls here, and there are texts. What are these? They are signs of the right way ... They are signs on the right road ... This chapel is the meeting place for all men of any form of religion, where they can come together to hear the truth that embraces all, and makes all religions one—the truth that religion is an all-embracing experience. That is the basic teaching that we call Vedanta.[2]

The final speaker was the author and poet, Christopher Isherwood. He spoke of the universal appeal of Vedanta and humbly shared some of his personal experiences. Devotion and deep spiritual feeling pervaded the dedication service.

A Temple Fund was strongly suggested at this time, which was to have results later on, in 1964. A significant need to renovate the library also resulted in a library fund. In 1953 the library was improved and dedicated. However, the singular event of 1953 was the celebration of the birth centenary of Holy Mother, Sarada Devi. The Society gave its homage in a morning of devotional worship and inspired meditation.

PUBLIC INTEREST IN THE ACTIVITIES
OF THE SOCIETY GROWS

During this period, the Society's activities were steadily becoming known to the general public, which increased public interest in Vedanta. In 1953 the *New York Times* and the *Herald Tribune* published articles about the Vedanta Society in America and the Ramakrishna Order in India. The Swami was invited by *Voice of America* to give two radio talks in 1954, one on Sri Ramakrishna and one on Mahatma Gandhi. Outside guests were also invited to the Society's pulpit. New York's ambassador to India, Mr. Mehta, spoke on "The Spirit of India," and Mrs. K. Menon of the United Nations spoke on "The Women of India." Other guest speakers included Norman Cousins, editor of the *Saturday Review*, and Gertrude Emerson Sen, historian and journalist. Ravi Shankar, the renowned performer on sitar, gave an evening recital.

Swamis from other Centers in America were invited to speak, including Swami Akhilananda and Swami Vandanananda. In 1955 and 1956 the Society was visited by Swami Madhavananda, the Ramakrishna Mission's general secretary, and Swami Nirvanananda, its treasurer.

Swami Pavitrananda was invited to speak before audiences at New York University, Columbia University, Bryn Mawr College in Pennsylvania, Temple Emanuel in Lynbrook, New York, the West Center Church in Bronxville, The Broadway Temple – a Methodist church in Manhattan, Brooklyn's Union Church, and The Laymen's Movement in Rye, New York.

Groups of students and visitors interested in Vedanta came to the Society, sometimes by special arrangement and sometimes to attend the lectures. Students of comparative religion and their teachers came from New York University, Union Theological Seminary, Willimantic Teachers College in Connecticut, and Transylvania College in Kentucky.

1958 TO 1962: YEARS OF QUIET, STEADY GROWTH AT THE SOCIETY

Swami Pavitrananda had long anticipated a pilgrimage to India. In 1958 his journey was realized and lasted from

April to December. During his absence from the Society, Swami Vivekananda's lectures were read to the congregation on Sundays, and recordings of Swami Pavitrananda's lectures were attended on Tuesday evenings. During this period, the guest Swamis included Swami Sarvagatananda, Swami Akhilananda, who gave a memorable account of his reminiscences of Swami Brahmananda, and Swami Nityaswarupananda, of the Institute of Culture in Calcutta who lectured on "The Indian Way of Life" and also gave his reminiscences of the leaders of the Ramakrishna Movement. A member of the Indian Parliament gave a talk on Mahatma Gandhi. Swami Madhavananda, the general secretary of the Ramakrishna Math and Mission, came in 1961 for medical reasons. Other Swamis came from the United States to visit him. Swami Madhavananda and the Swamis all graciously and informally met with the members in question-and-answer sessions.

During this period, Swami Pavitrananda spoke before audiences at the First Presbyterian Church in Ridgewood, New Jersey and at the Twenty-third Street YMCA in New York. Student groups visiting the Society to learn about Vedanta came from New York University, Alfred University, Finch College, The New School for Social Research, Dyer University, New York State University at Queens College, Bayside High School, Bellevue Hospital, and from Drew University in New Jersey. Guest speakers included Rabbi Asher Block Minister Emeritus of the Little Neck Jewish Center; Professor Harlow Shapley, the well-known scientist; Mr. Arthur Lall, the United Nations representative from India; and Reverend Donald Szantho Harrington, minister of the Community Church of New York.

A new second edition of *The Sayings of Ramakrishna* was again published by the Society in 1961. In 1962 the Society began a new tradition: the Fourth of July Vivekananda Celebration at the home of Erik Johns and Jack Kelly at Moss Hill Farms, New York. In 1962 the Society also began its kitchen and living room renovation program.

The year 1960 marked the passing away on Good Friday of Miss Rolande Genêt, who had served the cause of Vedanta with exemplary and heroic devotion for more than twenty-five years. The preceding chapter relates how Rolande was inexorably led by Sri Ramakrishna and Swami Vivekananda to the Society while it was under the leadership of Swami Bodhananda. She was survived by her mother, *Maman*, and Jeanne, who became a beacon of light of the Society.

1963: THE CENTENARY OF THE BIRTH OF SWAMI VIVEKANANDA

The year 1963 marked the 100th anniversary of the birth of Swami Vivekananda. The Swami focused on Swamiji's life as the dominant theme in his Tuesday evening discourses. A Centenary fund was raised and the proceeds sent to India. Swami Pavitrananda was invited to speak at the Ramakrishna-Vedanta Society in Boston and at the Centers in San Francisco and Hollywood. During his absences, the guest speakers included Swami Nityaswarupananda of the Institute of Culture in Calcutta, and Professor Lee Belford of New York University. By 1963 the Society's membership reflected the increased interest in Vedanta and had expanded to about eighty members.

Up to this time, the Society had made many physical improvements. The Chapel was reconstructed, the library rebuilt, and the upstairs bedrooms furnished. The members generously responded to cover these necessary expenses.

1964 TO 1970: THE SOCIETY CONTINUES TO EXPAND AND RENOVATE

In 1964 the Society recognized and approved of necessary and additional annual expenditures, including a floral fund, and the cost of the annual Members' Dinner. In April 1966 seventy members attended the Members' Dinner. Towards the end of this period, rumors were circulating about the potential of municipal construction on the street of the Society. The executive board became concerned about the potential effects upon the Society, and established a special Vivekananda Temple fund and a financial reserve of twenty-one thousand dollars to prepare for this possibility.

Swami Pavitrananda was invited to speak at New York University, Cardozo High School, the Indian Association of Stamford, Connecticut, The National Conference of Christians and Jews at Tenafly, New Jersey, and the Rotary Club of Nanuet, New York. The Swami was also invited when the cornerstone of the Temple of Understanding in Washington, D.C. was laid. At the Fourth of July Vivekananda Celebration at Moss Hill Farms, John Schlenck of the Society presented part of his trilogy on Swamiji.

Students interested in Vedanta came from New York University; Queens College; Nyack Missionary College in New York; Dwight Girls School of Englewood, New Jersey; Muskingum College in Ohio; and Franklin College in Indiana. Church and synagogue groups also came from New York, New Jersey, and Connecticut.

1971 TO 1977: THE SOCIETY GAINS A NOT-FOR-PROFIT STATUS

In 1971 the Vedanta Society of New York gained its present status as a not-for-profit religious organization. The achievement of tax-exemption came through the initiative of Swami Pavitrananda and the diligent help of two members of the Society: Courtenaye Olden, who succeeded Mrs. Ruth Rieger as the Society's treasurer in 1972, and Susan Salm. Mr. Nathan Shapiro, the Society's president, helped to establish it free of tenants. Despite Swami Pavitrananda's gradually failing health from 1974 onwards, the Swami continued to give the Friday classes for members and the Sunday lectures. Taped recordings of the Swami's earlier series of lectures on the Bhagavad Gita and the Upanishads were played at Tuesday night classes. In 1976 the library classes were changed to Thursday evenings, for the study of Swami Vivekananda's *Jnana Yoga*. The annual Members' Dinner of 1975 included devotional music offered by Miss Y. G. Srimati. Songs by great Indian saints also were performed.

Guest Swamis came from the United States and abroad, including Swami Gambhirananda, the general secretary of the Order in 1972. Swami Vidyatmananda from the Centre Vedantique Ramakrichna in Gretz, France and Swami Bhavyananda of the Ramakrishna Vedanta Centre in London, England also came to the Society.

THE LAST YEARS OF SWAMI PAVITRANANDA

SWAMI TATHAGATANANDA IS CHOSEN TO ASSIST THE SOCIETY

In 1976 Swami Pavitrananda did not travel to lecture during the summer recess but did attend the Fourth of July Vivekananda Celebration at Moss Hill Farms and stayed on for a brief rest. In August he visited the Boston Center's retreat, Sarada Ashrama, at Marshfield, Massachusetts. He was a guest of Swami Sarvagatananda and participated in the celebration of Sri Krishna's birthday. The Vedanta Society of New York opened on September 19, 1976. Shortly thereafter the members received the long-anticipated news of an assistant Swami for the Society.

At that time, I was the head of Ramakrishna Mission, Baranagore. Swami Gambhirananda, the then general secretary, asked me to proceed towards the New York Vedanta Society to assist Swami Pavitrananda. After obtaining my Visa,

I arrived at the New York Vedanta Society on February 15, 1977. I began my work on March 8, 1977 with the Tuesday evening lectures on the Isa Upanishad and continued until the end of the season. I made a tour of most of the Vedanta Centers in the United States during that summer. In the beginning of the fall, due to the failing health of Swami Pavitrananda, I received the full responsibility of the public activities of the Society. Later that fall, Swami Pavitrananda recovered a little during October and early November, and was able to receive members and friends in his room after the Sunday service.

SWAMI PAVITRANANDA PASSES AWAY

Swami Pavitrananda passed away suddenly on November 18, 1977. His body was taken to a funeral home near the Society, then to New Jersey, where the Swami was cremated. Swami Sarvagatananda and I chanted the Upanishads. The ashes were sent with a member of the Society to Belur Math. They were consigned to the Ganges by senior Swamis of the Order performing the sacred rites.

Thirteen days later, the Society held a memorial service at 8 P.M. in the Chapel on December 1, which was reported in the March 1978 issue of *Vedanta Kesari* and the April 1978 issue of *Prabuddha Bharata*. The memorial service was attended by nine Swamis from various Ramakrishna Vedanta Centers in America and abroad: Swami Aseshananda, Swami Nihshreyasananda, Swami Shraddhananda, Swami Sarvagatananda, Swami Swahananda, Swami Swananda, Swami Prabuddhananda, Swami Adiswarananda, and Swami Bhaskarananda. Reverend Donald Szantho Harrington and Rabbi Asher Block also attended and spoke warmly about the Swami. I chanted the concluding prayer.[3]

In December 1977 *Prabuddha Bharata* reported his passing: "He was much-loved and respected by his brother-monks, by devotees, and by his disciples. He maintained a spirit of independence and aimed at precision and perfection in every thing he said or did ... He was easily accessible to young and old, and he scrupulously practiced the lofty principles of the monastic life ... He was very capable, responsible, and much-venerated."

Swami Pavitrananda, by nature, was gentle, suave, and simple. Self-effacement, serenity, and humility were his forté. Austere by nature, unassuming by temperament, asceticism was the prominent characteristic of his integral life. He always extolled the fundamental universal spiritual values of life before his close associates, and meticulously followed those ideals in his personal life. People coming in close contact with him felt the silent influence of his saintly character. They sincerely loved and respected him.

Pavitranandaji represented the ideal and philosophy of inward living in everything he did and said. This is character. The core of his character lay in his one-pointedness. Saintliness of his introspective life, his loving, forgiving nature, and his peaceful, simple life of contentment are the most persuasive testimony of his deep spiritual life. He took keen interest in the development of the inner life of his close associates, holding many classes in the library during the week, and kept a sharp eye on them. Many of the close devotees of our Society today came in his time.

7

THE VEDANTA SOCIETY OF NEW YORK FROM 1978 TO 2000

1978 TO 1985: THE RHYTHM CONTINUES WITH SOME NEW PROJECTS

The general rhythm of the Society is being continued by Sunday lectures and two evening classes on Scriptures. In 1978 non-members were invited to participate in our library reading classes held on Mondays, Wednesdays, and Fridays. After five or six years, the library classes were discontinued due to some time inconveniences on the part of the members. From 1978 to this day, the entire congregation is served food in our Chapel after Durga Puja and the birthday celebrations of Sri Ramakrishna, Holy Mother, and Swami Vivekananda. Since 1983, food continues to be brought to the annual Members' Dinner by Indian devotees.

SOME BEAUTIFUL PAINTINGS AND PHOTOGRAPHS ARE BROUGHT INTO THE SOCIETY

At my suggestion, in 1979 a beautiful photographic image of Swami Vivekananda was installed in the entrance hall of our Society on Sri Ramakrishna's birthday. At my request an exquisite oil painting of Holy Mother's likeness was installed and now graces our "Sarada Home." It was rendered by Swami Tadatmananda of Trabuco Monastery in California, whose oil portrait of Swami Vivekananda also adorns the study. Over the years, many beautiful photographs have found their niche in our Society. Moving photographic portraits of Swami Brahmananda, Swami Abhedananda, Swami Bodhananda, and Swami Pavitrananda appear in the study.

In 1993, Revered Swami Gahanananda, vice president of the Order, was a guest at our Society between September 30 and October 4, 1993. He spoke on October 3 on "Swami Vivekananda's Advent in the West." He visited Ridgely Manor and expressed a keen interest in having the property obtained as a place of pilgrimage for the followers of Ramakrishna-Vivekananda. During his stay, he hung Swami Tadatmananda's oil portrait of Swami Vivekananda and a photograph of Swami Abhedananda in our Society's study.

An exquisitely charming photograph of Belur Math also hangs reverently above the stairwell entrance that leads to the Swami's living quarters and study and can be appreciated while descending the stairs from that level.

In 1980, I visited the Centre Vedantique Ramakrichna in Gretz, France and during my visit, I admired a large and particularly beautiful photograph of Belur Math in their Center. They graciously sent me a copy of it and it was immediately installed in our library. The dining hall and hallway of "Sarada Home" are also graced with many charming photographs of Swamiji and his disciples, and of Sri Ramakrishna, Holy Mother, and Sri Ramakrishna's birthplace.

SOME ADDITIONAL NEW PROJECTS AND EVENTS

In 1980 I began a new project, of the free distribution of Vedanta literature, to more than fifty libraries in the New York area. The books that were chosen for this project were *Vedanta for Modern Man*, a collection of essays by well-known writers, and the English translation of the biographies of Sri Ramakrishna and Swami Vivekananda by Romain Rolland. A bimonthly class for the informal religious instruction of the children whose parents attended the Sunday lectures was also inaugurated. Dr. Betty Robinson generously undertook this responsibility in the Society's Vivekananda Room.

In December 1980, the second international Convention of the Ramakrishna Math and Ramakrishna Mission took place at Belur Math, for a periodical review of its future plans and patterns of work to help "lead humanity to its cherished goal as visualized by Swami Vivekananda." The first Convention had been held in 1926. According to their suggestion, the senior-most member of our Society, Miss Jeanne Genêt, whose name was forwarded by me, was accepted as one of the vice-presidents of the General Committee for this work. Five Society members suggested by me were also accepted to serve as members of the General Committee: Mr. C. H. MacLachlan, Mr. Erik Johns, Mr. William Conrad, Mr. John Schlenck, and Mr. Marc Olden. Their names were printed in the Convention booklet that was published for that occasion.

During Swami Pavitrananda's time, the Society printed an advertisement of the Sunday lectures in the *New York Times* and *The New York Herald*. Some time after my arrival, the ads were suspended, for perhaps a year or so, as there had been little benefit from them. One day in 1980, an elderly devotee, unknown to me, called and inquired about the existence of the Vedanta Society in New York. Because the ads had been discontinued, she thought that the Society was no longer in New York. More than a year later, on April 27, 1981, we again began to publish a weekly ad in *The New York Times*.

In 1983, during a brief visit to Canada, I conducted a three-day retreat in Toronto. On June 29, 1989 I conducted another one-day spiritual retreat in Washington, D.C. with a focus on the topic of the Upanishads.

In 1984 I made a pilgrimage to India—the first since my arrival at the New York Vedanta Society in 1977. During my stay in India, I was invited to address the students of the Indian Institute of Technology (I.I.T.) at Kharagpur, West Bengal, Calcutta University, and the Institute of Culture at Gol Park. I visited India again in 1989 via Japan and Singapore.

In 1987, I participated in the Golden Jubilee Celebration of the Ramakrishna-Vedanta Society of Massachusetts in Boston.

In 1996, from May 22 to August 8, I visited England and India. I gave talks at various centers of the Ramakrishna Order and conducted the annual retreat at the Ramakrishna Vedanta Centre in Bourne End, England. In India, I gave a number of talks in Calcutta and places nearby—at the Vivekananda Society, the Ramakrishna Mission Institute of Culture, and the Ramakrishna Mission Sevapratisthan—a large hospital, in Calcutta. The annual meeting of the hospital was held in its spacious auditorium. The meeting was attended by more than a thousand persons, and was presided over by Dr. Sushil Kumar Mukherjee, the former vice chancellor of Calcutta University. I also spoke at a training center of the Order and Vidyamandir—a Ramakrishna Mission college in Belur Math.

Also in 1996, we recorded with sorrow the passing of three senior Swamis in America. I was able to participate in the memorial services for Revered Swami Bhashyananda of the Chicago Center and Revered Swami Aseshananda of the Portland Center, the last living monastic disciple of Holy Mother. I was out of the country and unable to participate in the memorial service of Revered Swami Shraddhananda of the Sacramento Center.

ONGOING RENOVATIONS AT THE SOCIETY

The building that is home to our Society was purchased in 1921 and is now almost 100 years old. Since 1981 the Society has undertaken major renovations and restoration from time to time. In 1982, the sagging stairways on the second and third landings in the Society's building were repaired. At my initiative a building renovation fund was established and a letter of appeal in my name was sent out to members and friends of the Society in October 1983. As a result, nearly seventeen thousand dollars in building costs were covered, when the first major renovations were completed in September 1983. The word "Men" in the message on the Chapel wall was changed to "Sages" in 1993, during renovations to the Chapel. The message now reads: TRUTH IS ONE, SAGES CALL IT VARIOUSLY. In 1995 the aging structure of the Society's home again required major interior and exterior repairs and several major appliances were replaced.

1986 TO 1993: THE SOCIETY HOSTS AND PARTICIPATES IN CELEBRATIONS OF AUSPICIOUS AND HISTORICAL EVENTS

1986: SRI RAMAKRISHNA'S 150TH BIRTH ANNIVERSARY

In 1986 the 150th anniversary of the birth of Sri Ramakrishna was observed on Sunday, March 9. I spoke on "The Message of Sri Ramakrishna." After the service, lunch was served to the entire congregation. The anniversary celebration also included two guest lecturers. Swami Ranganathananda gave a talk on May 23 and Rabbi Asher Block spoke on "Sri Ramakrishna: An Interfaith View." The celebration continued into 1987.

1987: 100TH ANNIVERSARY OF THE FOUNDING OF THE RAMAKRISHNA ORDER

On January 5, 1987 our Society celebrated the special occasion of the birth anniversary of Sri Ramakrishna and the

100th anniversary of the founding of the Ramakrishna Order of monks. Our Society hosted six visiting Swamis. I requested Swami Aseshananda, head of the Vedanta Society of Portland, a disciple of Holy Mother and the most senior monk of the Order in America, to preside over the service. The revered Swami gave the first talk of the evening, which included personal reminiscences of Holy Mother and disciples of Sri Ramakrishna. Swami Sarvagatananda, Swami Swahananda, Swami Prabuddhananda, Swami Adiswarananda and Swami Aparananda all spoke. It was a memorable and moving evening, attended by more than could be seated, and so noteworthy that a Christian minister who was there remarked that any Christian that was present should have come away a better Christian.

1988: SWAMI VIVEKANANDA'S 125TH BIRTH ANNIVERSARY

Swami Vivekananda's 125th birth anniversary was celebrated in 1988. Distinguished guest speakers were invited to the Society throughout the year, including Revered Swami Hiranmayananda, the general secretary of the Order, Revered Swami Nityaswarupananda, founder and former head of the Ramakrishna Mission Institute of Culture in Calcutta and a direct disciple of Holy Mother, and Revered Swami Bhuteshananda, the vice president of the Ramakrishna Math and Mission. The Swamis also shared personal reminiscences of the disciples of Sri Ramakrishna.

Two other distinguished speakers were invited as part of the celebration of Swami Vivekananda's birth anniversary. Rabbi Asher Block spoke on "Swami Vivekananda: An Interfaith Perspective." Rev. Donald Szantho Harrington Minister Emeritus of the Community Church of New York spoke on "Vivekananda and the Soul's Struggle for Enlightenment." Rev. Harrington's father was a minister who had twice heard Swami Vivekananda speak at the Chicago Parliament of World Religions in 1893 and was deeply impressed. Three Society members, John Schlenck, William Conrad and William Davis also gave talks on aspects of Vivekananda's life and work.

1992: THE FOURTH INTERNATIONAL CONGRESS OF VEDANTA: CENTENNIAL CELEBRATION OF SWAMI VIVEKANANDA'S SOJOURN IN AMERICA

On April 2-5, 1992 I was invited to the Fourth International Congress of Vedanta, sponsored by the Departments of Philosophy and Religion at Miami University, Oxford, Ohio. It is the major conference on Indian Philosophy held outside India and attracts the world's leading scholars in Indian Philosophy. The Congress of 1992 was dedicated to the centennial celebration of Swami Vivekananda's sojourn in America and his participation in the Parliament of World Religions. One hundred twenty scholars from the United States, Canada, Europe and India and more than two hundred people participated in this Congress. On the opening day, at the request of the Congress, I unveiled a large photograph of Swami Vivekananda, after which the conference began. I spoke on "Swamiji's Practical Vedanta" at the Inaugural Plenary chaired by Dr. P. T. Raju of the College of Wooster. My expanded version of this talk was published in the October 1992 issue of *Prabuddha Bharata*. An extract may be found in Appendix A for the interested reader.

Several others also spoke at the Inaugural Plenary: Hal W. French of the University of South Carolina spoke on "Vivekananda and his Western Followers: Patterns of Relationships." Glynn Richards of the University of Stirling, Scotland, spoke on "Vivekananda and Universal Religion."

1993: THE SOCIETY PARTICIPATES IN THE CENTENARY OF THE PARLIAMENT OF WORLD RELIGIONS IN CHICAGO AUGUST 28 TO SEPTEMBER 4, 1993

The Parliament of World Religions was held from August 28 through September 4, 1993 at the Palmer Hilton Hotel in Chicago to celebrate the centenary of the original Parliament of 1893 at which Swami Vivekananda spoke. I was invited to speak with eight other Swamis of the Order, including Swami Gahanananda, the vice president of the Order. I spoke on August 29 at the religious service and again at two major presentations with the other Swamis. I participated in a series of talks on "Swami Vivekananda's Message to the West" on August 31 and in a series of talks on "Swami Vivekananda—The Awakener to Service of God in Man" on September 1.

A performance of *Seek the Eternal: an Interfaith Cantata Celebrating the Spiritual Life* was given, the evening of September 1. It was composed by John Schlenck, music director of the Vedanta Society of New York, and performed at St. Peter's Roman Catholic Church in downtown Chicago as an offsite event of the Parliament. The performance, made possible through the generosity of the composer's sister, Josephine S. Gumbiner, featured the Halevi Choral Society, conducted by Judith H. Karzen. The hour-long work was performed by a chorus of twenty-three, accompanied by an orchestra of seventeen. Three members of the chorus performed vocal solos. This performance—by a Jewish chorus in a Catholic church of a musical work by a Vedantist composer drawing on texts from major religious traditions—celebrated the spirit of the Parliament and of Swami Vivekananda.

On this occasion, I published a booklet, "Swami Vivekananda's Impact at the Parliament of Religions," containing two articles with reference to Swami Vivekananda's powerful impact on the Parliament.

1993: THE SOCIETY PARTICIPATES IN OTHER
CENTENARY EVENTS IN THE U.S. AND CANADA

During the summer of 1993, I was invited to participate in various centenary events in the United States and Canada. On September 18, I was invited by the Indian Embassy in Washington, D.C. to speak and participate in their centenary celebration. Ambassadors to the United States from India and Sri Lanka and leaders of various faiths also spoke. I conducted a seminar at William Paterson College in Wayne, New Jersey on December 2. Professor Marie Friquegnon, the dean of the School of Philosophy, and other professors of that college also attended together with many students. On December 4, I lectured at the State University of New York at Stony Brook.

Outside Speakers Are Invited To The Podium On Sundays

As part of these centenary celebrations, the Society invited others to speak about Vivekananda and Vedanta. The contributions of Vedanta and Jewish thought to the 1893 Parliament were the subjects of "Truth is One," a talk given by Rabbi Asher Block. Reverend Donald Harrington spoke about Swami Vivekananda and the Parliament.

1993: A BOOK IS PUBLISHED FOR
THE CENTENARY CELEBRATION

My book, *Meditation on Shri Ramakrishna and Swami Vivekananda*, was published in 1993 by the Standard Literature Company of New Delhi as part of the centenary celebration.

1894 TO 1994: THE SOCIETY CELEBRATES
ITS 100TH ANNIVERSARY

1994: YEARLONG CENTENARY CELEBRATIONS

In 1994 the Society honored the 100th anniversary of its founding by Swami Vivekananda by sponsoring a yearlong observation through various programs at the Society and around New York City. From May to December, the head Swamis of Vedanta Centers in the United States and Canada and their assistants were invited to the Society. All attended except one Swami, who could not come.

The Society's centenary celebration began in April with a four-act play, *Arise! Awake!*, and continued with a special service in the Chapel of the Vedanta Society in early May. The Vedanta Society of New York celebrated the centenary of Swami Vivekananda in conjunction with the Bengal Studies Conference at New York State University College at Old Westbury in late May. The conference was followed by the Convocation of Global Religions at Queens College in July, the Fifth International Congress of Vedanta at Miami University in August, and the centenary concert, *A Mission to the World*, at Lincoln Center in October.

In honor of its centenary, the Society published my book, *Meditation on Swami Vivekananda*, containing essays on the many aspects of Swami Vivekananda's life and teachings.

THE CENTENARY CELEBRATION BEGINS
ON APRIL 30, 1994: ARISE! AWAKE!

On Saturday, April 30 Vivekananda Vidyapith, an academy of Indian philosophy and culture at Wayne, New Jersey, presented the play, *Arise! Awake!*, at New York City's Martin Luther King Jr. High School. This was a very dedicated performance by a cast of one hundred, with ages ranging from pre-school through college levels. I requested our guest Swamis, Swami Swahananda of Hollywood, Swami Prabuddhananda of San Francisco, and Swami Adiswarananda of the New York Ramakrishna-Vivekananda Center, to give the opening benediction. The audience was charmed and very receptive to the academy's devotional and ambitious undertaking, presenting events from the life of Swami Vivekananda.

The play began with Sri Ramakrishna's vision predicting the advent of Swami Vivekananda, then emphasized the qualities of Swamiji evinced from boyhood that revealed his fearlessness, compassion and leadership, and went on to present Swamiji's intimate spiritual relationship with Sri Ramakrishna in the second act. The third act was dedicated to Swamiji's days as a wandering monk throughout the length and breadth of India and was beautifully enhanced with slides. The fourth act was set in America. Swamiji's full stature, his thrilling and rousing speech at the Parliament of World Religions, and two of his messages on the Harmony of Religions were dramatically presented, significantly moving the audience. The performance concluded with the entire cast singing Swamiji's song, *Arise! Awake!* The play produced a standing ovation of appreciation.

THE CENTENARY CELEBRATION:
THE VEDANTA SOCIETY OF NEW YORK
HOLDS A SPECIAL SERVICE MAY 1, 1994

A special two-hour service was held on Sunday, May 1 at the Vedanta Society of New York. It was attended by more than two hundred devotees from the United States and Canada. Several messages of eulogy on the occasion of the Society's 100th anniversary were read. Revered Swami

Bhuteshanandaji Maharaj, the president of the Ramakrishna Math and Mission, described the centenary as a "Matter of Joy," and proffered, "May the blessings of Swamiji and Sri Ramakrishna be showered on the centre, and by their grace may all activities ... be continued effectively during the years to come." Revered Swami Ranganathanandaji, the vice president, conveyed his "Best wishes for the success of the centennial celebration," and recalled "with joy the several occasions of my stay at this Society and speaking at its Sunday services."

Swami Aseshanandaji, spiritual leader of the Portland Center, sent his message that the Society may "continue to enjoy the benediction of Swamiji and the Divine Grace of Sri Ramakrishna and Holy Mother in giving spiritual solace to those who are associated with it." Swami Shraddhanandaji, spiritual leader of the Sacramento Center, conveyed his "Deep congratulations and best wishes on the occasion of your celebration." He concluded his letter with the blessing that "The inspiration of Swami's message to the West" will bring "new interest, hope and courage for the practice of Vedanta in your lives." Swami Sarvagatanandaji, spiritual leader of the Boston and Rhode Island Centers, noted that the Society has rendered "valuable service all these one hundred years ... May Sri Ramakrishna, the Holy Mother and Swami Vivekananda bless this Society."

Commendatory letters were also received from the Archbishop of New York, India's Ambassador to the United States, and the representative of His Holiness the Dalai Lama.

The guest Swamis, Swami Swahananda, Swami Prabuddhananda, Swami Adiswarananda, and Rabbi Asher Block were then invited to address the congregation. Rabbi Block spoke of the Society's unique and singular dedication in spreading the eternal message of Swamiji given at the Parliament: "Accept all Religions." He also expressed his own understanding of Vedanta as that which links philosophy with practice to produce what is known as practical religion.

16

Swami Prabuddhananda spoke of Vedanta's influence in the West and of Vedanta's increase in strength over the last one hundred years, that can be "measured by its influence on the lives of people." He invoked Swamiji's blessings and the Great Power behind him as the background reality of the successful efforts of the Society.

Swami Adiswarananda spoke about the universal principles of Vedanta as a way of life. He stressed Swamiji's understanding of the reciprocal relationship between the East and West that must be founded on the best aspects of both. The Swami's address invoked the eternal power behind Swami Vivekananda's promise to "continue to inspire men and women everywhere."

Swami Swahananda spoke of the unique appeal of Vedanta for the Western world: the West, recognizing its love of freedom and expression, loves the vast, boundless message of Vedanta. Swamiji gave this freedom to the West when he planted the seed of Vedanta into the nation's consciousness.

At my initiative, a centenary fund of about $18,000 was also collected.

THE CENTENARY CELEBRATION: BENGAL STUDIES CONFERENCE MAY 27 TO 29, 1994

On May 27 to 29 the Bengal Studies Conference joined the Vedanta Society of New York to participate in our Centenary program, together with Swami Shantarupananda, the assistant minister of the Portland Center. We went to the Bengal Studies Conference at the State University of New York City at Old Westbury. The visiting Swami and myself spoke, Professor Jayanta Sircar of the University of Maryland at College Park, gave a lecture accompanied by slides, and papers were presented by William Davis, Ph.D., and Mr. George Dean, members of our Society. The Vedanta Society Choir performed songs describing Swamiji's life and works.

THE CENTENARY CELEBRATION: CONVOCATION
OF GLOBAL RELIGIONS JULY 9 TO 10, 1994

Many are requested, a few express their sympathy, but only one or two come forward to give their whole heart. When I requested that something be done on a grand scale for our centenary, Mr. Swapan Ganguly of Long Island responded enthusiastically. Mr. Ganguly was one of the chief initiators and organizers of the Convocation of Global Religions. He worked hard to enlist the cooperation of other religious leaders of the city. In this connection, Father Louis M. Dolan, New York's acting executive director of the Temple of Understanding, showed interest and worked sincerely for its success. Mr. Harendra Sevak was the treasurer. John Schlenck and William Conrad, members of the New York Vedanta Society, also rendered organizational assistance.

The Convocation of Global Religions was held on July 9 to 10 at Queens College in New York. It had a twofold purpose: to celebrate the centennial of the 1893 Parliament of World Religions and to mark the centennial of the founding of the Vedanta Society of New York. This was also the first interfaith conference organized by the New York Hindu community. A series of lectures and cultural activities, and an interreligious dialogue chaired by Father Dolan were held simultaneously. Twenty-two spiritual leaders representing the major religions of the world were present with fifteen hundred in attendance.

At the opening plenary session, I gave a benediction for the success of the conference: "Enlightened men and women, I hope you will hear Swamiji's message with reverential attitude. We spiritual leaders are expected to enrich our lives in the light of tolerance and fraternity ... so our practitioners can learn from us. Swami Vivekananda accepted wholeheartedly the coexistence of all religions and also recognized the uniqueness of each of the traditional faiths. He envisioned the harmony of religions on the basis of One Reality behind

244   THE VEDANTA SOCIETY OF NEW YORK

all faiths." Later in the conference, I addressed the assembly
with the topic, "Peace Within."

The keynote speaker was His Holiness Dada J. P. Vaswani,
spiritual head of Sadhu Vaswani Mission in Pune, India.
Greatly inspired by Sri Ramakrishna and Swamiji, Dadaji
Vaswani spoke movingly of both. He appealed to all for "heart
unity," for the harmony of all religions in the vision of the
beautiful truths taught by Holy Master and boldly disseminated
by Swamiji.

A disciple of Swami Bodhananda and senior nun of the
Ramakrishna Order, Hollywood Convent, Pravrajika
Bhaktiprana, spoke about Swamiji's legacy. Daniel Gomez
Ibanez, the executive director of the 1993 Parliament of the
World's Religions in Chicago, a Vedantist, spoke about Swamiji
and the Parliament. Professor Aurobind Sharma also spoke.

The Vedanta Society Choir and the New York Concert
Singers performed two musical works on Swami Vivekananda:
the cantatas, *The Universal Gospel and Epistles 1893 - 1894.*
These were composed by the music director of the New York
Vedanta Society, John Schlenck, and directed by Judith
Clurman. The text of *The Universal Gospel* was taken from the
major world scriptures. *Epistles* was composed of excerpts from
Swamiji's letters of 1893 to 1894, with a connective narrative
by Erik Johns of the Vedanta Society of New York. Many
Indians assisted in this function in various ways. Dr. Braja Dulal
Mookherjee was president of the committee.

THE FIFTH INTERNATIONAL CONGRESS
OF VEDANTA: ONE HUNDRED YEARS OF
VEDANTA IN AMERICA AUGUST 10 TO 14, 1994

On August 10 to 14, 1994 I was invited to the Fifth International Congress of Vedanta at Miami University in Oxford,
Ohio. The Congress was attended by more than one hundred

scholars from various universities. It was dedicated to Veda and Vedanta, Vedanta and Buddhism, and the philosophy of Sri Aurobindo. The Special Plenary, "One Hundred Years of Vedanta in America," was a symposium celebrating the 100th anniversary of the founding of the Vedanta Society in New York by Swami Vivekananda and was chaired by Professor S. S. Rama Rao Pappu of Miami University. I spoke at the Special Plenary about Swamiji's contribution to Indian philosophy and world thought.

Prabuddha Bharata reported the Congress:

> One hundred scholars and professors from Canada, USA, and England read papers. A large photograph of Swami Vivekananda was placed in the hall where the deliberations took place. A special feature of this five-day Congress was a plenary session held on August 11, entitled, "One Hundred Years of Vedanta in America." The symposium's objective was to celebrate the 100th anniversary of the founding of the Vedanta Society of New York by Swami Vivekananda. Speakers were: Swami Tathagatananda, Vedanta Society of New York; Robert N. Minor, University of Kansas; K. Sundaram, Lake Michigan College; and Tim Bryson, Harvard University, whose Ph.D. thesis was on Swami Vivekananda at Harvard. Each speaker addressed different aspects of Swamiji. Swami Tathagatananda spoke about Swamiji's contribution to Indian philosophy and world thought.[1]

THE CENTENARY CELEBRATION: *A MISSION TO THE WORLD* OCTOBER 16, 1994:

On October 16 the Vedanta Society of New York gave its last public homage to Swami Vivekananda during its centenary celebrations. The New York Concert Singers and Orchestra performed the centenary concert, *A Mission to the World*, under

the direction of Judith Clurman at Lincoln Center's Alice Tully
Hall, with well-known music commentator Martin Bookspan
as narrator. In all, seventy-eight performers participated. For
an entire month the full-size portrait of Swami Vivekananda
in his Chicago pose was displayed on a large billboard outside
the Hall. The oratorial trilogy on Swami Vivekananda's life in
America was composed by the Society's music director, John
Schlenck, and the narrative text with quotations from Swamji
was written by Erik Johns, also of the Vedanta Society of New
York.

Part One of the trilogy began with Swami Vivekananda
on the podium at the Parliament of Religions, ready to begin
his talk. The orchestra imitated the sound of applause from
the vast audience. With a sudden change of key the waves of
applause became the waves of the ocean at Kanyakumari;
Swamiji was back on the rock at India's southern tip, pondering
his mission. The events leading up to Swamiji's appearance
at the Parliament were recalled—his travels throughout India,
his intense feeling for the misery of the Indian masses, the
encouragement he received from friends to go to America.
His mission clear to Swamiji, the orchestra brought forth the
sound of applause in Chicago once more, with Swamiji back
on the podium ready to give his message to the West.

Part Two of the trilogy was a summary of Swamiji's
message: the truth of all religions with a call for an end to
bigotry and bloodshed, the outline of the main tenets of
Vedanta, the divinity of the soul, the paths of knowledge and
devotion, and the rousing call to realize the Divine in this life.
Part Three of the trilogy told the story of Swamiji's strenuous
life in America up to the founding of the Vedanta Society of
New York in the fall of 1894.

India Abroad reviewed the concert in its October 17, 1994
issue. Professor Jayanta Sircar ("Ananda") also reviewed the
hallmark event through the perspective of Swamiji's mission
to the West with his opening words at the first Parliament of
World Religions in 1893 in Chicago, "Sisters and Brothers of

America!" In an article published in the January 1996 issue of *Prabuddha Bharata*, he traced the foundational events during December 1892 to November 1894—the period covered in *A Mission to the World*. Two events were highlighted in the article: the September 1893 debut of Swami Vivekananda-Vedanta in the modern world at the Parliament in Chicago, and the November 1894 founding of the first Vedanta Center in the West. This is the Vedanta Society of New York, the zenith of Swamiji's efforts during those first two years. The tradition of Swamiji's message of inspired giving, resulting in the construction of the headquarters in Belur Math and the founding of numerous Vedanta Centers throughout the world was acknowledged.[2]

Mrs. Josephine Schlenck Gumbiner, the composer's sister, gave a gift of one hundred thousand dollars to fund this concert and an earlier one, also composed by her brother and performed at the 1993 Parliament of World Religions in Chicago. Mrs. Gumbiner's generous gift was recalled in an obituary published in 1997 in the summer issue of the journal *American Vedantist*:

> As part of the Centenary celebrations of the Vedanta Society of New York, Mrs. Gumbiner funded a concert at Lincoln Center in New York, at which the oratorio trilogy *A Mission to the World*, composed by two of our editors, Erik Johns and John Schlenck, was premiered with chorus, soloists, narrator and orchestra ... Josephine (as Mrs. Gumbiner preferred to be called) was a social worker by profession, working for many years at the Department of Adoptions in Los Angeles County and at the United Way's Project on Aging. As a young woman working towards her Master's degree in social work, she did volunteer work with American Friends Service Committee in Indianapolis, where she grew up. Her volunteer work later in life included service on the boards of the YWCA of Long Beach (California) and the Long Beach Stroke Foundation.

THE CENTENARY CELEBRATION:
DISADVANTAGED CHILDREN RECEIVE
A BOOST-UP OCTOBER 1994

As part of its homage to Swami Vivekananda in October 1994, the charitable organization, Street Children International, funded a banquet to feed more than two hundred disadvantaged children and youth at the Mount Nebo Baptist Church in Harlem. Louise Riskin, a friend of the Society, organized it. Tapan Sarkar, M.D., of Street Children International, donated five hundred dollars. I was present at this function, together with Mr. William Conrad.

The January 1995 issue of *Prabuddha Bharata* published an article written by Joan Shack, a member of the Society. It reviewed all the Society's activities during the 1994 centenary celebration.

1995: THE SOCIETY'S SPECIAL BIRTHDAY SERVICE
FOR SWAMI VIVEKANANDA

On January 12, 1995—on the auspicious day of the birth of Swami Vivekananda—a large shipment by sea arrived at the Vedanta Society of New York. Six hundred hardcover copies of my book, *Meditation on Swami Vivekananda*, were deposited at the doorstep. The total number of books published was eleven hundred: six hundred in hardcover and five hundred in paperback. His Excellency K. L. Agarwal Deputy Consul General of India formally released *Meditation on Swami Vivekananda* on January 22, during the Society's special birthday service for Swami Vivekananda. More than one hundred copies were sold on that day.

The service was attended by more than one hundred seventy people. Three distinguished guests spoke on "The Message of Swami Vivekananda." Rabbi Asher Block, long-standing friend of the Society, highlighted the spiritual uniqueness of the Vedanta Society. Dr. Robert J. Meinke, a retired sociology professor long associated with the Society, spoke about the historical Swami Vivekananda. Mr. Agarwal spoke on the significance of Swami Vivekananda in his personal life. Professor Jayanta Sircar gave a lecture and slide presentation on the role of the Vedanta Society in spreading the message of Swami Vivekananda to the Western world. A review of this service, "The Vedanta Society of New York: Centenary Events, January 1995," appeared later in the August 1995 issue of *Prabuddha Bharata*.

THE ONGOING IMPORTANT ROLE OF THE NEW YORK VEDANTA SOCIETY IN THE COMMUNITY

LECTURES AT UNIVERSITIES, COLLEGES AND SCHOOLS

From the time of my arrival at the New York Vedanta Society on February 15, 1977, I have been invited to lecture at academic and religious education institutions throughout New York State, Connecticut, New Jersey and Maryland. The lectures are scheduled in addition to conferences, seminars and other special events and are held occasionally on an annual basis—sometimes including multiple courses, over a period of years. My lectures at New York University; Southern Connecticut State University (sponsored by the Asian Studies and Asian Academic Society) for a consecutive ten years— sometimes twice a year, and later on for two more years; Pace University in Pleasantville, New York; the Department of Religion at Syracuse University; Trenton State College for two consecutive years with four courses each year; the Alliance Theological Seminary at Nyack College for a consecutive ten years (1981-1990), and several years afterward; the Birch Wathen School, New York City for five years; and the local

Trinity School, where I gave the annual introductory class on Hinduism for a consecutive seven years, fall into this category.

I have also delivered lectures to undergraduate students in comparative religion at Columbia University, and to students at Fordham University; the State University of New York at New Paltz and Stony Brook; before a distinguished gathering at the Hall of New York State University at Albany; Rutgers University; the Divinity School of Yale University; The Cooper Union for the Advancement of Science and Art; the Philosophy Department of the University of Maryland; the Philosophical Society of Long Island University; Sarah Lawrence College; Marymount College; Packer Collegiate Institute; William Paterson College; St. Mary of the Woods College in Indiana; St. Regis High School; and Loyola School, a Catholic school for boys.

INTERFAITH AND PEACE CONFERENCES, SEMINARS AND SYMPOSIUMS, AND INAUGURATION PROGRAMS: A SUMMARY

I have also been invited to lecture in the academic and religious communities through the broader framework of conferences and seminars.

In 1982 I was invited to give a seminar at Pace University on "The Concept of Soul or Self in Vedanta." The reader who wishes to have a deeper understanding on this concept may refer to Appendix B.

On March 12, 1984 the Humanities Institute at Brooklyn College of the City University of New York sponsored a seminar, "Is There Reincarnation?" chaired by Professor Viscuse. I was invited together with the co-speaker, Dr. Paul Edwards, professor of philosophy, Guggenheim Fellow and editor in chief of the *Encyclopedia of Philosophy*, to debate and explore the intercultural ideas about reincarnation.

I participated at several interreligious events: the 1983 Washington, D.C. Interfaith Centenary Celebration at the

Indian Embassy; the United Nations Interfaith Peace gathering at Dag Hammerskjold Auditorium on November 23, 1984, with Mr. N. Krishnan, the U.N.'s permanent representative to India; and the 1986 Peace Conference at the Cathedral of St. John the Divine, sponsored by the Temple of Understanding.

In the summer of 1987 I was invited to participate in a special Vedanta Convention sponsored by the Vivekananda Vedanta Society of Chicago. It was held at the Vivekananda Monastery and Retreat in Gangestown, Michigan. Eighteen Swamis and more than 800 people attended from the U.S. and Canada and abroad. John Schlenck of our Society also led the choir in a musical performance.

In 1988 I was invited to speak at the Embrace Foundation's Interreligious Dialogue Conference at the Waldorf-Astoria Hotel. In 1990 I participated in a seminar on World Spirituality at Fordham University, The Bronx. I was requested to guide a group of thirty people in meditation. Distinguished speakers from the United States and Canada also participated in this seminar.

In April 1991 Rev. Father Louis M. Dolan invited me to speak at a peace program at his Orthodox Christian Church in New York City. Other dignitaries of various faiths were also invited, including the dean of the St. John the Divine Cathedral and the imam of the New York Mosque. When the United Nations celebrated Father Dolan's birthday in 1997, I was invited and pleased to participate. Father Dolan had made a considerable contribution to the 1994 centenary celebrations of our Society and the 1993 Parliament of Religions as an organizer of the 1994 Convocation of Global Religions at Queens College.

On September 20, 1994 I was invited to offer the Hindu prayers and to speak at the Interfaith Prayer Breakfast at UNICEF House for the annual United Nations International Day of Peace. I spoke about Swami Vivekananda as a unique messenger of peace. Jacques Boisson, the ambassador of

Monaco to the U.N., presided over the meeting. On October 17, 1994 I spoke at an interfaith service with a broad international participation at the Cathedral of St. John the Divine in New York.

In 1995 New York University invited me to participate with two Buddhist monks and a Christian leader in an interreligious seminar. I conducted a seminar on Hinduism at the Alliance Theological Seminary in 1996. During 1996 and 1997 I conducted two seminars consisting of two courses each on Indian Philosophy at Trenton State College in New Jersey.

On July 12, 1998, I participated in the dedication ceremony of a bronze figure of Swami Vivekananda that was installed in the Hindu Temple of Greater Chicago. Swami Atmasthananda, vice president of the Order, dedicated the statue, which stands at a height of ten feet, two inches and is over one ton in weight.

My participation at the Fourth International Congress of Vedanta at Miami University in Oxford, Ohio in 1992 and at the Chicago Parliament of the World's Religions in 1993 have been detailed earlier in this chapter.

NEW JERSEY CLASS STARTED

At the earnest request of Dr. Sudeb and Chanda Das of New Jersey, I agreed to hold a monthly course on Vedanta at the Ved Mandir in Milltown, New Jersey. The class began in March 1998 and continues as of this writing. Dr. Goutam Sen kindly drives me back and forth from the Center to Ved Mandir.

PUBLIC LECTURES AT VARIOUS PLACES OF WORSHIP

I have been invited to speak at various places of worship, including the Princeton Unitarian Church, the Unitarian

Church in Summit, New Jersey, the Flatbush Jewish Center in Brooklyn, and various Hindu Temples.

STUDENTS OF COMPARATIVE RELIGION COME TO THE SOCIETY TO LEARN MORE ABOUT VEDANTA

Large numbers of students in comparative religion have arranged to meet with me at the Society. They often come with their professors in small or large groups. In 1978 I gave a scheduled talk in our Center to a group from the National Institute for Lay Training. In the early 1980s Dr. Norma Thompson brought her students from New York University to the Society to hear me speak about Vedanta. Rabbi Gilderman of New York, who was training students in ecumenical ministry, sent twenty of them to the Society in 1985 to learn about Vedanta.

For several years Columbia University students of comparative religion and art visited the Society to speak with me about Vedanta. They came throughout the year in 1989 and also attended the services. That same year sixty students from Pace University arranged to attend one of our Sunday services. Students from Fordham University arranged to have me lecture to them at the Society in 1992 and 1995. Fordham's Professor A. M. O. Brain brought her students to the Society on two occasions in 1992, for lengthy discussions about Vedanta. In 1997, thirty-four students of religion came from Columbia University with their professor, Dr. Jack Hawley, to attend one of my evening classes.

Students continue to come to learn about Vedanta, individually and in small and large numbers. Sometimes, individual students realize the benefit and attend the evening classes also. Groups and individuals also visit our Society often, to learn about Vedanta and the spiritual heritage of India. A Unitarian church group from Princeton, New Jersey visited the Center and attended our annual public celebration of Sri Ramakrishna's birthday in 1978.

GUEST LECTURERS AT THE SOCIETY

Throughout the years, the Society has occasionally invited guest lecturers and Swamis to speak on Sundays. Some who have spoken on auspicious occasions have been mentioned earlier. A few others may be mentioned here. In 1978 a veteran social and political worker of India and a close associate of Mahatma Gandhi, Mr. R. R. Diwakar, gave a talk on Sri Ramakrishna. A former governor in one of the states of India and a former minister of the central government, he also has written a book on Sri Ramakrishna.

In 1989 Revered Swami Lokeswarananda, the head of the Ramakrishna Institute of Culture in Calcutta, visited the Society from June 24 to 26 and spoke on "Sri Ramakrishna's Message to the West."

Several distinguished guests visited and lectured at the Society during 1991. Revered Swami Shraddhananda was our guest on May 21 to 22 and spoke on "The Spiritual Life." On June 23 a distinguished professor of Indian philosophy at Calcutta University, Dr. Nirodbaran Chakravarty, spoke on "Swami Vivekananda in the East and West."

On June 6, 1998 Revered Swami Atmasthananda, the vice president of the Order, visited our Society and gave a lecture on "The Centenary of the Ramakrishna Mission" at a special service commemorating that occasion.

TELEVISED INTERRELIGIOUS DIALOGUES

In 1987 I was invited to participate in two interreligious conferences that were televised. On July 24 I participated with a Carmelite nun in a dialogue on "Prayer" that was sponsored by the Embrace Foundation and televised in New York. I took part in an interreligious dialogue on December 2, with a Rabbi, a Muslim imam, and a Catholic priest. The dialogue was televised on December 6 and broadcast by Paragon Cable Manhattan.

BOOKS ON VEDANTIC THOUGHTS ARE PUBLISHED

In 1989 the Society published my book, *Glimpses of Great Lives*, a collection of articles written earlier and previously published in *Prabuddha Bharata*, *Vedanta Kesari*, and other Indian journals.

In 1991 Sontosh Kumar Chakraborty, the nephew of Swami Ramakrishnananda, who was a direct disciple of Sri Ramakrishna, published my book, *Healthy Values of Living*. The book was published in deference to the wishes of devotees and friends of the Society. It is a collection of thirty articles on a variety of useful topics that were all previously contributed to eastern and western periodicals, excepting one. Most were published in the *Yuba Bharati* of the Vivekananda Rock Memorial and the journal *Bhavan* between 1966 and 1987. Emma Martierena, a sincere devotee of the Ramakrishna Ashrama in Argentina translated *Healthy Values of Living* into Spanish. In 1993 our Society's secretary, Miss Jeanne Genêt, published a revised, enlarged second edition.

In 1993 Mr. S.K. Chakraborty also published my book, *Albert Einstein: His Human Side*. This small book is meant for the general public interested in knowing Einstein the man. The book is now being freely distributed among friends and interested parties whose contributions will be used for the Ramakrishna-Ramakrishnananda Ashrama at Ichapur, which has been accepted by Belur Math. Emma Martierena chanced across the book at the ashrama in Argentina, was inspired, and immediately translated it into Spanish within fifteen days.

In October 1997 my book, *Ramayana Katha*, was published by Udbodhan, the Order's Bengali publishing center in Calcutta. The book was well received by the Bengali reading public. On Holy Mother's birthday, December 10, 1998, my book, Mahabharata Katha, was also published by Udbodhan.

In addition, I contribute articles to *Prabuddha Bharata* and other Indian journals. In 1987 I was invited by Dr. Norma Thompson, professor of religion and philosophy at New York

University, to contribute an essay on Hinduism to the book
Religious Pluralism and Religious Education. Dr. Thompson
edited the book, which was published in 1988 by the Religious
Education Press, Birmingham, Alabama.

THE TRADITION AT MOSS HILL FARMS CONTINUES

In 1961 a tradition was started with only four or five
members of the Society at Moss Hill Farms which continues to
this day. At the upstate New York farm of Erik Johns and Jack
Kelly, the Vedanta Society's members gather together to
celebrate the passing away of Swami Vivekananda on the fourth
of July. The day was originally spent reading about
Vivekananda.

Gradually, more and more members came to Moss Hill
Farms. Musical works on the theme of Swami Vivekananda or
the *Kathopanishad* were performed. They were composed by
John Schlenck, the Society's music director and the librettos
were written by Erik Johns. Swami Sarvagatananda, our dear
friend of the Vedanta Society of Boston, also attended the
fourth of July celebration many times. Erik Johns and Jack
Kelly took the initiative to create this event, which our members
and friends love to attend each year.

RIDGELY MANOR, OUR NEW NEIGHBOR

It is well known to our devotees that Ridgely Manor was
sanctified three times by the presence of Swami Vivekananda.
On June 27, 1981, I went there along with seventeen of our
Society's devotees for a one-day spiritual retreat. Since then I
have gone many times with our devotees.

Mary Ann Lucker, a devotee of Swami Pavitranandaji,
spent some years in India. As a student of Vedanta, she
developed some interest in the spiritual welfare of American

women. In her old age she sought the advice of John Schlenck and William Conrad of our Society as to how she might promote that welfare in a concrete way. She was informed about the work of Joan Shack, head of the Sri Sarada Society of Albany, a college teacher, and a sincere, long-standing devotee, who shared her interest. Miss Lucker left $100,000 in her will to the Sri Sarada Society.

When the Society received the money in 1994, Joan Shack became very enthusiastic about the possibility of purchasing Ridgely Manor to be used by women as a place of retreat and spiritual development. Joan Shack, along with many devotees far and wide, did the spadework to generate publicity about the project. She made a tireless attempt to move heaven and earth to involve many known and unknown friends. The Sri Sarada Society made a videotape and campaigned to raise funds. Some of our devotees gave money. Joan Shack showed the videotape after our Center's birth anniversary celebration for Sri Ramakrishna on March 5, 1995. Ultimately, Ridgely was taken over by the Ramakrishna Mission.

Since the inception of Ridgely Manor, the New York Vedanta Society has participated in all major programs held there. In 1998, Swami Atmasthananda, vice president of our Order, came to Ridgely. On June 26 to 28, 1998 I was invited to participate in the inauguration of the Vivekananda Retreat at Ridgely Manor, which had recently been purchased by the Vedanta Society of Southern California for that purpose. The New York Vedanta Society Choir performed an original work by John Schlenck on Swami Vivekananda's life. Robert Gupta, the gifted ten-year-old son of two of the Society's members, performed on the violin with the Choir. Other Society members, including John Schlenck, William Conrad, William Davis, and Robert Alexander, rendered valuable service to Ridgely. That Society and ours continue to enjoy a very cordial relationship. It may be recalled that the Leggetts had been host to Swami Vivekananda in their manor at Ridgely during his sojourns in America.

1977 - 2000: THE SOCIETY LOSES SOME
TREASURED AND DEDICATED MEMBERS

During my years at the Society, I met and became intimately acquainted with members who have been loyal and dedicated to the Society from Swami Bodhananda's time— Miss Gwendolyn Thomas, who is now known as Pravrajika Bhaktiprana, Mrs. Victoria Hugo Hollister and her husband, Mr. Harold I. Cole, Mrs. Ruth Rieger, Mr. Alec Burgess, Miss Marie Russell and Miss Mercedes Mendoza. All have passed away but for Pravrajika Bhaktiprana, Miss Russell and Mr. Burgess. We record their passing along with others in appreciation of their various contributions to the work of the Society.

In February 1978 Mr. Reynold Gandolfi, an active, humble and steadfast member for nearly forty years, who had attended classes since Swami Bodhananda's time, passed away.

In 1981 Mrs. Ruth Rieger passed away. She had served as treasurer of the Society for more than twenty years, since the time of Swami Bodhananda. I was invited by her friends to conduct a simple burial service and was accompanied on the train to the cemetery near Pleasantville by the Society's secretary, the treasurer, and a friend.

In 1985 Mr. C.H. MacLachlan, the Society's vice president for almost ten years and a member since 1958, passed away serenely. He contributed several thoughtful articles to *Prabuddha Bharata*. He was a pillar of our Society, serving on the board of directors for many years and faithfully attended classes with his wife as long as their health permitted. He was also a journalist and the editor of *The Long Islander*, a paper started by the poet Walt Whitman.

Miss Tyyne Hakola also passed away in 1985. She had been a member since Swami Bodhananda's time and was an artist by profession. Thirty years before her death she had rendered two beautiful interior wall paintings for the Society. One, of the temple at Belur Math, is in our "Sarada Home" and the other, of the banyan tree under which Sri Ramakrishna meditated, is to be found in our library.

Four of the Society's loyal members passed away in 1987. Mr. Harold I. Cole, who was associated with the Society from Swami Bodhananda's time, served as a trustee for more than thirty years and gave legal counsel. For a number of years during his service as a trustee he was vice president of the Society. After attending his first service in the Society's Chapel with his wife in 1951, they both felt they had "come home."

Mrs. Indu Marathe first came to the Society from India, as a newly arrived young wife with her husband. They were devoted to the Society from the time of Swami Bodhananda, and began a tradition that continues to this day, of cooking and bringing halva for the entire congregation to the annual birthday celebration of Swami Vivekananda. After her passing in 1987, her friends, Mr. and Mrs. Shakundala, were inspired by this devotion and continue to bring sweets for Swamiji on the yearly auspicious occasion.

Mrs. Rosa Widmaier, a professional nurse, came in contact with the Society during Swami Bodhananda's time, through her interest in yoga. Though unable to travel very often from Connecticut to the Center, her correspondence with Swami Pavitrananda and steadfast striving helped her to develop serenity in her life. She had been a member for 22 years before passing away in 1987.

Mrs. Victoria Hugo Hollister also passed away in 1987. She first came to the Society with her husband in 1933, during Swami Bodhananda's time. Mrs. Hollister knew Helen Keller intimately and wrote a biography of her. She dedicated the biography to Swami Vivekananda and Swami Bodhananda and asked me to write the "Foreword." The book was published by the Ramakrishna Mission Ashrama in Narendrapur, West Bengal. The entire proceeds from the book were donated to the ashrama's Academy for Blind Boys.

In June 1989, Mr. Jack Perry Kelly, a member of the Society since 1955 and an enthusiastic devotee of Vedanta, passed away. It may be recalled that it was at his initiative that the annual Swami Vivekananda July Fourth festival began to be celebrated in 1962 at Moss Hill Farms, co-hosted by him and Erik Johns at this property, which they jointly owned.

In 1991 Alice Cook, a member of the Society for thirty-five years, passed away. She was a dedicated worker with the Center, especially in the treasury work up to the time of her retirement in 1973. In 1967 she collaborated with two other members of the Society on a libretto for a cantata on the life of Swami Vivekananda, that was performed three times at the July Fourth Festival at Moss Hill Farms over the years. She sustained her meditation and Vedantic study until her death.

In 1992 the Society lost several treasured members. Arnold Elkie, a disciple of Swami Yatiswarananda, had been a member of the Society during Swami Bodhananda's last years, and again for several years until 1971, before moving to California. Mrs. Bella Cole had been a member of the Society for more than forty years and served as a board member for much of that time.

Nariman Dhalla, a student of Swami Aseshananda, had been a member of the Society since 1979 and also passed away in 1992. He spent the last eleven years of his life in France and visited the New York and Portland Centers each year. He was a Zoroastrian by birth and came to Vedanta after reading *The Way of a Pilgrim*. His character was extraordinary and his devotion to Sri Ramakrishna was exemplary. I stayed a few days with him at his Paris residence in 1992 and I returned to see him again with four Swamis from the Gretz Centre before he passed away. Though Mr. Dhalla was bedridden, he remained alert. All of us took books from his library collection before leaving. Mr. Dhalla donated his house in Brooklyn to the Society. At my request, William Conrad negotiated the sale, and the Society received approximately $38,000 from the proceeds.

The year 1994 marked the passing away of Mercedes Mendoza, a steadfast and loyal member under three Swamis at the Society since 1942. Though she had retired to Florida, her membership and service remained enthusiastic, and she maintained her correspondence with me and other members.

Dr. Anil Saha, a dean and professor at Rutgers University and a member of the Society since 1979, passed away in 1995. He is remembered for his exquisite spring and fall flower offerings at the Society's altar every week from his own garden, cultivated exclusively for his devotion to Sri Ramakrishna. A good tabla player, he also accompanied the Society's choir on special occasions. He was a generous donor.

The year 1996 marked the passing away of Mr. Nathan Shapiro, the president of the Society for nearly twenty years and a member of the board for nearly forty. He was a distinguished attorney who served devotedly under Swami Pavitrananda and myself and rendered legal counsel to the Society. Mr. Shapiro placed all his abilities and experience at the disposal of the members always without a fee, with kindness, humor and love for the Center.

The Society also recorded with sorrow in the same year, the loss of Patricia Bankert, on March 18, 1996. She was a student of Swami Nikhilananda who had been associated with our Center since 1957, minding the book table before and after the Sunday services, and preparing meals for Swami Pavitrananda, sometimes. Especially devoted to Swami Shantaswarupananda, she had retired shortly before her death to Lucknow, India, to be near him. Once, during an earlier period, she had lived and worked for a number of years in Lucknow, as a lay volunteer at the Ramakrishna Mission Hospital. She is remembered for her virtues of steadfastness, devotion, and common sense.

In 1997 Ethel de Turck, a long-time devotee of Vedanta associated with the Society, passed away in India.

THE SOCIETY LOSES ITS SECRETARY

In 1998 the Society lost its secretary and revered senior-most resident member, Miss Jeanne Genêt. We all know she was exposed to the life-giving message of Ramakrishna-Vivekananda when she was just 26, in 1932. From that time they became the cry of her life, the song of her soul. Ramakrishna-Vivekananda lit a beacon of hope for her. She took firm determination and stern resolve to follow the idealism of these twin stars in the firmament of modern life. Her entire life, as it appeared to me, was one of humility, self-effacement and an ungrudging labor of love. She had never lived an embittered, immolated, resentful and self-pitying life. On the contrary, she was consciously and intelligently committed to the philosophy of work as spelled out by Swamiji. She committed her life in unreserved obedience to him. It is conspicuously different from the mild, conventional religious life known to us all. She lived an amazingly simple life with a singleness of purpose. Miss Genêt passed away on 28 August 1998. She was almost 93. She lived and worked in the Society premises for almost half a century. What a saintly life she lived! Her value should not be measured by the years she has lived or by the work she has done. Her value can be partially estimated by the spiritual attitude behind her life and work. What a magnificent epic of devotion to Sri Ramakrishna and Swamiji we saw in her life!

A Special Memorial Service For Miss Jeanne Genêt

On September 13, we had a memorial service for Miss Jeanne Genêt in our Chapel. One hundred forty devotees were assembled. I read the condolence messages of Revered Swamis Ranganathananda, Gahanananda, Atmasthananda and Sarvagatananda. I spoke about her noble life. Courtenaye Olden and her husband, George Olden, were long-time associates of the Genêt family, since the early fifties. Courtenaye knew each one of the Genêts intimately and rendered service to them in various ways; she also spoke. She was followed by John Schlenck, William Conrad and Susan Salm, who came to the Society in 1958, 1955 and 1968, respectively. Rabbi Asher and Mrs. Hilda Block were close friends of the Genêt family; Mrs. Block related her cherished memories.

The accompanying speakers were Professor Jayanta Sircar of Maryland University, College Park; Uma (Carmen Gauci), a graduate student who lived with Miss Genêt in the Society for seven years, from 1978 to 1984, who later joined the Santa Barbara Convent in 1985; and Joanne Kilgour, Ph.D., who lived with Miss Genêt at the Society, during two-and-a-half years of her undergraduate years at The Julliard School from 1986 to 1989, and is now a professor at Atlanta University, Georgia. Robert Alexander and his wife, Paula, have been close devotees of the Center since 1982; Paula spoke. They were followed by Maria Barbosa, for two years one of Miss Genêt's four personal attendants, and Helen Manolatos, who rendered signal service for Miss Genêt's well being in every possible way, especially during the last two years of her illness. Everyone was given sumptuous food.

Eleven hundred copies of a booklet containing my article, "The Genêts: A Legacy of Dedication," with a charming photograph of Miss Genêt on the cover, were printed for this occasion. Copies were freely distributed to all. It had been previously published in the September 1989 issue of *Prabuddha Bharata*. As a symbol of Miss Genêt's loving renunciation and unceasing service, two fruits were offered to everyone. Everybody was immensely happy.

Dr. Tapan Sarkar of Syracuse University, a longtime and dear friend of the Society, spontaneously came forward to donate $8,000 for the construction of a dispensary at Jayrambati. The Swami in charge agreed to place there a marble plaque upon which, "In Honour of the Genêts, Donated by The Vedanta Society of New York" is to be carved.

I wrote two additional booklets, *The Genêts: A Legacy of Dedication*, and another booklet in Bengali about the Genêts. Both were published by the Vedanta Society of New York in 1998 and 1,100 complimentary copies of each were distributed.

The Society also recorded with sorrow the passing away of Sara Massuque in January, one month preceding her 100th birthday. She was very devoted to Sri Ramakrishna and a member of the Vedanta Society of New York since 1981. Because she resided in Connecticut, she could only come to have interviews with me, and in 1976, seeking a spiritual environment and daily spiritual companionship, she moved to Santa Barbara, California and spent her last years at the Vedanta Society of Southern California.

IN CONCLUSION

Modern civilization is passing through a great crisis, which is prominently reflected in our chaotic society. We are rootless and aimless; restless activity is the hallmark of our age, or, to quote Einstein, "the perfection of the means and the confusion of the goal is the characteristic of the age." The advancement of knowledge has awakened a new attitude about life and its aspirations. The prejudice of religions, the tyranny of the herd instinct and deeply rooted ethnic, gender, racial, and color consciousness have penetrated into our thought and life. The phenomenal progress of science and technology has not touched upon the fundamental weakness of mankind. The modern world, in comparison with the ancient world, is not made poorer by one superstition. The more problems we solve, the more problems our solutions create.

Our age forcefully demands that we meet the challenge of life with the challenge of an adequate and rational philosophy. We cannot have a meaningful life with enduring peace until we have a philosophy of life more adequate to the cosmic and psychological facts. The modern scientific concept of "a single universe" or "unbroken wholeness of the universe" cannot accept division of mind and matter, of matter and spirit, of God and man. Many of our biggest, gravest problems arise from a piecemeal approach, from the lack of a larger picture of man and nature. The emergence of a global society impelled by science and technology demands a new, holistic paradigm with which to establish harmony and peace.

The unitary vision of Vedanta is integral and inclusive, whereas modern thinking based on dualism, is dialectic and exclusive. An intregral approach will bring about a higher level of consciousness in humanity. Of all ideas and thoughts, Vedanta is the only philosophy—the science of Reality—that is characterized by deep and vast scholarship, penetrating analysis, and fearless critical thinking. To those who have carefully followed the spirit of Vedantic ideas and thoughts expressed throughout this book, it may be evident that Vedanta is altogether unique in its breadth of vision and comprehensive grasp. Its main concepts—the divinity of man; the non-dual spiritual character of ultimate Reality; the basic solidarity of all existence; realization, not mere belief or creed, as the criterion of religion; and the harmony of religions—these concepts, realized by the mystics, breathe the spirit of the universal and human, marking human culture at its best and highest. They give rise to the values of tolerance, peace, gentleness and non-aggressiveness that are the most cherished values of modern persons. As Romain Rolland anticipated, this is "the fruit of a new autumn, a new message of the Soul, the symphony of India, bearing the name of Ramakrishna."

Vedanta provides a synthetic view of life that brings harmony between religion and science, reason and faith, spiritual aspiration and secular life. In Vedanta, all objects are anchored in God. True spiritual life is based on an integral vision of life and the world. It provides a soul to the growing world-consciousness. The doctrine of the unity of the spiritual essence of the universe and the diversity of its manifestation introduces a tremendous dynamism in life.

Philosophy inspires us, motivates us, and carries us to the gate of the Promised Land, but cannot let us in. True followers of Vedanta, through their exalted character, will have to bring enlightenment among the people.

The Society has been steadily maintaining the integral character of the Movement. We interpret the facts in the light of our knowledge of Vedanta and against the background of history. Shri Ramakrishna's insight is expressive of a timeless spiritual fact. He is the great world teacher who exemplified the noblest characteristic of manhood. He revealed profoundest Truth, brought home to us the ideal of human excellences by embodying them visibly in himself.

The main distinguishing feature of our Society is the quietness and steadiness of our spiritual ministration, without being tempted, in the least, to succumb to cheap popularity and inordinate publicity.

In these days of meaningless noise and perversion, hankering after obsessive identification with the fleeting opinions about religion, we have maintained the breadth and vigor of our goal, kept our Society on a spiritual and intellectual level, exhorted the seriousness of the vocation and avoided the danger of having sensation-seeking members.

We keep our eyes on timeless Truth, on values which are perennial, universal, paramount, and rational and intelligible. We are not curators of outmoded religious ideas and practices, which are but lifeless mockeries. We are disseminators of healthy and creative ideas of spiritual life. Vedanta is not culture-oriented but it is humanity-oriented. Universal religion hardly attracts the masses. Swamiji says: "A ... large crowd of people does not mean a propagation of the message of Shri Ramakrishna."

With the conviction deeply implanted in our heart, the epochal new dispensation is full of promise to usher in a cosmopolitan attitude in our spiritual thoughts. The matchless beauty and redeeming power of Vedantic ideas are being gradually appreciated among the rational-minded people all over the world.

We are humble, small in numbers, but sincere in our quest. We are pure and hence strong. We have got an honored place in society.

"Growth is slow when roots are deep. But those who light a little candle in the darkness will help to make the whole sky aflame."

AT A GLANCE

Homes of the Vedanta Society of New York
(As accurately as can be traced)

Year	Address Source*	Swami in Residence
1895	54 West 33 St. MLB, III:574	Swami Vivekananda
1895/96	228 West 39 Street MLB, III:578	Swami Vivekananda
1896	509 Fifth Ave/42 St. MLB, IV:345	Swami Saradananda
1897	117 Lexington Ave. AJ, 138	Swami Abhedananda
1897	170 Lexington Ave. CWSA, X:15	Swami Abhedananda
1899	146 East 55 Street[1] Apostle, 290	Swami Abhedananda
1900	102 East 58 Street MLB, V:145; VI:266, 307	Swami Abhedananda
1905	62 West 71 Street[2] VMB (Apr. 1905) I:cover	Swami Abhedananda
1907	135 West 80 Street[3] VMB (Apr. 1907) III:14, 61 VMB (Mar. 1908) III:12:207	Swami Abhedananda
1915	236 Central Pk. West VQ (Oct. 1915) 236	Swami Bodhananda
1921	34 West 71 Street[4] PB (Jul. 1922) 280	Swami Bodhananda Swami Pavitrananda Swami Tathagatananda

*Source Key: AJ: Swami Abhedananda, *Amar Jivankatha*
                Apostle: Sister Shivani, *An Apostle of Monism*
                CWSA: *Complete Works of Swami Abhedananda*
                MLB: Marie Louise Burke, *Swami Vivekananda in the West: New Discoveries*
                PB: *Prabuddha Bharata* (Awakened India)
                VMB: *Vedanta: Monthly Bulletin*
                VQ: Vedanta Quarterly, *Message of the East*

[1] The address was located between Lexington and Third Avenues.
[2] The Vedanta Society of New York was located here up to April 1907.
[3] The Vedanta Society of New York was located here from April 25, 1907.
[4] The Vedanta Society of New York's permanent and current home.

GLEANINGS

VEDANTA IN AMERICA: 1905

"Many have thought that the philosophy and religion of Vedanta, which thrives so rigorously in India, would not bear transplanting; those who know its teachings have never doubted that it was a world-plant of perennial growth. Yet even to these the rapid spread of Vedanta, especially in America, is a source of constant surprise... Strangely enough one of the most active among these new centers of interest is a thickly settled mining district of South Dakota. Less than a year ago frequent orders for our publications began to come from there, each a little larger than the previous one; then we received a letter asking whether in buying Swami Vivekananda's Raja Yoga and Jnana Yoga by the dozen a discount would be allowed; and soon followed an order amounting to $25.00. This led us to write and beg some information regarding what was being done. The response to our question ran thus: 'Vedanta Philosophy was brought to us by Dr. _____ (an American physician), whom you already know. We like it and accept it to be the clearest explanation, and whenever we can get someone interested, we are glad to spread the Advaita idea. We are all laboring men, and most of our earnest men are married men, but there are some who are single, who may eventually be brought to the point of renunciation. In such case I would like to know if the Society has a branch of the order of Sannyasins established in this country? Or if it makes any provision for those who are willing to devote their time to distributing literature and lecturing? One grand feature of Vedanta is that it gives a clear explanation of the New Testament, without which explanation many things written in it are too dark and veiled for the ordinary mind. I anticipate some radical changes in the churches of this country, dropping off of many fetichistic ideas and appealing to the intelligence of humanity. Ramakrishna says: 'When the lotus unfolds the bees come of their own accord to gather honey; but the bee can travel only so far in a day, so when lotuses are scattered, some bees can obtain honey that might otherwise go without.' There must be many who long for an explanation of the phenomena of life, and Jnana is as clear as can be had. Write me of your method of reaching people; it is sometimes a little awkward to approach those outside of one's own circle of acquaintances.' It was suggested in the answer to this letter that a co-operative community might be formed and a Swami brought from India. To this our correspondent replied: 'As I wrote before, most of our men, in fact most of the men of the town, are laboring men, and we will have to increase our number very much before we could think of having a Swami come. We are dependent upon the mining industry almost entirely. An agricultural district would be better suited for a co-operative move and I have thought much of conducting a cattle-raising business along these lines. Our season is too short to do much tilling [of] the soil. There are but two things for us to do, increase our number to what would insure a living for a Swami or those who are interested to move to where they could be with an instructor.'

"This is only one of the many instances which are constantly coming up to disprove the prevailing belief that Vedanta is only for the few, that it appeals only to those who have the leisure and opportunity to study all that the world has to offer. On the contrary, experience shows that it draws with equal power those who have been less favored by fortune, whose knowledge has come from a hand-to-hand encounter with the stern conditions of actual life, in the farms, factories and mines. One man from northern New York, recently writing for advice about the study of Vedanta, closes his letter with the sentence: 'I am only a poor laboring man and cannot afford expensive books.' Another from a town in Pennsylvania tells us that he works nine hours a day as a trackman and only earns $1.32 a day and asks how much he can accomplish in the Yoga training under such conditions. Still another sends us a weekly order for some book with such regularity that we suspect that it is thus that he marks pay day. Here in New York one of our most persistent customers at one time was a motorman on the Eighth Avenue line, and he assured us that 'there were a lot of boys at the car-house reading the books,' which was the reason he bought so many.

"One Sunday in the early summer a man was seen walking up and down before the Society House casting an occasional furtive glance towards the windows, evidently not daring to venture in. At last, picking up his courage, he slid sidewise through the half-open door, dragged a dollar out of his pocket and asked for as much literature as could be had for that sum. 'But what special subject will interest you?' we asked, pointing to the row of pamphlets on the table. 'Oh, I don't know,' he replied with a broad Scotch accent, 'but the man who talked to me about it told me I ought to read the Bag _____ something, only he said I'd have to read it fifty times before I'd understand it.' So we gave him the Bhagavad Gita with some single lectures and he turned to go. But as he reached the door, he paused and said, 'If Mr. Hadelin ever comes to you just tell him that Mac, the ship's carpenter on the Ward line, was here.'

"In the face of such facts can one doubt the practical usefulness of the teachings of Vedanta in our busy bread-earning American life?"

(*Vedanta Monthly Bulletin*, October 1905, 108-110)

VEDANTA IN AMERICA: 1907

"Any teaching which appeals so uncompromisingly to man's higher nature as does Vedanta can never hope to spread rapidly. In summing up the year's record of work, therefore, too much must not be expected, for the foothold which Vedanta has gained in this country is shown less by the number of its direct followers, or the extent of its book sales, than by the way it has everywhere modified and transformed existing modes of thought; and this can never be set down in figures.

" ... The publication department of the Society is the one which must always play the most important part in all work of propaganda. No matter how vast the public hall, the voice of the Swamis can never reach beyond the limits of its doors; and there are hundreds beyond the limits of its doors; and there are hundreds sitting by lonely firesides far away, who are hungering for what that voice would tell them could they but hear. Only through the printed page can the message reach them and if we who live here near the heart of the teaching would share with the world at large the great blessing we enjoy, we should do all we can to extend this section of the Society's work."

(*Vedanta Monthly Bulletin*, Extract from the
Report of the Vedanta Publication Committee,
February 1907, 220-221)

THE VEDANTA PHILOSOPHY

"Mr. Charles Johnston, the well-known Theosophist, has an interesting article on "The Vedanta Philosophy" in a recent number of *The Open Court*. The Editor, Mr. Paul Carus, says of Mr. Johnston: "A long sojourn in India and careful study of the original scriptures has made him thoroughly conversant with the ancient Brahmin thought, and I agree with him that we Western people ought to be more familiar with Indian Philosophy and Indian modes of thinking." We have therefore selected a few passages from the article, feeling that Mr. Johnston's testimony, being the result of careful reflection, must have value. "Two things," he writes, "seem to me to distinguish our philosophy in the West from the philosophy of India, especially in its golden age. Without disrespect one may say of Western philosophy that it has always held a somewhat subordinate and secondary position; it has leaned for support against some other teaching or science to study, drawing its color therefrom. This is even so of Plato, great and august though he be, for Plato's philosophy is entangled amid dialects and rests thereon... In the early Church, and on through the Middle Ages, philosophy leaned upon theology, and was deeply tinged with theologic coloring. Philosophy did not for itself seek out the heart of the mystery, but accepted, as firmly fixed and established, what theology gave it. The schoolmen and the whole scholastic system illustrate this, and their work now suffers from the very relation which once gave it power and popularity.

"In India it is, and in the Golden Age it was, strikingly otherwise. There, philosophy, *Vidya*, wisdom, stood boldly on its own feet, and begged support and countenance from no fashionable science or belief. Philosophy was not a recreation for the student, it was the supreme end of life.

"The other difference between Western and Eastern philosophy is even more fundamental. Western philosophy, almost without exception, draws all its conclusions from our waking consciousness, and treats other modes of consciousness either as non-existent, or as mere vagaries and reflections, almost as morbid conditions of bodily life... Every one of us Western folk, if we are pushed, will admit that we believe not so much in the communion of saints, as in the solid universe of matter, which geologist and chemist tell us of, and we bank on its reality, so to speak, in the practical conduct of our lives. To judge from our acts, we assuredly believe that, 'when the brains are out, the man is dead.' Yet through all this tacit materialism runs a warp of something quite different; something which for a generation or more, since Darwin ceased to be a startling novelty, has been slipping into the popular consciousness, something which makes the Indian position much more intelligible. Almost imperceptibly, we are beginning genuïnely to believe in other modes of consciousness beside our waking state, which, to Locke, was all in all. We are feeling our way through a mass of contradictory data concerning the trance state of mediums, clairvoyance telepathy, and the like, and if all goes well, we may presently reach the point at which the Indian wisdom began.

"In antique India they studied science. They had certain sound conclusions in astronomy, they had pushed far in geometry and mathematics, and even today we are using the numerical system of India. They had even a very suggestive evolutionary theory, in some things, foreshadowing Laplace and Darwin. But the followers of the higher way, the seekers after wisdom, made no great concern of these preliminary matters; they pushed on boldly toward the great Beyond, and we might say that they held the visible world as useful chiefly for its imagery, making it yield symbols to express the world ordinarily deemed invisible.

"Waking consciousness, so far from being the whole matter with the sages of India, is held to be merely the region outside the threshold. The sun is for them a good symbol of the spirit; the moon is a handy image for the changing mind; the atmosphere, with its storms and lightnings, does well to represent the emotional realm; fire typifies vitality, the rivers and seas are the tides of life. But the real world lies beyond and must be sought with other eyes."

(*Vedanta Monthly Bulletin*, Review, May 1906, 34-36)

BISHOP POTTER'S RELATIONSHIP WITH VEDANTA

It is interesting to know that Bishop Potter was very friendly to the Vedanta Movement. In 1909 the *Vedanta Magazine* reported his influence as well as his support: "The Students' Meeting ... was conducted by Mrs. C. G. Kelley who explained the origin of her beautiful little book *For the Union of All Who Love, in the Service of All Who Suffer*. Surely our dear secretary wrote from her heart for the title is a reflection of her own lovely soul. Bishop Potter, who was so keenly interested in all things pertaining to India, inspired the author through his lectures along these lines. The late bishop himself distributed many of the booklets among his fellow clergymen and friends."

(*Vedanta Magazine*, Jan/Feb 1909, 106)

CHRISTMAS SERVICE: 1908

"On Sunday afternoon (Dec. 27) a throng of students who realize the Christ through Vedanta gathered at the lecture rooms and listened with reverence while the Swami Abhedananda read from St. Mark and St. Matthew chapters relating to the birth of the Savior. The altar was draped in white, while Christmas candles and flowers illumined the portrait of the Divine Mother and Child, which hung above. The Swami knelt before the altar saying "Salutations to Thee" and offered up a silent prayer. He asked us to meditate for a few moments upon the divinity of Christ, to look for His image in the cave of our hearts, and try to realize in Him the manifestation of the Lord of All. He asked us to think of the Savior's seven beautiful examples, comparing them with flowers of Purity, Humility, Self-Denial, Truthfulness, Patience, Self-Sacrifice, etc., after which he read some notes he had carefully prepared from the pens of Socrates and other historians as to the actual date of the birth of Jesus the Christ, closing with meditation upon the Lord's Prayer, and offering the benediction as in the service of the Christian Church."

(*Vedanta Magazine*, Jan/Feb 1909, 104)

APPENDIX A:

PRACTICAL VEDANTA
SWAMI TATHAGATANANDA

Practical Vedanta

SWAMI TATHAGATANANDA

Swami Vivekananda gave a new direction to philosophy and religion, and made Vedanta a practical system to be espoused by the common people. God-centered philosophy was made man-centered. The system, which was confined to a few seekers of Truth, began giving the eternal bread of life to the millions. The traditional Vedanta has now become, through new interpretation, a source of inspiration for everyday life, and has been labelled the Neo-Vedantic Movement. This Neo-Vedantic Movement of Swami Vivekananda not only opened a new and vital chapter of our spiritual life, but also enhanced the prestige of this life-giving system. The very call of Swami Vivekananda—"Back to the Upanishads!"—ushered in an era of new vitality and dynamism in Hinduism. The constructive genius of Swami Vivekananda gave this new gospel of living a universal, catholic and non-sectarian voice, unlike the voice of previous movements that are negative, destructive, condemning and abusive. One of the brilliant landmarks of this progressive and creative message is that it is geared to the all-round happiness of the people, and thus paves the way for modernism. It bridges the gulf between science, religion and philosophy. Besides all the achievements, it freed Vedanta from lifeless scholastic arguments and the narrow groove of academic discussion in which it lay buried for many centuries. The new Vedanta eschews abstract reasoning and discussion of mere intellectual faith. It has become a new gospel of work

284   THE VEDANTA SOCIETY OF NEW YORK

and creative progress, fertilizing every aspect of human life. The life-giving ideas of Vedanta have to be practiced in life.

Swamiji said, "My ideal, indeed, may be put into a few words, and that is to preach unto mankind their divinity and how to make it manifest in every movement of life." The Swami threw a flood of light on certain basic tenets of Hinduism. The two doctrines of Karma and maya had proved to be a double noose on the neck of the Hindu race for centuries. These theories practically ruined the nation's life with their deadening fatalism and intellectual bankruptcy. Karma and maya, like two powerful vampires, were sucking the blood of national life, making the Hindu race weak, inactive, isolated and fatalistic. By his magnetic personality, dynamic spirit and inspired attitude, Swamiji gave new insight about these concepts. It was the singular achievement of the Swami to have interpreted them in a creative manner, bringing back their original significance and vigour, thereby making a very powerful, fresh vehicle for the dynamic development of national life. He was able to rejuvenate national life through his soul-stirring message of robust enthusiasm. To make India well equipped for her all-round growth, to enable her to discover her hidden potentialities and her glorious past, and to emancipate her mind from pessimism and a narrow mould, Swamiji worked vigorously. The Swami expounded the concept of Karma and rebirth from a rational point of view, bringing in a new and fresh world of joy and creativity. This theory was proved to be the very opposite of a negative attitude.

With a rare insight, Swamiji identified the idea of relativity as the substance of maya, the Hindu Sphinx. God appears as matter due to maya. Maya creates division; One appears as many. The world of maya will persist so long as the mind, which is itself maya, is not purified through spiritual insight. Maya will lose its charm, and its puzzle will be solved, when the mind is made pure. Maya can be transcended.

Swamiji was the very embodiment of courage. With a remarkable insight, he equated Courage with Reality and viewed Courage, Strength or Virility as one of the most distinguishing attributes of Divinity. This is a completely new interpretation, hitherto unknown to India. We know from our study of the Upanishads (Br. Up., 4.4.25) that the Divine is fearless; that we should have Courage stems from that great idea. But the concept of Courage is conspicuously absent from our philosophical system and moral vocabularies. Therefore, the word "courage" is not in vogue in our moral tradition. Swamiji projected before us the concept of dynamic Divinity— rather than static Divinity, which hardly evokes enthusiasm in human minds. It may be remembered that Swamiji made Strength a pivot on which other virtues turn. He said: "It is weakness, says the Vedanta, which is the cause of all misery in this world. Weakness is the one cause of suffering. We become miserable because we are weak. We lie, steal, kill and commit other crimes, because we are weak. We die because we are weak. Where there is nothing to weaken us, there is no death nor sorrow" (C. W., II, 198). The Gita made courage a central plank to support the moral edifice. In Swamiji's considered opinion, the real message of the Upanishads is Strength. He thundered: "If there is one word that you find coming out like a bomb from the Upanishads, bursting like a bomb-shell upon masses of ignorance: it is the word "fearlessness," and the only religion that ought to be taught, is the religion of fearlessness" (C. W., III, 160).

THE CONCEPT OF SOUL OR SELF IN VEDANTA

SWAMI TATHAGATANANDA

APPENDIX B

THE CONCEPT OF SOUL OR SELF IN VEDANTA

SWAMI TATHAGATANANDA

THE CONCEPT OF SOUL OR SELF
IN ADVAITA VEDANTA

SWAMI TATHAGATANANDA

*No books, no scriptures, no science, can ever imagine the glory
of the Self that appears as man, the most glorious God that ever was,
the only God that ever existed, exists, or ever will exist.*
                              —Swami Vivekananda, *Complete Works*

Right understanding about our life is the most valuable
wisdom for the right way of living. This was hinted at by Jesus
Christ who said, "What shall it profit a man, if he shall gain
the whole world, and lose his own soul?" The soul is the datum
of all experience and wisdom. The proper understanding of
the nature of the soul will make our life better, clearer, wider,
and deeper. Modern mind craves to know about the Self.
(Atman, Brahman, Absolute, Self, Soul, Impersonal God, Pure
Consciousness, and Spirit, are names of the same Being.)
"Being should be understood, when used as a general noun,
to mean *potentia*, the source of potentiality; "being" is the
potentiality by which the acorn becomes the oak or each of us
becomes what he truly is." Being is the foundation of all
existence. Being posits everything but Itself is not posited.
There can be only one such Being and that is God.

The innate divinity, infinitude, luminosity and blissfulness
of the soul was experienced by the sages of the Upanishads.
Max Müller, in his *Three Lectures on the Vedanta Philosophy*, gives

19

his opinion as to why this supreme wisdom about healthy human living was not available to the Greeks, or to the Medieval or modern philosophers: "But if it seem strange to you that the old Indian philosophers should have known more about the soul than the Greek or Medieval or modern philosophers, let us remember that however much the telescopes for observing the stars of heaven have been improved, the observatories of the soul have remained much the same ... the rest and peace which are required for deep thought or for accurate observation of the movements of the soul, were more easily found in the silent forests of India than in the noisy streets of our so-called centres of civilization" (Max Müller, *Three Lectures on the Vedanta Philosophy* [London: Longmans, Green, and Co.: 1894], 7-8).

All-pervading Supreme Consciousness underlying every form of existence, animate and inanimate, is manifest within every living being as the Self. God or Supreme Being is the Soul of all souls. He is the sum total of all souls and is their inner controller. Both the soul and God belong to the same category of Self—the former is the individual self (*Jivatman*), whereas the latter is the Supreme Self (*Paramatman*). The individual self or embodied soul is regarded as a manifestation of the other. The one has a body and is subject to many limitations; the other is free from all limitations. The distinction between the soul and the body or the mind is fundamental in Vedanta.

The word used in Indian scriptures for Self is Atman. The Atman in Vedanta is Self-existent as well as Self-luminous. Divine power is not a mere formless, impersonal material principle. It is a living dynamic conscious force that can assume a concrete personal form. It is the source of all Existence, Knowledge and Bliss. These are not qualities of the Soul, but Its essence. It is identical with Pure Consciousness or Intelligence. It is the sole support and substance of the manifold. The Reality or Self understood intuitively is the Supreme Spirit, and understood outwardly, is the physical world. It precedes everything, for everything is manifested or projected by the Self. "This *Brahman* is without a prior or a posterior, without interior or exterior, this *Atman is Brahman*, the experiencer of everything" (*Brihadaranyaka Upanishad*, 11.5.19). The changeless Reality (Brahman) that upholds the manifold is identical with the same changeless Reality (Atman) that indwells in the human being.

The entire universe originates from, is manifested, and is sustained by It. The self-luminous Atman (Self) is the sole spiritual entity; all else belongs to the realm of matter, gross or fine, being devoid of intrinsic Consciousness. Therefore, primordial nature and all its modifications constituting the world, physical and psychical, come under the category of matter. None of them have self-intelligence and self-consciousness as their essence. Vedanta does not accept the idea of secular scholarship that the universe, life and consciousness come out of dull, insentient matter. Physical processes can produce physical light but not the light of spirit marked by self-awareness. This alone distinguishes spirit from matter. No human ingenuity can create life out of lifeless matter.

Each of us has two consciousnesses, as it were, individual and universal, or lower self and higher Self. It is not the case that there are two selves in a man, one empirical and the other noumenal. Rather, the same self has different characters. The term "Self" includes both the Atman and its reflection or shadow, the ego. The Atman or God is the same in everybody; it is our diehard inveterate attachment for an egocentric life or psychophysical organism or simply the ego that differs from individual to individual. It is the ego that separates us from our higher Self, from other beings and ultimately, from God, and thereby produces insecurity, fear and dread in us. The higher Self of the individual is called the Atman. Atman is defined in the Brihadaranyaka Upanishad 4.3.7: "That which manifests Consciousness in the organs." Sankara says, "It is so called because it pervades, it receives, and it experiences objects in the world, and because from it the world derives its existence." We see, hear, smell, speak and taste through Consciousness or Atman. The common man calls it life; the mystic calls it Atman.

This Atman (Self within) is Brahman. The individual self is only an "abridged edition," as it were, of Brahman. The Supreme Self, chained to a body-mind consciousness, appears to be limited, weak and finite. Although the individual is one with the Divine, each person is a partial manifestation of the Divine.

The Self is revealed in every state of consciousness. Every thought, every physical act, produces a flash of Self-revelation in us. The ego is transcended only when the luminous Atman manifests in our conscious mind in the wake of strenuous spiritual struggle. The supreme object, according to Vedanta, is to know the Reality through direct intuitive knowledge, which is superior to discursive reasoning. This immediate knowledge unites the knower with that which is known.

The essence of knowledge is self-shining consciousness. Vedanta denotes Supreme Reality as *sat-chit-ananda* (being-consciousness-bliss absolute). Through Consciousness (*chit*) we are aware of our existence (*sat*) and happiness or bliss (*ananda*). The whole universe is a projection of consciousness. The luminous Self requires no proof. An individual's self-awareness is immediate and direct. Here is the foundation of human knowledge. From here the entire cognitive process starts. It is the luminosity of Consciousness that manifests all objects, physical and psychical. Each and every act of cognition is but an expression of Pure Consciousness through mental modes.

Consciousness or Intelligence is at the root of life, which is ever associated with sentiency, purposiveness, and the power of cognition. Life presupposes sentiency. Purposiveness is implicit in livingness because we notice an innate plan of self-preservation and self-development in all living beings. Unconscious things like the three forms of energy of nature, which are themselves mechanical, cannot organize themselves and work purposively unless there is a conscious principle to furnish the goal and purpose. Consciousness is intrinsic in the cognizer, while the object cognized is devoid of it. The cognizer and the cognized cannot be identical. The knower per se and the objects known are of contrary nature, like light and darkness. The Self illuminates everything and is not illuminated by anything else. The Real Self is the single constant factor in human personality. This Self is the changeless immortal in a changeful psychological garb. The Atman as the immutable and eternal Consciousness is the witness of the changing states. This knowing Self integrates all physical and psychical factors into a coherent whole, and coordinates the diverse functions of the mind, the organs, and the body. In fact, the organs, the mind and the *prana* (vital force) are like so many attendants of the Self (Atman) to carry out specific functions. The Self maintains the identity of the man in spite of all changes within and without. Our ideas of the Self are that (1) It is Consciousness, (2) There is continuity in Consciousness, and (3) It is associated with all activities as the knower and experiencer. The existence of the Self (Atman) is Self-evident. Though the Self permeates every pore of our being, the real nature of the Self is not self-evident to us. The famous argument of Descartes, "I think; therefore, I exist," can be remembered. Nothing is indubitable in this universe, except the fact of Self-existence. Vedanta reverses this statement: "I exist; therefore, I think." Descartes also says, "Mind is a self-knowing principle," which, also, is not accepted by Vedanta. S. Radhakrishnan observes, "There is a tendency especially in the West, to overestimate the place of the human self. Descartes attempts to derive everything from the certainty of his own isolated selfhood. It is not realized that the thought of the self which wants to explain everything, the will of the self which wants to subjugate everything, are themselves the expression of a deeper whole, which includes the self and its object. If the self is not widened into the universal spirit, the values themselves become merely subjective and the self itself will collapse into nothing" (S. Radhakrishnan, *An Idealist View of Life, Being the Hibbert Lectures for 1929*, 2nd ed. [London: George Allen & Unwin Ltd., 1937], 274).

Existence precedes thinking or doubting. One can never doubt the existence of one's Self. The body is compared to a cart and the soul to its driver. Coordination between the body, the mind, the organs, and *prana*, is possible due to conscious spirit, the knowing Self. All living bodies possess a tripartite personality with soul, mind and body. There cannot be a living organism without the coordination of these three.

The individual self represents finite, small consciousness. Every human being is individualized Universal Consciousness, the Self of the universe. All individual minds are parts of a Cosmic mind. Just as the microcosm is held, sustained, and controlled by the individual self, so is the macrocosm by the Universal Self. One Supreme Self is individualized or particularized by each finite mind, just as one sun reflected in the ocean appears as millions of suns. When the transcendental entity appears through the screen of matter in a particular way, we call it the individualized expression of the Infinite Being. It is something like a solar light or the sky. The light or the sky is infinite in its own being, but when we open the door of a room and look at the infinite sky or the light beyond through the door, they appear in the shape of the door. Various golden ornaments such as bangles, rings, and so on, though outwardly different, partake in essence of the same substance; that is, gold. We may number the various waves in the sea as separate lines of force, but they all actually represent unfoldings of the same tidal wave. Maya or ignorance obliges us to see things as separate rather than as unified in a single field. The individual is a creature, not a creator. The soul is being and God is the Supreme Being.

Vedanta holds that Self is beyond the intellect, mind, and ego. Life and nature are very limited expressions of Self and dependent on it. From the aforesaid study it can be concluded that (1) The Self is eternal, immortal, infinite Consciousness, one and non-dual. It is transcendental as well as immanent Entity; (2) It is Self-evident. Its existence and its unchanging continuity are fact; (3) It is identical with the Absolute Reality; (4) Pure Consciousness is ever the subject and hence the Absolute Reality is never objective; (5) The objective world is a projection of the Self and hence is only apparently real; (6) It is the datum of all experience and knowledge; and (7) It is Existence, Knowledge, and Bliss Absolute.

The Greek religion was, essentially, worldly and pragmatic. Though Socrates raised the religious attitude above the positivistic level, it was never pursued by the Greeks beyond the social level. Protagoras, most famous among the Sophists, formulated the dictum, "Man is the measure of all things." The well-known historian, Stace, explains: "By man he did not mean mankind at large. He meant the individual man ... Each individual man is the standard of what is true to himself" (Stace, *Critical History of Greek Philosophy*, 113). Protagoras lived nearly five centuries before Christ. Socrates, who is known by the scholars as the finest flower of Sophistic culture, gave the world a new dictum—"Know Thyself." In that statement, "Know Thyself," he gave special emphasis to the first word, "Know," and dedicated his entire life in the dissemination of knowledge. To him, "knowledge is virtue." He thought that right knowledge will easily help people to get an insight about right conduct. Western scholars never bothered about the real concept of the Self.

Plato only said that there were three kinds of Soul, the plant, the animal and the rational, without making the attempt Aristotle made to explain that this difference ultimately referred to a difference in the degree of consciousness. But he too finally upheld the contradictory notion that these different degrees of consciousness constituted the different kinds of Souls.

A vast body of scholarship has been produced through the untiring efforts of many Western scholars during the last two and a half millennia. But the result is disappointing. In his lecture, "Origin of the Vedanta," Max Müller quotes the remarks of the German philosopher, Frederick Schlegel: " ... 'It cannot be denied that the early Indians possessed a knowledge of the true God; all their writings are replete with sentiments and expressions, noble, clear, and severely grand, as deeply conceived and reverentially expressed as in any human language in which men have spoken of their God. Even the loftiest philosophy of the Europeans, the idealism of reason, as it is set forth by the Greek philosophers, appears, in comparison with the abundant light and vigour of Oriental idealism, like a feeble Promethean spark in the full flood of heavenly glory of the noonday sun—faltering and feeble, and ever ready to be extinguished.' And with regard more especially to the Vedanta Philosophy, he says: 'The divine origin of man is continually inculcated to stimulate his efforts to return, to animate him in the struggle, and incite him to consider a reunion and reincorporation with divinity as the one primary object of every action and exertion.' ..." (*Three Lectures on the Vedanta Philosophy*, 10-11).

Western thought cannot give us a concept like the Vedantic Self, which is self-luminous Atman, the sole spiritual entity. According to Vedanta, all else belongs to the realm of matter, gross or subtle, being devoid of intrinsic Consciousness. Change cannot be cognized unless there is an unchanging observer to relate the succeeding with the preceding condition. According to Vedanta, the mind is subtle matter, the finest of all material substances, and it is basically pure. It is distinct from the physical body and the knowing Self as well. It is intermediate between the two. It has been the prevailing tendency in the West to identify mind either with the soul or with the body. There is a good deal of vagueness in the writings of Western philosophers and psychologists. From Plato onward, philosophers in the West have held that the mind has three faculties—the cognitive (knowing), the conative (willing), and the affective (feeling). Will being only a special function of the mind and the mind itself being influenced by thoughts and desires—how can the will ever be free? The sense of freedom in our life is due to the presence of the higher Self in us. (Western scholars, denying the existence of Soul, consider human personality to be an offshoot of matter. The concept of Soul in the West is something like the concept of the subtle body in Vedanta.) Swami Vivekananda says, "The West never had the idea of soul until they got it through Sanskrit philosophy, some twenty years ago" (*C. W.*, III, 126).

Any age or country that produces a Plato, Aristotle, Kant or Hegel may be justified in its pride of their exceptional perception and scholarship. Despite their deep erudition, however, their view of life was not a universal view. Though they were notable philosophers, they never achieved a universal philosophy of life that can be accepted by all. European philosophers, in general, excepting a few, take an objective attitude to comprehend the Self. They labor hard to explain the subjective in terms of the object, the inner in terms of the outer. This inherent and predominant bias for objectivity is at the root of all the failures that spoil the Western theories of Self. Yet despite their objectivism, they naturally recognize, almost invariably, that the Self is unique—that the Self cannot be interpreted or understood through objectivity, regardless of their desire to do so. This objective attitude of the West fails to explain the important problem of human experience— the relation of the one and the many, changelessness and change, unity and plurality. The objective attitude of the western philosophers failed to give a satisfactory solution to the perennial problem of Self.

The tragedy of human life stems squarely from our metaphysical ignorance about —our divinity. "A more serious source of resistance," says Rollo May, "is one that runs through the whole of modern western society—namely, the psychological need to avoid and, in some ways, repress, the whole concern with 'being'." In contrast to other cultures, which may be very concerned with being—particularly the Indian and Oriental—the characteristic of our period in the West, as

Marcel rightly phrases it, is precisely that awareness of "the sense of the ontological—the sense of being—is lacking. Generally speaking, modern man is in this condition; if ontological demands worry him at all, it is only dully, as an obscure impulse" (Gabriel Marcel, *The Philosophy of Existence* [1949], 1).

In the Western view, man consists of body and soul. Here soul is synonymous with mind, ego, and consciousness. In the West, generally, no distinction is made between mind and soul. Soul refers only to the different forms of experience of a normal human being. This is the general idea in all non-Hindu spiritual traditions. The Self as a real entity distinct from body, mind, and ego has never been satisfactorily established. In Vedanta, Atman or Self is beyond body and mind, ego, intellect, and all physical appearances. It transcends everything. The Self is Self-existent, pure and immortal. In the West, each soul is created by God individually. In Vedanta, the human being consists of Atman, mind, and body; in the West the human being consists of body and mind which are created by God. Western scholars study only what the Vedantins call attribute consciousness, not existential consciousness.

According to Vedanta, the human being is divine, as the Pure Self is the inmost essence of man. God is not extra-cosmic or distant, He is immediate, direct and the nearest. Two concepts—the non-divine nature of man and the distance of God—are not accepted in Vedanta. In the Western view, God being the Creator, is therefore the subject, while the created soul is the object; the two can never be the same. God is not only ultimate but also intimate, according to Vedanta. God is nearer than our arteries, our inmost being. God, in Vedanta, is not only the Creator but also the created.

In summing up, the transcendent character of the ever-pure and immortal Self is never tainted by the impurities of mind, nor is it saved by the grace of a savior. When impurity is removed, the bliss of the Self is spontaneously experienced. In the West, soul is not a transcendent entity, it is created.

Hence the impurities of the mind taint the soul, which is mind, and hence it requires the grace of a savior. The Self of Vedanta is not a created entity; soul in the West is created. The doctrine of the eternal, pure, self-luminous and infinite Self was developed in Vedanta alone.

PRACTICAL RELEVANCE

The pressing need for the real conception of human life is the main key not only to right living but also to right knowledge of the universe. Practical points are: (1) The microcosm and macrocosm (the individual and universal) are built on exactly the same plan. The infinite is the support of the finite. Behind the world of multiplicity there is essential unity and interconnectedness; (2) The wisdom of the unity of existence provides a holistic view of life and the universe. This insight can make our life contemplative, spiritual, and dynamic; (3) The infinite glory of the human personality can be experienced by those who are really convinced of the divinity within. "Religion is the manifestation of the divinity already in man." This idea of Swami Vivekananda will be more appealing to humanity in the future. It is the expression of divine qualities in our life and not the subscription to a creed or a dogma. Religion essentially unites us with God; and (4) Swami Vivekananda's idea that in the future the thought of immanent God—God manifest in human beings, will impel us to serve them as God. This future vision of Vivekananda will be immensely fulfilled.

DEDICATED MEMBERS OF THE SOCIETY

DEDICATED MEMBERS OF THE SOCIETY

The Vedanta Society expresses its heartfelt gratitude to all our dear, long-standing members who supported our cause through various ways at different times. We are mentioning only a few names of those who are actively participating in our daily activities. The year they joined the Society is also given.

Miss Courtenaye Olden, 1951, Treasurer
Erik Johns, 1955, Vice President
William Conrad, 1955, Board Member
John Schlenck, 1958, Secretary
Stanley Quinn, 1961 (retired)
Marc Olden, 1967, Vice President
Susan Salm, 1968
Dianne Crafford, 1970, Board Mmeber
William Davis, 1972, Board Member
Richard Murphy, 1977
Robert Alexander, 1978, Board Member
Paula Alexander, 1978
Mary Hoffman, 1981 (retired)
Dora Barbera, 1986
Helen Manolatos, 1987
Jeanne Brady, 1987

APPENDIX D

THE NATURE OF THE SOCIETY'S ACTIVITIES

THE NATURE OF THE SOCIETY'S ACTIVITIES

In the flier reproduced below the interested reader may find the nature of the activities of the Society in 1912.

The Vedanta Society of New York
Founded by Swami Vivekananda in 1894
Lecturer and Teacher, since 1912
Swami Bodhananda
A direct disciple of Swami Vivekananda
and member and Trustee of the
Ramakrishna Order, India.
LECTURES
Sunday—11 A. M.—All are welcome
CLASSES—Open to all
Tuesday, 8 P. M.—Discourses upon the
BHAGAVAD GITA or Song Celestial
and the Upanishads alternately
Friday, 8 P. M.—Concentration Lessons and
Explanation of HATHA-YOGA and
RAJA-YOGA — For Members
Daily Noonday Meditation—12 o'clock
Objects of the Vedanta Society:
(1) To disseminate the Ethics and Religion of
the Vedas through Logic and Reason.
(2) To inculcate the Oneness of the Origin
and Goal of all Religions.
(3) To promote sympathy and harmony
among mankind on the basic principle
of Unity of Life and God.
Vedanta is not identical with any "isms."
It embraces them all and transcends them.
For all information apply to the Secretary
of the Vedanta Society.
34 West 71st Street, New York, U. S. A.

In the two fliers reproduced below the interested reader may find the nature of the activities of the Society during Swami Pavitrananda's time.

THE VEDANTA SOCIETY OF NEW YORK
34 WEST 71st STREET
NEW YORK, N. Y. 1023

SWAMI PAVITRANANDA, LEADER

THE VEDANTA

According to the Vedanta, man is potentially divine and the purpose of human life is to realize this truth through prayer, meditation, spiritual inquiry or unselfish work. Thus Vedanta represents the essence of all religions and recognizes different religions to be different paths to the same Goal. It does not believe in proselytizing: it believes in the spiritual transformation of lives.

HISTORY

The Vedanta Society of New York was founded in 1894 by Swami Vivekananda. He was the first teacher of Vedanta in the West and made history by his triumphant address at the Parliament of Religions held in Chicago in 1893. After that a group of eager students gathered about the Swami and started the first Vedanta Society in the United States in New York City. At present there are eleven such centers in America.

MEMBERSHIP

Membership in the Vedanta Society is open to all irrespective of creed or religious affiliation, provided they are genuine seekers after Truth. The privilege of membership includes spiritual guidance under the direction of the Swami, use of the library and admission to members' classes.

SERVICES

There is a service every Sunday at 11 A.M., and a Scriptural class with meditation on Tuesdays at 8:15 P.M. except dueing the period of vacation. There are also special classes for the members only.

INTERVIEWS

The Swami is glad to give interviews to those who are interested in Vedanta. Appointments may be made with the Swami after the services, or by telephone any weekday morning.

PUBLICATIONS

The book table has large numbers of publications dealing with Vedanta. Books may be purchased before 10:45 A.M. on Sundays or before 8 P.M. on Tuesdays as well as after the services.

Vedanta Society of New York
34 West 71st Street, New York, N. Y. 10023

EASTER SERVICE

Sunday, April 18, 1965 at 11 A.M.
Swami Pavitrananda
Will speak on:

"THE ILLUSION OF DEATH"

Devotional Music
Tuesday evenings at 8:15
Meditation and Discourse on "Bhagavad Gita"
You and your friends are cordially invited.

In the flier reproduced below the interested reader may find the nature of the Society's activities in the year 2000.

THE VEDANTA SOCIETY OF NEW YORK

Founded by Swami Vivekananda in 1894
34 West 71st Street, New York NY 10023
(212) 877-9197, 873-7439
e-mail: vedanta@mail. com, website: http://www.westved.org
Leader: Swami Tathagatananda
Ramakrishna Order of India

April 2000
SUNDAY SERVICES — 8 PM

April 2	"Pain and its Relief"
April 9	"Prerogatives of Devotees"
April 16	"Spiritual Life"
April 23	"The Message of Easter"
April 30	"Hidden God"

EVENING CLASSES — 8 PM

Tuesdays—Meditation; Study of the Gospel of
Sri Ramakrishna
Fridays—Meditation; Discourse on Bhagavad Gita
Group Devotional Singing—Saturdays and Sundays at 6 PM

INTERVIEWS

Swami Tathagatananda is glad to give interviews to spiritual seekers who wish to know more about Vedanta or the practice of meditation. Appointments must be made in advance.

MEMBERSHIP

Anyone who is in sympathy with the principles of Vedanta is welcome to become a member of the Society, subject to the approval of the Swami. The privilege of membership includes spiritual guidance under the direction of the Swami and use of the lending library.

BOOKS

The bookstall at the rear of the chapel is open to the public before and after services and classes. Books may also be purchased by mail. Our Book and Price List is available on request.

God is our very own. We should say to him, "O God, what is Thy nature? Reveal Thyself to me. Thou must show Thyself to me; for what else hast Thou created me? . . . One must take the firm attitude: "What? I have chanted the Mother's name. How can I be a sinner any more? I am Her child, heir to Her powers and glories." . . . Force your demands on God. He is by no means a stranger to you. He is indeed your very own. . . . God will certainly listen to your prayers if you feel restless for Him. He is our own Father, our own Mother. We can force our demands on Him.

—*The Gospel of Sri Ramakrishna*,
pp. 96, 147, 384

The kingdom of Heaven suffereth violence, and the violent take it by force.

—*The Gospel according to St. Matthew*,
11:12

Swami Tathagatananda gives a class on the Bhagavad Gita one
Saturday a month at Ved Mandir, 1 Ved Mandir Drive, Milltown,
NJ 08850. Tel: (732) 821-0404.
There will be classes on March 25 and April 22
Time: 4:00 P.M.
For further details, please contact Dr. Sudeb Das
Phone: (732) 329-8087

ENDNOTES

ENDNOTES

NOTES

Works frequently cited appear in their abbreviated form as shown:

Apostle

Sister Shivani, *An Apostle of Monism: An Authentic Account of the Activities of Swami Abhedananda in America* (Calcutta: Ramakrishna Vedanta Math, 1947).

C. W.

The Complete Works of Swami Vivekananda, 9 vols., 4th–11th editions. (Calcutta: Advaita Ashrama, 1972-1979).

C. W., S. A.

The Complete Works of Swami Abhedananda (Calcutta: Ramakrishna Vedanta Math, 1970), vol. X.

Compr. Bio. S. V.

S. N. Dhar, *A Comprehensive Biography of Swami Vivekananda*, 2 vols. (Madras: Vivekananda Prakashan Kendra, 1975-1976).

Life, II

The Life of Swami Vivekananda by His Eastern and Western Disciples, 5th ed., rev. and enl. (Calcutta: Advaita Ashrama, Volume II, 1981).

N. D.

Marie Louise Burke, *Swami Vivekananda in the West: New Discoveries*, 6 vols. [individual subtitles] (Calcutta: Advaita Ashrama, 1984-1987).

PB

Prabuddha Bharata.

316   THE VEDANTA SOCIETY OF NEW YORK

Reminiscences (1961)	*Reminiscences of Swami Vivekananda*, by His Eastern and Western Admirers, 1st ed. (Calcutta: Advaita Ashrama, 1961).
VD	*Vedanta Darpana.*
VK	*Vedanta Kesari.*
VM	*Vedanta Magazine.*
VMB	*Vedanta: Monthly Bulletin.*
Varieties	William James, *The Varieties of Religious Experience: A Study in Human Nature*, 1st ed. (London and Bombay: Longmans, Green, and Co., 1902).
With the Swamis	Swami Atulananda, *With the Swamis in America and India* (Mayavati: Advaita Ashrama, 1988)

Chapter One: After the Parliament: Swami Vivekananda's Work in America

[1] *Compr. Bio. S. V.*, 580.
[2] *N. D.*, 2:42.
[3] Ibid., 5:147-148; the reader may also refer to *N. D.*, 2:18-19.
[4] *N. D.*, 3:21-2.
[5] Ibid., 2:17.
[6] Ibid., 2:48-49.
[7] *Reminiscences(1961)*, 254-255.
[8] *Western Women in the Footsteps of Swami Vivekananda*, Pravrajika Atmaprana, ed. (New Delhi: Ramakrishna Sarada Mission, 1995), 96.
[9] *Swami Vivekananda: A Hundred Years Since Chicago, A Commemorative Volume* (Belur, West Bengal: Ramakrishna Math and Ramakrishna Mission, 12 January 1994), 133. [Hereafter, *Commem. Vol.*].
[10] Ibid., 133.

[11] Ibid., 133-134.

[12] SV to the Hale sisters, 11 August 1894, *C. W.*, VIII:318.

[13] *N. D.*, 2:136.

[14] Ibid., 2:150.

[15] Ibid., 2:159-160.

[16] Marie Louise Burke, *Swami Vivekananda in America: New Discoveries*, 1st ed. (Calcutta: Advaita Ashrama, 1958), 429. [Hereafter, *SV in America*].

[17] *N. D.*, 2:138.

[18] Ibid., 2:138.

[19] *C. W.*, VI:267.

[20] *PB* (September 1986): 382.

[21] *N. D.*, 4:554.

[22] *Commem. Volume*, 137-138.

[23] Ibid., 138-139 (quotation from *American Mysticism*, 73).

[24] *Varieties*, 513-514.

[25] *N. D.*, 2:187.

[26] *Varieties*, 400.

[27] *C. W.*, VIII:302-303.

[28] Ibid., V:50.

[29] *SV in America*, 333.

[30] Ibid., 338-339.

[31] Ibid.

[32] *N. D.*, 3:524.

[33] Ibid., 2:226.

[34] Ibid., 2:227.

[35] Ibid., 2:20.

[36] Ibid., 3:7.

[37] Ibid., 2:382-383.

[38] Ibid., 3:8.

[39] Ibid., 2:230.

[40] *N. D.*, 2:254.

[41] Ibid., 2:330.

[42] "Swami Vivekananda and the American Women: A Study of Their Contacts (1893-1896), *PB*, (January 1999): 303.

[43] *N. D.*, 2:261.

[44] *Compr. Bio. S. V.,* 1:674.

[45] *N. D.,* 3:9.

[46] Ibid., 2:52-53.

[47] Ibid., 3:18-20.

[48] *Letters of Swami Vivekananda,* 4th ed. (Calcutta: Advaita Ashrama, 1976), 219-220.

[49] *Reminiscences (1961),* 166.

[50] *N. D.,* 3:39-40.

[51] Ibid., 4:96; the reader may also refer to Burke's resource, *The Complete Works of Sister Nivedita, Birth Centenary Publication* (Ramakrishna Sarada Mission, Sister Nivedita Girls' School: 1967), 254.

[52] *Life,* II:11-12.

[53] *Compr. Bio. S. V.,* 1:713.

[54] *N. D.,* 3:392

[55] *Life,* II:4-5.

[56] *N. D.,* 3:44-45.

[57] Ibid., 3:45.

[58] *C. W.,* VI:308.

[59] *N. D.,* 3:103.

[60] Ibid., 3:63.

[61] *C. W.,* V:82-83.

[62] *Life,* II:19.

[63] *C. W.,* VI:302.

[64] *Reminiscences (1961),* 127-128.

[65] *N. D.,* 3:25.

[66] *Reminiscences of Swami Vivekananda,* by His Eastern and Western Admirers, 2nd ed. (Calcutta: Advaita Ashrama, 1964), "Reminiscences by Sister Devamata," 132-133. [Hereafter, *Reminiscences (1964)*].

[67] *N. D.,* 3:9-10; the reader may also refer to *C. W.,* V:48.

[68] *Life,* II:10-11.

[69] *N. D.,* 3:97-98.

[70] *Life,* II:85-86.

[71] Swami Tathagatananda, *Meditation on Swami Vivekananda* (New York: The Vedanta Society of New York, 1994), 166-167.

72 Ibid., 167.

73 *N. D.*, 3:117.

74 *Compr. Bio. S. V,* 1:747.

75 *Life*, II:38-39.

76 Ibid., 39.

77 *N. D.*, 3:183-184.

78 Ibid., 2:53-54.

79 Ibid., 3:334.

80 Ibid., 144.

81 Ibid., 3:332.

82 "Conquest by Other Means: Vivekananda's Approach," *PB* (September 1993), 420; the reader may refer to note 22, *Brahmavadin* (March 28, 1896).

83 *Life, II*, 66-67.

84 *N. D.*, 3:392-393.

85 Ibid., 3:527.

86 *Reminiscences (1964)*, 136-137.

87 *N. D.*, 3:491-492.

88 *C. W.*, VIII:364.

89 *Life, II*, 67.

90 *N. D.*, 3:529-533; the reader may refer to Ibid., 3:540-542 for Burke's additional research regarding the lecture "My Master" and also to "Sunday Lectures," 23 February 1896, Ibid., 3:577.

91 Ibid., 3:531-2; see note 90.

92 W. H. Starick to Sister Shivani, 1 September 1944, *Apostle*, 230; see note 90.

93 *N. D.*, 4:316.

94 Ibid., 3:14.

95 Ibid., 3:525.

96 Ibid., 3:528.

97 Ibid.

98 *N. D.*, 3:387.

99 Ibid., 3:528.

100 Ibid., 4:134.

101 Ibid., 4:341.

[102] Ibid.

[103] *N. D.*, 4:337.

[104] *C. W.*, VI:376-377.

[105] *N. D.*, 4:339.

[106] *Brahmavadin* (June 1903): 328-333.

[107] Swami Vivekananda, introduction to *The Vedanta Philosophy* (New York: Vedanta Society, 1896).

[108] New York students to Swami Vivekananda's brother disciples in India, 3 May 1896, *N. D.*, 4:133 (for entire letter, Ibid., 4:560-561).

[109] *N. D.*, 4:135.

[110] Ibid., 3:375.

[111] Ibid., 3:538.

[112] *Life*, II:211.

Chapter Two: Swamiji's Second Trip to America

[1] *With the Swamis*, 59-60.

[2] *Life*, II:487-488.

[3] *With the Swamis*, 292.

[4] *Vivekananda: A Biography in Pictures* (Calcutta: Advaita Ashrama, 1977), 58.

[5] *N. D.*, 3:347-348.

[6] *N. D.*, 5:159.

[7] "Swami Vivekananda as I Saw Him," *PB* (January 1989): 18-21.

[8] *Life*, II:488-489.

[9] Ibid., 489.

[10] Ibid., 489-490.

[11] *N. D.*, 6:266.

[12] *N. D.*, 6:271-273.

[13] Ibid., 6:270-271.

[14] Ibid., 2:134.

[15] Ibid., 6:291.

[16] *With the Swamis*, 45-54.

[17] *N. D.*, 6:293.

[18] *Life*, II:534.

[19] *PB* (1925): 2-4.

[20] *N. D.*, 6:276-277.

[21] Taped message of 1955 to members of N.Y. Vedanta Society, *N. D.*, 6:277-282.

[22] Ibid., 6:283.

[23] Ibid., 6:284.

[24] Office for Metropolitan History, 246 West 80 Street, New York, NY 10024, Christopher Gray, Dir.

[25] Christopher Gray, "Dad's House, Stanford White Design, Swami's Visit," *New York Times*, Sunday, 7 March 1999, Special: Manhattan Real Estate Offerings, "Streetscapes/ Readers' Questions," p.5.

[26] *N. D.*, 6:307-308.

[27] Ibid., 6:307.

[28] Ibid., 6:308.

[29] *C. W.*, VII:204.

[30] *Life*, II:535.

[31] *N. D.*, 6:306.

[32] Ibid., 6:309.

[33] *Life*, II:536.

[34] *SV in America*, 611.

[35] Marie Louise Burke, *Swami Vivekananda: His Second Visit to the West, New Discoveries*, 1st ed. (Mayavati: Advaita Ashrama, 1973), 611. [Hereafter, *SV, Second Visit to the West*].

Chapter Three: Swami Saradananda: 1897 - 1897

[1] Swami Aseshananda, *Glimpses of a Great Soul* (Portland: The Vedanta Society of Portland, 1982), 20. [Hereafter, *Glimpses of a Great Soul*].

[2] *N. D.*, 4:314.

[3] Ibid., 4:314-315.

[4] Ibid., 4:315.

[5] *The Apostles of Sri Ramakrishna*, edited and compiled by Swami Gambhirananda (Calcutta: Advaita Ashrama, 1967), 259.

[6] *N. D.*, 4:345-346.

[7] *With the Swamis*, 58.

[8] *Glimpses of a Great Soul*, 24-25.

Chapter Four: Swami Abhedananda: 1897 - 1910

[1] *C. W., S. A..*, X:12.

[2] Ibid.

[3] *With the Swamis*, 24-25.

[4] Swami Abhedananda, *Amar Jivankatha* (Calcutta: Ramakrishna Vedanta Math, 1964), 135. [Hereafter, *Amar Jivankatha*].

[5] *C. W., S. A.*, X:12.

[6] Ibid., X:15.

[7] Ibid., X:19.

[8] *Apostle*, 126.

[9] *C. W., S. A.*, X:20-21.

[10] Ibid., X:27.

[11] Ibid., X:26.

[12] Ibid., X:39.

[13] *Apostle*, 290.

[14] *C. W, S. A.*, X:27.

[15] Ibid., X:82.

[16] Ibid., X:86.

[17] *Brahmavadin* (March 25, 1899); *Amar Jivankatha*, 66, 203.

[18] *VK* (March 1978): 109-110.

[19] *PB* (May 1902): 89-90.

[20] *VMB* (April 1905): 9-11.

[21] Swami Gambhirananda, *History of the Ramakrishna Math and Mission* (Calcutta: Advaita Ashrama, 1957), 181. [Hereafter, *History*].

[22] Sister Gargi (Marie Louise Burke), *Swami Trigunatita: His Life and Work* (San Francisco: The Vedanta Society of Northern California, 1997), 287.

23 Swami Prajnanananda, *The Philosophical Ideas of Swami Abhedananda, A Critical Study: A Guide to the Complete Works of Swami Abhedananda* (Calcutta: Ramakrishna Vedanta Math, 1971), 415-417. [Hereafter, *Philosophical Ideas, S.A.*].

24 *With the Swamis*, 34.

25 *PB* (May 1899): 79.

26 *C. W., S. A.*, X:91.

27 Ibid., X:90.

28 *N. D.*, 5:145-146.

29 Ibid., 5:146.

30 *Apostle*, 104-106.

31 Ibid., 292.

32 *Life*, II:485-486.

33 *N. D.*, 6:267.

34 *Life*, II:531-532.

35 *N. D.*, 4:552-553.

36 *VMB* (November 1907): 146-7.

37 *Brahmavadin* (January 1903): 54-57.

38 Ibid., 56.

39 *SV, Second Visit to the West*, 602.

40 *Vivekananda The Great Spiritual Teacher: A Compilation* (Calcutta: Advaita Ashrama, 1995), 565-566; "Swami Vivekananda and His Work," *Brahmavadin* (June 1903): 329-330; *Philosophical Ideas, S. A.*, 313-315.

41 *VMB* (February 1906): 167-169.

42 Ibid., (February 1907): 222-223.

43 Ibid., 223-224.

44 Ibid., (February 1908): 185-188.

45 Ibid., (April 1905): I, no. 1:1.

46 *Apostle*, 121-122.

47 *VMB* (February 1906): 167.

48 Wendell Thomas, *Hinduism Invades America* (New York City: The Beacon Press, Inc., 1930), 115. [Hereafter, *Hinduism Invades America*].

49 *VMB* (February 1906): 167.

50 Ibid., (October 1905): 108.

[51] *PB* (March 1906): 57-58.

[52] *VMB* (February 1907): 221.

[53] Ibid.

[54] "New York Vedanta Society," *PB* (March 1904): 53-54.

[55] *Amar Jivankatha*, 338.

[56] *Apostle*, 122.

[57] "Vedanta in America," *VMB* (April 1905): 11-12; *PB* (April 1905): 76-77.

[58] "Swami Abhedananda Addresses Clergymen," *VMB* (April 1905): 7-8.

[59] *Brahmavadin* (June 1905): 347-348.

[60] *VMB* (May 1906): 31.

[61] Ibid., (June 1906): 56.

[62] *Apostle*, 137.

[63] *VMB* (April 1907): 14.

[64] Ibid., (August 1907): 96.

[65] *Apostle*, 175.

[66] *PB* (January 1991): 47.

[67] Moni Bagchi, *Swami Abhedananda: A Spiritual Biography* (Calcutta: Ramakrishna Vedanta Math, 1968), 351-353.

[68] *VMB* (March 1908): 204-205.

[69] Swami Ranganathananda, *A Pilgrim Looks at the World* (Bombay: Bharatiya Vidya Bhavan, 1974), 406-408.

[70] *VM* (January/February 1909): 99.

[71] *VMB* (August/September 1908): 71-72.

[72] "News and Notes," *VM* (May 1909): 140.

[73] *VM* (January/February 1909): 105.

[74] *With the Swamis*, 28-29.

[75] Ibid., 36-38.

[76] Ibid., 44-46.

[77] *VMB* (August/September 1908): 72.

[78] *VM* (January/February 1909): 105; Ibid., (March 1909): 118.

[79] *VM* (January/February 1909): 106; Ibid., (April 1909): 130; Ibid., (July/August 1909): 161.

[80] *VMB* (February 1908): 193.

[81] Ibid., (August/September 1908): 72.

[82] *VM* (January/February 1909): 107.

[83] Ibid., (March 1909): 117.

[84] *History*, 178-179; *Amar Jivankatha*, 400.

[85] *History*, 180.

[86] "Religion and Social Service," *The Literary Digest* XLV, New York, No. 2 (13 July 1912).

[87] *Philosophical Ideas, S. A.*, 420.

Chapter Five: Swami Bodhananda: 1912 -1950

[1] *VK* (May 1924).

[2] *VMB* (July 1906): 72.

[3] Ibid., 59-68.

[4] *VMB* (January 1907): 14-16; Ibid., (February 1907): 207-217.

[5] *VMB* (February 1907): 225; Ibid., (April 1907): 15.

[6] *VMB* (February 1908): 191-192.

[7] *VM* (July/August 1909): 158.

[8] "Notes of Interest," *Voice of Freedom* (May 1909): 31.

[9] "Notes of Interest," *Voice of Freedom* (September 1909): 95.

[10] "The Message of the East," *VMB* (October 1915): 236.

[11] *PB* (June 1950); *New Encyclopedia Britannica*, s.v. "Morton, Levi Parsons," 8:344.

[12] "News and Notes" and "Miscellany," *PB* (December 1923): 478-480.

[13] "News and Notes: 'Srimat Swami Bodhananda Back to India'," *PB* (January 1924): 47-48.

[14] "An Interview with Swami Bodhananda," *PB* (March 1924): 126-129.

[15] "News and Notes: 'Swami Bodhananda Back to New York'," *PB* (January 1925): 47-48.

[16] "News and Notes: 'Swami Bodhananda's Tour in the Pacific Coast'," *PB* (August 1926): 377-379.

[17] John Yale, ed., *What Vedanta Means to Me: A Symposium* (New York: Doubleday & Co., 1960), 88.

[18] *PB* (February 1936): 272.

[19] "Message of the East," *VMB* (January 1927): 32.

[20] *Hinduism Invades America*, 95-102.

[21] "Vedanta Society, New York," *PB* (May 1929): 260.

[22] *VD* (November 1932): 16.

[23] Ibid., (April 1933): 14-16.

[24] Ibid., (February 1931): 2-3.

[25] *Life*, II:539.

[26] Ibid., II:549-550.

[27] *PB* (March 1977): 101.

[28] "How I First Met Swami Vivekananda," *PB* (October 1934): 500-502.

[29] "News and Reports: 'A New Centre at Boston'," *VK* (September 1942): 158.

Chapter Six: Swami Pavitrananda: 1951 - 1977

[1] "News and Reports: 'Vedanta Society of New York: Dedication of a New Chapel'," *VK* (August 1952): 205-206.

[2] "Notes and Comments: 'Vedanta and the West'," *PB* (July 1952): 311-313.

[3] *VK* (March 1978): 135; "News and Reports: 'Vedanta Society, New York, Report: January-December 1976 (with some later information)'," *PB* (April 1978): 199.

Chapter Seven: The Vedanta Society of New York: 1978 - 2000

[1] "News and Reports: 'Vedanta Society, New York: Anniversary Commemorated'," *PB* (January 1995): 412.

[2] "A Sister's Tribute to 'A Mission to the World' (A Centennial Celebration of the Vedanta Society of New York—Swami Vivekananda's First Mission to the West)," *PB* (January 1996): 65-67.

SELECTED BIBLIOGRAPHY

(The journals, *The Brahmavadin, Vedanta Monthly Bulletin, Vedanta Magazine, Vedanta Darpana, Prabuddha Bharata,* and *Vedanta Kesari* have been cited in the endnotes).

Abhedananda, Swami. *The Complete Works.* Vol. X. Calcutta: Ramakrishna Vedanta Math, 1970.

—— *Amar Jivankatha.* Calcutta: Ramakrishna Vedanta math, 1964.

Aseshananda, Swami. *Glimpses of a Great Soul.* Portland: The Vedanta Society of Portland, 1982.

Atmaprana, Pravrajika, ed. *Western Women in the Footsteps of Swami Vivekananda.* New Delhi: Ramakrishna Sarada Mission, 1995.

Atulananda, Swami. *With the Swamis in America and India.* Mayavati: Advaita Ashrama, 1988.

Bagchi, Moni. *Swami Abhedananda: A Spiritual Biography.* Calcutta: Ramakrishna Vedanta Math, 1968.

Burke, Marie Louise. *Swami Vivekananda: His Second Visit to the West, New Discoveries.* First ed. Mayavati: Advaita Ashrama, 1973.

—— *Swami Vivekananda in America: New Discoveries.* First ed. Calcutta: Advaita Ashrama, 1958.

Swami Vivekananda in the West: New Discoveries, 6 vols. (individual subtitles) Calcutta: Advaita Ashrama, 1984-1987.

Dhar, S. N. *A Comprehensive Biography of Swami Vivekananda.* 2 vols. Madras: Vivekananda Prakashan Kendra, 1975-1976.

Eastern and Western Admirers. *Reminiscences of Swami Vivekananda.* First ed. Calcutta: Advaita Ashrama, 1961.

Eastern and Western Disciples. *The Life of Swami Vivekananda.* 2 vols. Fifth ed., rev. and enl. Calcutta: Advaita Ashrama, 1979 and 1981.

French, Harold W. *The Swan's Wide Waters: Ramakrishna and Western Culture.* Port Washington, New York and London: Kennikat Press, 1974.

Gambhirananda, Swami, ed. and comp. *The Apostles of Sri Ramakrishna.* Calcutta: Advaita Ashrama, 1967.

—— *History of the Ramakrishna Math and Mission.* Calcutta: Advaita Ashrama, 1957.

Gargi, Sister (Marie Louise Burke). *Swami Trigunatita: His Life and Work.* San Francisco: The Vedanta Society of Northern California, 1997.

Jackson, Carl T., *Vedanta for the West: The Ramakrishna Movement in the United States.* Bloomington & Indianapolis: Indiana University Press, 1994.

Kapoor, Satish K. "Swami Vivekananda: A Study of His Sojourns and Impact on the West, 1893-1896." Ph.D. Thesis, Punjab University, Chandigarh, 1980.

Prajnanananda, Swami. *The Philosophical Ideas of Swami Abhedananda, A Critical Study: A Guide to the Complete Works of Swami Abhedananda.* Calcutta: Ramakrishna Vedanta Math, 1971.

Ranganathananda, Swami. *A Pilgrim Looks at the World.* 2 vols. Bombay: Bharatiya Vidya Bhavan, 1974.

Rolland, Romain. *The Life and Gospel of Vivekananda.* Calcutta: Advaita Ashrama, 1979.

Rolland, Romaine. *The Life of Ramakrishna.* Calcutta: Advaita Ashrama, 1947.

Shivani, Sister. *An Apostle of Monism: An Authentic Account of the Activities of Swami Abhedananda in America.* Calcutta: Ramakrishna Vedanta Math, 1947.

Swami Vivekananda: A Hundred Years Since Chicago, A Commemorative Volume.

Belur, West Bengal: Ramakrishna Math and Ramakrishna Mission, 12 January 1994.

Tathagatananda, Swami. *Meditation on Swami Vivekananda.* New York: The Vedanta Society of New York, 1994.

Thomas, Wendell. *Hinduism Invades America.* New York City: The Beacon Press, Inc., 1930.

Vivekananda, Swami. *The Complete Works.* 9 vols. Fourth - eleventh eds. Calcutta: Advaita Ashrama, 1972-1979.

Vivekananda The Great Spiritual Teacher: A Compilation. Calcutta, Advaita Ashrama, 1995.

Yale, John, ed. *What Vedanta Means to Me: A Symposium.* New York: Doubleday & Company, Inc., 1960.

INDEX

Abbreviations used in the index:

RK   Sri Ramakrishna
SV   Swami Vivekananda
SA   Swami Abhedananda
Ved.   Vedanta
VM   Vedanta Movement
VSNY   Vedanta Society of New York

INDEX

VSNY after her birth anniversary services, 230; Frank Dvorak paints her likeness, 179; her birth centenary at VSNY, 222; her image in new Chapel at VSNY, 220; oil painting of her likeness installed in "Sarada Home" at VSNY, 231; SA seeks and receives her advice, 137; Swami Bodhananda initiated by her, 191; Swami Pavitrananda writes book, *Holy Mother*, 215; Swami Aseshananda her disciple, 233, 235; Swami Nikhilananda her disciple, 201; Swami Nityaswarupananda her disciple, 235; Swamis give personal reminiscences of her at 100th anniversary of founding of Ramakrishna Order at VSNY, 235
Hooper, Prof. Franklin W., 174
Huntington, Helen F., 92
Huxley, Aldous, 23

I

India-America Friendship Dinner, 200
Ingersoll, Miss Anna J., 153
Ingersoll, Robert, 56
Iowa University, 151
Isherwood, Christopher, 42, 47, 222

J

Jackson, Prof. A. V. W., 157
James, Prof. William, 57, 61-64, 132

Janes, Dr. Lewis G., 58, 60, 143
Jesus Christ, 58, 155, 289
Jnaneswarananda, Swami, 198-201
Johnston, Charles, 276
Jung, Prof. Carl, 215-219

K

Kant, Immanuel, 297
Kripananda, Swami (*see also* Landsberg, Leon), 90, 91, 96, 113

L

Landsberg, Leon (*see also* Kripananda, Swami), 54, 65, 71, 72, 78, 79
Lanman, Prof. Charles Rockwell, 57, 61, 157, 158
Le Page, Mr. 176
Le Page, Mrs. Mary. *See* Shivani, Sister
Leggett, Francis H., 144
Leggett, Mrs. Bessie MacLeod (Sturges), 140
Lesseps, Ferdinand de, 193
Liberal Congress of Religions, 141
Lokeswarananda, Swami, 254
Low, Professor Seth, 157

M

MacLeod, Josephine, 72, 81-82, 86, 159
Madhavananda, Swami, 223, 224
Madison Square Garden Hall, 96, 100
Marcel, Gabriel, 298
Markham, Edwin, 180
May, Rollo, 297

Prabhavananda's lectures and Swami Bodhananda's lectures at Theosophical Lodge and Congress of Religions, 196; televised interreligious dialogues, 254; Vedanta work at religious schools and academic institutions continues, 249-250;

Ved. and Christianity: at Parliament, 47; Christian view at the Parliament of World Religions, 36-37; RK's spiritual practices, 30; SV on Jesus Christ, 58

children's classes in Ved., 153-156

Ved. literature, at 1904 World's Fair, 170; removes prejudice, 173

100 years of Ved. in America: 100th anniversary of founding of VSNY, 239; 100th anniversary of Parliament of Wrold Religionss, 237; Bengal Studies Conf., 242; Convocation of Global Religions, 243-244; Fifth Int'l Congress of Vedanta, 244-245; Fourth Int'l Congress of Vedanta, 236; Special Service at VSNY, 240-242

Vedanta Center of Greater Washington, D.C., 170

Vedanta Convention, 251

Vedanta Movement in London: revived by SA, 175-176

Vedanta Movement in New York (see also Ramakrishna Movement): a "Great Movement," 169; a "Neo-Vedantic Movement", 283; American Mysticism reports on Ved. Movement, 62; Bishop Potter its

supporter, 278-279; Dr. Lewis G. Janes its strong supporter, 60, 143; followers recognize importance of VSNY in it, 156; permanent center needed for its supporters, 66; SV's decision for free lectures to maintian its purity, 100; Swami Atulananda's impressions of movement in New York, 182-184; Swami Nirmalananda assists the movement in VSNY, 169; VSNY becomes SV's chosen vehicle for it, 100

Vedanta Society of New York (VSNY):
at 228 West 39 St., 79
at 509 Fifth Ave., 133
at 117 Lexington Avenue, 139
at 170 Lexington Avenue, 139, 140
at 146 East 55 St., 107, 152
at 102 East 58 St., 113, 116, 157
at 62 West 71 St., 150, 165, 170
at 135 West 80 St., 175, 192
at 236 Central Park West, 192;
at 34 West 71 St. (present and permanent home), 193
a vehicle for Ved. in the West, 100
anniversary celebrations: 12th anniversary, 161; 13th anniversary, 162-164; centenary anniversary, 238;
birth anniversary services for Holy Mother: 100th anniversary, 222;
birth anniversary services for RK: 100th anniversary, 203; 150th anniversary, 234; 98th anniversary, 202